Let There Be Light

Selected excerpts
from
The Book of Zohar

LAITMAN
KABBALAH PUBLISHER

Compiled by Yaniv C

Let There Be Light
Selected excerpts from The Book of Zohar

Copyright © 2012 by Michael Laitman
All rights reserved
Published by Laitman Kabbalah Publishers
www.kabbalah.info   info@kabbalah.info
1057 Steeles Avenue West, Suite 532, Toronto,
ON, M2R 3X1, Canada
2009 85th Street #51, Brooklyn, New York, 11214, USA

Printed in Canada

ISBN: 978-1-897448-74-8

Library of Congress Control Number: 2012936446

Translation: Chaim Ratz
Associate Editor: Noga Burnot
Editor: Debra Rudder
Layout: Baruch Khovov
Cover: Inna Smirnova
Executive Editor: Chaim Ratz
Publishing and Post Production: Uri Laitman

FIRST EDITION: JANUARY 2013
First Printing

TABLE OF CONTENTS

FOREWORD

"Looking was I at that eternal world..."

The Book of Zohar, VaYera [The Lord Appeared]

Next to the Bible, *The Book of Zohar* [*The Book of Radiance*], also known as *The Zohar*, is the most enchanted and mysterious composition ever written. No other composition has aroused such profound emotions of awe and reverence as did *The Zohar*. The book contains all the secrets of creation but until not long ago, the wisdom of *The Zohar* was locked behind a thousand doors. Now *The Zohar* is being disclosed in order to take humanity forward, as was written in it, "When the days of the Messiah draw near, even infants in the world will find the secrets of the wisdom" (*The Book of Zohar, VaYera* [The Lord Appeared], Item 460).

The great Kabbalist, Rav Yehuda Ashlag (1884-1954), built for us a key to unlock *The Zohar*—the *Sulam* [Ladder] commentary. The book you are holding contains selected excerpts from a series of books titled *Zohar for All*, which is a reader friendly version of *The Book of Zohar* with the *Sulam* commentary. The excerpts were selected with great care to make the reading easy and enjoyable. Each portion in *The Zohar* comes in its own chapter, and each item number is clearly marked at the beginning of the text.

The Book of Zohar holds within it a unique capability to usher us into the utmost good; it is a source of energy, of vital force, allowing us to connect with eternity. It is inspiring, fascinating, and so enthralling that it keeps readers coming back to it for more.

> "And the wise shall shine as the brightness of the firmament ... are the ones who exert in this brightness, called *The Book of Zohar*."
>
> *The Book of Zohar, BeHaalotcha*
> [When You Mount the Candles], item 88

The Experience of Reading in The Zohar

The Book of Zohar is a wondrous tool that can unlock an entire world before us, a world of astounding revelations. *The Zohar* is like a gate to the actual reality, which is currently hidden from our perception. However, to use the revealing power of *The Zohar* we must know how to read *The Zohar* properly. The five below guidelines will help us prepare for the great journey in the paths of *The Zohar*.

Rule One—the Heart Understands: Do not Study with Your Intellect

The Book of Zohar should be studied with the heart, by feeling and wanting. Unlike ordinary forms of study, which rely on processing information and analyses of data, with *The Zohar*, the approach is fundamentally different. The study of *The Zohar* is intended to invoke internal transformations, to qualify us to perceiving the hidden reality.

The student's success depends solely on the extent of our desire to discover and feel that reality. For this reason, there is no need for any prior knowledge, skills, or special talents for the study of *The Zohar*. All that is required is to have a genuine desire to open one's eyes and heart to a broad new world.

Rule Two—Man Is a Small World: Interpreting the Words Correctly

The Book of Zohar contains many descriptions and terms that we know from our world, such as sea, mountains, trees, flowers, animals, people, and road trips. Keep in mind that all the details, characters, and events mentioned in the book *do not* speak of the world around us, but only of what unfolds *within* us. Therefore, while reading *The Zohar*, we should interpret the words within it as expressions of what happens within us, in our souls. We should see the text as a bridge that leads to our deepest qualities and desires.

Rule Three—the Light in It Reforms: Seek the Light

We often hear about *The Zohar* having a special quality, known as *Segula*. *Segula* is the natural law of development operating within all of life's forces. It is not a mystical, imaginary power.

Kabbalists explain that our material world is dominated entirely by the egoistic desire to exploit others, while the spiritual world is dominated by the intention to give and to love. Therefore, we have been given a special means by which to tie those two opposite worlds together, that is, to make our own qualities similar to the quality of love and giving that governs the spiritual world. That special means is called "the light that reforms."

The light affects us during the reading in a manner we cannot currently perceive, and this is why we call it *Segula*, or "miracle." But for Kabbalists, who already perceive the spiritual world, there are no miracles at all here, but a completely natural process. All that we must do, they stress, is read *The Book of Zohar* and wish for the power within it to affect us during the study. Gradually, we will begin to feel a change developing within us. This will be the reforming effect of the light. Then the spiritual world will open and what seemed to us as a *Segula*, a miracle, will become a clear and vivid natural law.

Rule Four—Everything Depends on the Desire

We know what tremendous efforts babies are required to make to take their first steps in life, how diligently they exert for it, never giving up, trying time and time again until they succeed. We, too, must persist with the study of *The Zohar* patiently and diligently until we begin to "walk" on our own two feet and discover the spiritual world. The system required for our progress has been prepared in advance, and all that is required is that we provide the great desire to attain it.

Rule Five—As One Man in One Heart: Bonding Is the Key

The Book of Zohar was written by a group of ten Kabbalists who created among them a complete *Kli* [vessel]—a unified desire to discover reality's supreme force, the Creator. It was only the profound connection among them, the love, and the bonding that enabled them to break through the barriers of the material world and rise to the eternal level that *The Zohar* narrates. If we wish to follow them, we must try to build a similar connection among us, to search for the power of bonding that existed among the students of

Rabbi Shimon Bar Yochai. *The Zohar* was born through love. Hence, its rediscovery in our time will be made possible only out of love.

"When we stand before Rabbi Shimon, the fountains of the heart are open to all directions and everything is revealed."

The Book of Zohar, Yitro [Jethro], item 412

INTRODUCTION

OF THE BOOK OF

ZOHAR

Introduction of The Book of Zohar

1) **The 613 *Mitzvot* [commandments] in the Torah are called *Pekudin* [commands/ deposits], as well as *Etzot* [counsels/tips].** This is so because in all things there is the preparation for attainment, which is the *Achor* [back] and the attainment of the matter, *Panim* [front/face]. Similarly, there are "We shall do" and "We shall hear" in Torah and *Mitzvot*. When keeping Torah and *Mitzvot* in "we shall do," prior to being rewarded with hearing, the *Mitzvot* are called "613 counsels," preparation, *Achor*. When rewarded with hearing, the 613 *Mitzvot* become *Pekudin*, from the word *Pikadon* [deposit]. This is so because in each *Mitzva*, the light of a degree is deposited opposite a unique organ in the 613 organs and tendons of the soul and of the body. It follows that by performing the *Mitzva* he extends the light that belongs to that organ and tendon through his soul and body. This is the *Panim* of the *Mitzvot*, hence the *Panim* of the *Mitzvot* are called "deposits." (Excerpt taken from "General Explanation for All Fourteen Commandments

and How They Divide into the Seven Days of Creation.")

8) **"Since man asked and researched, to observe."** "To observe" refers to the *Zivug de AVI*, called *Histaklut* [looking] of *AVI* at each other through their ascent to *Rosh de AA*. At that time, the *Bina* returns to receive illumination of *Hochma* for the *ZON*. This is because while *YESHSUT*, *ZAT de Bina*, do not need illumination of *Hochma* for themselves—since in and of themselves, *ZAT de Bina* are similar to their *GAR* and do not need to receive *Hochma*—when *ZON* rise for *MAN* to *YESHSUT*, *YESHSUT* awaken for them to rise to *Rosh de AA* and receive *Hochma*. However, *ZON*, too, do not rise for *MAN* to *YESHSUT*, except by raising *MAN* from the lower people to the *ZON* in a way that the souls of people rise for *MAN* to *ZON*, then the *ZON* rise for *MAN* to *YESHSUT*, and *YESHSUT* rise to *AA* and become one *Partzuf* with upper *AVI*. At that time, *AVI* look at each other and extend *Hochma* for the *ZON*.

"And since man asked" means that he raised *MAN*. "And researched" means scrutinizing his actions, to raise the *ZON* for *Zivug AVI* to look, so that *AVI* would look at each other and extend *Hochma*. "And to know from degree to degree through the end of all the degrees, the *Malchut*," since the illumination of *Hochma* that is drawn through raising MAN and the *Zivug* is called "knowing" or "*Hochma* through *Daat*" [wisdom through knowledge], for ZON that rise for MAN are regarded there as the *Sefira Daat* for AVI, as they cause their *Zivug*. Also, the *Zivug* is called "knowing," from the words, "And the man knew his wife, Eve."

"And to know" means to extend *Mochin* in *Daat* from degree to degree, from *Daat* of the degree of AVI to the *Mochin* of the degree of ZA. "Through the end of all the degrees" is from ZA to the *Nukva*, who is called "the end of all the degrees."

23) **The creation of the world means improvement and existence in a way that the world can exist and complete the aim for which it was created.** It is known that God has made them one opposite the other. Opposite each force in *Kedusha* [holiness], the Creator made an equal force in the *Sitra Achra*, opposite from the *Kedusha*. As there are four worlds ABYA de [of] *Kedusha*, there are four worlds ABYA de Tuma'a [impurity] opposite them.

Hence, in the world of *Assiya* there is no distinction between one who serves God and one who does not serve Him, as there is no distinction whatsoever between *Kedusha* and *Tuma'a*. Accordingly, how can the world exist? How can we tell good from evil, *Kedusha* from *Tuma'a*?

However, there is one, very important scrutiny, which is that another god is barren and does not bear fruit. Hence, those who fail in him and walk by the path of *ABYA de Tuma'a*, their source dries out and they have no blessing of spiritual fruits. Thus, they wither away until they shut completely.

The opposite is those who adhere to *Kedusha*. Their works are blessed, as it is written, "As a tree planted by streams of water, which yields its fruit in its season and its leaf does not wither; and in whatever he does, he prospers."

This is the only scrutiny in the world of *Assiya* to know if he is in *Kedusha* or to the contrary, as it is written, "'And test Me now in this,' says the Lord of hosts, 'if I do not open for you the windows of heaven and pour out for you a blessing until it overflows.'" Afterwards it is written, "So you will again distinguish between the righteous and the wicked, between one who serves God and one who does not serve Him." Thus, it explains that it is impossible to tell one who serves the Creator from one who does not serve Him, but only in the blessing.

This is the heart of this commentary of the letters, since all the letters came to create the world according to the instruction of the degree in *Kedusha* that is unique to that letter, for the twenty-two letters are the elements of all the heads of the degrees in the four worlds *ABYA*. Each of them appreciated its own merit, indicating that by obtaining her degree, the people of the world would be able to make the *Kedusha* prevail over the *Klipot*, to reach the desired end of correction. But the Creator replied to each of them that opposite here is that same force in the *Klipot*, as well, hence, people will not obtain any scrutinies through her.

Then came the *Bet*, whose instruction in her degree is *Beracha* [blessing], opposite which there are no *Klipot* whatsoever, since another god is barren and does not bear fruit. Then the Creator told her, "Indeed, I will create the world with you," since only in her was there scrutiny and distinction, telling between a servant of the Creator and one who does not serve Him, since she did not have an opposite in the *Sitra Achra*. Hence, the world will indeed exist in her, to scrutinize and to enhance the *Kedusha* over the *Merkavot* [chariots/structures] of *Tuma'a*, until death is swallowed up forever and they arrive at the end of correction.

54) **Who is so wise among you as to turn darkness into light,** for whom the bitter tastes as sweet even before he comes here, while he is still alive in this world? Who among you awaits the light each day, shining when the King visits the doe, at which time the glory of the King increases and He is called "the King of all the kings of the world." And one who does not expect it each day while he is still in this world has no part here.

56) **When a corporeal person fills with compassion and love over one's friend, he sheds tears, for it extends from the above-mentioned root of the spiritual tears,** since anything spiritual that occurs in the upper ones strikes and finds a branch in the corporeal creations. This is so because the upper light kicks and strikes the *Masach* to breach its boundary, since the upper light always extends only from *Ein Sof*, above the world of *Tzimtzum*, where no boundary is discerned.

Also, the upper light craves and longs to expand in the lower one, as it is written, "The

Creator craved to dwell in the lower ones." We also learn, "Divinity in the lower ones—a high need." Hence, He kicks and strikes the boundary in the *Masach*, to be drawn below its boundary, and the *Masach* repels it as *Ohr Hozer*, and in the meantime, tears fell outside.

These tears come out of compassion and love for the lower one. Hence, in the corporeal branch, too, the tears are always emitted when one's heart is moved with love and compassion for one's friend. Yet, spiritual tears do not vanish, as do corporeal ones.

The tears that are as boiling as fire fall into the great sea, as it is written, "For love is as strong as death, jealousy is as severe as the netherworld; its flashes are flashes of fire, the very flame of the Lord." This is so because those tears come out of compassion and love from the upper light to the lower one. And as you find in the corporeal branch, when one fills with love and compassion for one's friend, the tears are as boiling as the measure of his feelings for him.

So it is with the above-mentioned tears—they boil as fire, whose "Flashes are flashes of fire, the very flame of the Lord." This is why it was said, "And the tears are as boiling as fire and fall into the great sea." The quality of *Malchut* on the side of *Hochma* is called "the great sea," since great waters extend from it, breakers of the sea.

Through those tears, that appointee over the sea, called Rahav, stands and exists, meaning that minister of the sea who was killed at the time of the creation of the world. It is written, "And by His understanding He shattered Rahav," for when he was told, "Let the water ... be gathered together unto one place," he did not want to swallow the waters of *Beresheet*, and he stands and exists on those tears that fall into the great sea, for through them he is revived.

It was said that he sanctifies the name of the holy King and takes upon himself to swallow all the waters of *Beresheet*. This is so because at the time of the creation of the world, no correction reached *Malchut de Malchut*, since the Emanator corrected the worlds ABYA in MAN *de Bina* and not in MAN *de Malchut*, and this sufficed only for the first nine of *Malchut* and not for *Malchut de Malchut*.

It is written, "You are My people, you are in partnership with Me; I started the worlds, and you finish them." The entire correction of *Malchut de Malchut* is upon the lower ones.

Hence, when it was said to the minister of the sea, "Let the water ... be gathered together unto one place," he refused and did not wish to swallow all the waters of *Beresheet* because the *Klipot* would have overcome him for lack of the correction of *Malchut de Malchut*. This is why he was killed. However, those tears are the ones that sort and correct the *Malchut de Malchut*.

For this reason, they give vitality to the minister of the sea, so he may stand and sanctify the name of the holy King, to keep his Master's command and swallow all the waters of *Beresheet*. Then all the *Klipot* in the world and all the evil powers will annul, and all will gather unto one place—the world of *Atzilut*, since the world of *Atzilut* will expand equally with the *Raglaim* of AK down to this world. This will be the end of correction because BYA will return to being *Atzilut*.

61-62) **The Creator listens to the voices of those who engage in Torah**. With each word that is renewed in the Torah through a person who toils in the Torah, he makes one firmament. ZA is called "a voice," and *Nukva* is called "speech." When the righteous engages in Torah, he raises MAN to ZON with the voice and speech of his

Torah. A voice rises to ZA and the speech rises to the *Nukva*. The Creator listens to the voices of those who engage in Torah because the voice of Torah rises for MAN to ZA, who is called "the Creator." And in each word that is renewed in the Torah through the person who is exerting in Torah, he makes one firmament.

A word means speech. Each word that is renewed in the Torah of the one who engages in the Torah rises as MAN for the *Nukva*, who is called "word and speech." By that, one firmament is done. The firmament—the *Masach* on which the *Zivug* of the Creator with His Divinity is done—is carried out through the MAN that the righteous raise by their engagement in the Torah.

The reason why he says "In a word of Torah" and does not say "Innovation in the voice of Torah" is that the *Nukva* needs the construction of her *Yesod* anew for each *Zivug*, since after each *Zivug*, she becomes a virgin once again. And through the MAN of the righteous, the *Yesod* in her is always renewed, meaning the receptacle for the lights of ZA. This is why he says, "In each word that is renewed in the Torah," since the word, *Malchut*, is truly renewed by the righteous' word of Torah, for after every *Zivug* her receptacle disappears once more.

At the time when a new word of Torah comes out of the mouth of a man, that word rises and is introduced before the Creator. The Creator takes that word, kisses it, and crowns it with seventy decorated and engraved crowns. Then the new word of wisdom rises and sits on the head of the righteous one who lives forever. From there, it flies and sails through 70,000 worlds, rising to *Atik Yomin*, the *Keter*. All the words of *Atik Yomin* are words of wisdom in the high, hidden secrets. That is, when a person raises MAN with his word of Torah, the upper word, *Nukva de* ZA, rises and is introduced before the Creator for a *Zivug* with Him.

68) **The MAN that the righteous raise to bring contentment to their Maker, to benefit the upper one,** is called "innovated words of Torah." This is so because they are innovated by the upper *Zivug*, and through them ZON receive new *Mochin* until they are thus rewarded with establishing heaven and founding earth. By that, they become partners with the Creator because through their words, heaven and earth are renewed.

85) **The donkey driver who is leading the donkeys behind them is the assistance to the**

souls of the righteous, which is sent to them from above to raise them from one degree to the next. Had it not been for this assistance, which the Creator sends to the righteous, they would have been unable to rise from their degree and ascend higher. Hence the Creator sends a high soul from above according to the merit and degree of each righteous, and it assists him on his way.

In the beginning, the righteous does not know that soul at all. It seems to him that it is a very low soul which is accompanying him on his way. This is called "the impregnation of the righteous' soul." It means that the soul above has not completed her assistance, hence it is completely undistinguishable that it is her. But once she completes her assistance and brings the righteous to the desired degree, he recognizes her and sees her sublimity. This is called "the disclosure of the soul of the righteous."

119) **In the hall of the Messiah King, all the corrections that should be revealed at the end of correction—upon the arrival of the Messiah King—are already prepared and ready. Not a single detail is missing, and those souls in the hall of the Messiah King are all those who**

have already been rewarded with the end of correction from the root of their own souls.

120) **It was said about the upper King that he is sublime, hidden, and concealed, and He makes gates for Himself, one atop the other.** This is not an allegory. Rather, it is the lesson itself, since being a sublime, hidden, and concealed King, the thought cannot perceive Him whatsoever. Hence, He made many gates one atop the other, by which He made it possible to approach Him, as it is written, "Open for me the gates of righteousness." These are the gates that the Creator has made, making it possible for the righteous to approach Him through those gates.

At the end of all the gates, He made a gate with several locks. That gate is called *Malchut de Malchut*, the final point of all the upper gates. This last gate is the first gate for the upper *Hochma* [wisdom]. That is, it is possible to be rewarded with the upper *Hochma* only after the attainment of this last gate specifically, as for attainment of the upper *Hochma*, it is the first gate. This is why it is written, "Fear of the Lord is the beginning of wisdom," since "Fear of the Lord" is called the last gate, which is the first for the wisdom of the Lord.

121) The thought of creation is to delight His creatures and no pleasure is perceived by the creature while he must be separated from the Creator. Moreover, we learn that the Creator craves to dwell in the lower ones.

The common thing in understanding those two matters, which deny each other, is that the world was created in complete oppositeness from the Creator, from one end to the other, in every single point. This is so because this world was created with a desire to receive, which is the opposite form of the Creator's, in whom there is not even a shred of this desire, as it is written, "And man is born the foal of a wild donkey."

In that respect, all the issues of the governance of His guidance in this world are in total contrast to the thought of creation, which is only to delight His creatures, for it is according to the desire to receive in us, which is our standard and our tastefulness.

This is the meaning of the locks on the gates. First, all the many contradictions to His uniqueness, which we taste in this world, separate us from the Creator. Yet, when exerting to keep Torah and *Mitzvot* with love, with our soul and might, as we are commanded—to bestow contentment upon our Maker—all those forces of separation do not affect us into subtracting any of the love of the Creator with all our souls and might. Rather, in that state, every contradiction we have overcome becomes a gate for attainment of His wisdom. This is so because there is a special quality in each contradiction—revealing a special degree in attaining Him. And those worthy ones who have been rewarded with it turn darkness into light and bitter into sweet, for all the powers of separation—from the darkness of the mind and the bitterness of the body—have become to them gates for obtainment of sublime degrees. Thus, the darkness becomes a great light and the bitter becomes sweet.

Hence, to the extent that they previously had all the conducts of His guidance toward the forces of separation, now they have all been inverted into forces of unification, and sentence the entire world to the side of merit. This is because now each force serves for them as a gate of righteousness, by which they will come to receive from the Creator everything that He has contemplated for them, to delight them with the thought of creation, as it is written, "This is the gate of the Lord; the righteous will enter through it."

However, prior to being rewarded with inverting the desire to receive in us through Torah and *Mitzvot*, into reception in order to bestow, there are strong locks on those gates to the Creator, for then they have the opposite role: to drive us away from the Creator. This is why the forces of separation are called "locks," since they block the gates of approaching and drive us away from the Creator.

But if we overcome them so they do not affect us, cooling His love from our hearts, the locks become doors, the darkness becomes light, and the bitter becomes sweet. Over all the locks, we receive a special degree in His Providence, and they become openings, degrees of attainment of the Creator. And those degrees that we receive on the openings become halls of wisdom.

124) **Also, those who keep the Torah are seemingly the ones who make it** because all those forces of separation are inverted and become gates, each lock becomes a key, and each door becomes a hall of wisdom. By those who keep the Torah, all the sublime degrees that are included in the thought of creation to delight His creatures become revealed.

It follows that all the wisdom and the whole Torah are revealed only by those who keep the Torah, those in whom there is doing, in whom there is good and evil. This is why they are called "keepers of the Torah," for it appears only through them. The verse calls them "Those who do them," for they are seemingly the ones who make the Torah. This is so because were it not for their concealments, which have become gates through their prevailing, the Torah would not have been revealed.

125) **Rabbi Shimon was sitting and studying the Torah on the night when the bride, *Malchut*, unites with her husband.** On that night, after which—on the day of *Shavuot*—the bride is to be with her husband under the *Huppah* [wedding canopy], all the friends, who are the members of the bridal chamber, must be with her on that night and rejoice with her in the corrections in which she is corrected, meaning to engage in Torah, from Torah to Prophets, from Prophets to Hagiographa, the interpretations of the texts, and the secrets of the wisdom, for these are her corrections and adornments.

The Bride and her maidens come and stand on their heads, and she is corrected in them and rejoices in them all through that night. On the next day, the day of *Shavuot*, she comes to the *Huppah* only with them. And these friends, who engage in the Torah all night long, are called "members of the *Huppah*." And when she comes to the *Huppah*, the Creator asks about them, blesses them, and crowns them with the crowns of the bride. Happy are they.

Explanation: There are two meanings to it, which coincide.

1) The days of the exile are called "night," since this is the time of the concealment of His face from the children of Israel. At that time, all the powers of separation of the servants of the Creator dominate, and yet, precisely at that time the bride bonds with her husband–through Torah and *Mitzvot* of the righteous, who at that time are regarded as those who hold the Torah. All the sublime degrees called, "secrets of the Torah," are revealed by them, since this is why they are called "those who make them," for they seemingly make the Torah. It follows that the days of the exile are called "night," in which the bride bonds with her husband, and all the friends, who are the members of the bridal chamber, are those who hold the Torah.

After the end of correction and the complete redemption, it is written, "For there shall be one day, which is known to the Lord, neither day nor night, when in the evening time there will be light." This is why it is written that on the next day, the bride is to be with her husband under the *Huppah*, for then *BON* will return to being *SAG*, *MA* will be *AB*, and *AB* is regarded as the next day and a new *Huppah*.

At that time, the righteous are called "members of the *Huppah*," who engage in Torah, in whom there is no action, for then it is said, "And the earth shall be full of the knowledge of the Lord." And since those righteous—through their good deeds—raise *BON* to being *SAG* by their extension of the fear from the past, they are regarded as making this new *Huppah*, and this is why they are called "members of the *Huppah*."

2) The night of *Shavuot* is called "the night in which the bride bonds with her husband." This is so because on the next day, she is destined to be with her husband under the *Huppah*, on the day of *Shavuot*, the day of the reception of the Torah. However, it is the same matter as the first explanation because on the day of the reception of the Torah it was already the end of correction, in the form of "He will swallow up death forever,

and the Lord God will wipe away tears from all faces." It is as it is written in the verse, "*Harut* [carved] on the tablets"; do not pronounce it *Harut*, but *Herut* [freedom], since freedom from the angel of death has come.

126) In the end, when the great *Zivug* of *Atik Yomin*, *Rav Pe'alim uMekabtze'el*, appears, a great light will appear in all the worlds. By that, every flesh shall completely repent out of love.

128) *Huppah* is a gathering and assembling of all the *Ohr Hozer* [reflected light] that came out over the MAN that the righteous raised in all those *Zivugim* of the Creator and His Divinity, that appeared one at a time during all days and times of the 6,000 years. Now they have all become a great, single light of *Ohr Hozer* that rises and hovers over the Creator and His Divinity, who are now called "groom and bride." The *Ohr Hozer* hovers over them like a canopy [*Huppah*], and for this reason, at that time the righteous are called "members of the *Huppah*," for each has a part in this *Huppah*, to the extent of the MAN that he raised to the *Masach* in *Malchut* for raising *Ohr Hozer*. When it says, "the heaven," it is the bridegroom entering the *Huppah*. This refers to the time of the end of

correction, at which time the Creator is called bridegroom who then enters his *Huppah*.

138) ...**Know that this is the whole difference between this world, prior to the correction, and the end of correction.** Prior to the end of correction, *Malchut* is called "the tree of knowledge of good and evil," since the *Malchut* is the guidance of the Creator in this world. As long as the receivers have not been completed so they can receive His whole benevolence, which He had contemplated in our favor in the thought of creation, the guidance must be in the form of good and bad, reward and punishment. It is so because our vessels of reception are still tainted with self-reception, which is very limited in its measure, as well as separates us from the Creator.

The complete benefit, in the great measure that He had contemplated for us, is only in bestowal, which is pleasure without any boundary and limitation. But reception for oneself is limited and highly restricted because the satiation promptly puts out the pleasure. It is written, "The Lord has made everything for His own purpose," meaning that everything that occurs in the world was created from its inception only to bestow contentment upon

Him. Thus, people engage in worldly affairs in complete contrast to how they were initially created, since the Creator is saying, "The whole world was created for Me," as it is written, "The Lord has made everything for His own purpose," and "Everyone who is called by My name, I have created for My glory."

And we say the complete opposite because we are saying, "The whole world was created only for us." We want to devour all the abundance of the world into our bellies, for our own delights, and for our own glory. Thus, it is no wonder that we are still unworthy of receiving His complete benefit. For this reason, His guidance of good and evil has been prescribed for us, with guidance of reward and punishment, for they are interdependent because reward and punishment result from good and evil. When we use the vessels of reception contrary to how they were created, we necessarily sense evil in the operations of Providence in relation to us.

It is a law that the creature cannot receive disclosed evil from the Creator, for it is a flaw in the glory of the Creator for the creature to perceive Him as an evildoer, for this is unbecoming of the complete Operator. Hence, when one feels bad, denial of the Creator's guidance lies upon him and the superior Operator is concealed from him to that same extent. This is the greatest punishment in the world.

Thus, the sensation of good and evil in relation to His guidance brings with it the sensation of reward and punishment, for one who exerts to not part from faith in the Creator is rewarded even when he tastes a bad taste in Providence. And if he does not exert, he will have a punishment because he is separated from faith in the Creator. It follows that although the Creator does, is doing, and will do all the deeds, it still remains hidden from those who sense good and evil, since at the time of evil, the *Sitra Achra* is given the strength to conceal His guidance and faith. Thus, one comes to the great punishment of separation and becomes filled with heretical thoughts. And upon repentance, one receives the corresponding reward and can adhere to the Creator once again.

However, by the guidance of reward and punishment itself, the Creator has prepared it so that ultimately, we will be rewarded with the end of correction through it, that all the people will obtain the corrected vessels of reception in order to bestow contentment upon their Maker, as it is written, "The Lord has made everything for

His own purpose," as they were initially created. At that time, the great *Zivug* of *Atik Yomin* will appear, we will come to repentance from love, all the sins will be turned into merits, and all the bad into great good.

At that time, His private Providence will be revealed throughout the world, for all to see that He alone does, is doing, and will do all those deeds from before. This is because now, once the evil and the punishments have become benefits and merits, it will be possible to attain their Doer, for they have now become fitting for the work of His hands. Now they will praise and bless Him for those imaginary evils and punishments at the time.

This is the main point of the essay, for thus far the corrections, too, were regarded as the work of our hands because we received rewards or punishments for them. However, at the great *Zivug* of the end of correction it will be revealed that both corrections and punishments were all the work of His hands, as it is written, "The heavens tell the work of His hands." This is so because the great *Zivug* of the firmament will say that everything is the work of His hands and He alone does, is doing, and will do all the deeds.

140) This is so because prior to the end of correction, before we qualified our vessels of reception to receive only in order to give contentment to our Maker and not to our own benefit, *Malchut* is called "the tree of knowledge of good and evil." This is so because *Malchut* is the guidance of the world by people's actions. And since we are unfit to receive all the delight and pleasure that the Creator had contemplated in our favor in the thought of creation, we must receive the guidance of good and evil from the *Malchut*. This guidance qualifies us to ultimately correct our vessels of reception in order to bestow and to be rewarded with the delight and pleasure He had contemplated in our favor.

Our sensation of good and evil causes reward and punishment, too, since the sensation of evil causes separation from faith in the Creator. It follows that if one exerts during one's bad feeling to not blemish his faith because of that, and to keep the Torah and *Mitzvot* in wholeness, he is rewarded. And if he does not succeed in the test and receives separation, he is filled with evil thoughts.

It is known that for such thoughts the Creator punishes as for an act. It is written about it, "To lay hold of the hearts of the house of Israel."

It is also known that the righteousness of the righteous will not save him on the day of his transgression. However, this concerns only those who ponder the beginning.

Yet, sometimes the thoughts prevail over a person until he wonders about all the good deeds he has done and says, "What profit is it that we have kept His charge, and that we have walked in mourning before the Lord of hosts?" At that time, he becomes a complete wicked because he ponders the beginning and loses all the good deeds he had done by this bad thought, as it is written, "The righteousness of the righteous will not save him on the day of his transgression." This is why repentance is helpful, although this is already regarded as beginning to serve the Creator anew, as a newly born infant, whose righteousness from the past has completely vanished.

Often, the guidance of good and evil causes us ascents and descents, each according to what he is. You should know that for this reason, each ascent is regarded as a separate day because due to the great descent that he had, doubting the beginning, during the ascent he is as a newly born child. Thus, in each ascent, it is as though he begins to serve the Creator anew.

This is why each ascent is considered a specific day, and similarly, each descent is considered a specific night.

It is written, "Day to day pours forth speech," a holy day, from among those upper days of the King. In other words, on each ascent that a person had, when he clung to the upper days of the Creator, the friends are praised and each tells his friend that thing that he said. This is so because through the great *Zivug* at the end of correction they will be rewarded with repentance from love, for they will complete the correction of all the vessels of reception, so they will be only in order to bestow contentment upon the Creator. In that *Zivug*, all of the great delight and pleasure of the thought of creation will appear to us.

At that time, we will evidently see that all those punishments from the time of descents, which brought us into doubting the beginning, were the things that purified us and were the direct causes of all the happiness and goodness that have come to us at the time of the end of correction. This is so because were it not for those terrible punishments, we would never have come to this delight and pleasure. Then these sins will be inverted into actual merits.

"Day to day pours forth speech" means that each ascent prior to the end of correction is one of those upper days of the King, praising the friends. Thus, now it reappears in all the magnificence of its wholeness, which belongs to that day, and praises the friends who keep the Torah with that thing which each said to the friends, which is, "It is vain to serve God; and what profit is it that we have kept His charge," which at the time inflicted great punishments.

This is because now they have been turned into merits, since the entire wholeness and happiness of that day would not be able to appear now, in that grandeur and magnificence, were it not for those punishments. This is why those who speak those words are regarded as "Those who fear the Lord and who esteem His name," as actual good deeds. This is why it was said about them, too, "I will have compassion over them as a man has compassion for his own son who serves him."

It is said, "Day to day pours forth that speech" and praises it. This is so because all those nights are the descents, the suffering, and the punishments that arrested the *Dvekut* [adhesion] with the Creator until they became many days one after the other. Now, once the night and darkness have become merits and good deeds, as well, the night shines like the day and darkness like light, there are no more arrests, and all 6,000 years unite into a single great day.

Thus, all the *Zivugim* that came out one at a time and disclosed ascents and descents that were separate from one another have now assembled into a level of one, sublime, and transcendent level of *Zivug*, which shines from the end of the world through its end. It is written, "Day to day pours forth that speech" because the word that separated between one day and the next has now become a great praise and praises it, for it has become a merit. Thus, they all became one day for the Lord.

141) **We should know that in eternity, the order of time is not as it is in this world**. It follows that when the Creator contemplated creating the world, all the souls with all their conducts were already created in Him—through the end, in the complete wholeness that is required of them, to receive all the pleasure and delight that He had contemplated to delight them. In Him, the future is like the present, and future and past do not apply to Him.

Now you will understand the words, "The Creator showed Adam HaRishon each generation and its teachers," as well as to Moses. This seems perplexing. Since they have not been created yet, how did He show them? However, it is written that all the souls and all their conducts through the end of correction have already come out before Him in reality. They are all present in the upper Garden of Eden, and from there they come down, clothing bodies in this world, each in its time. The Creator showed them to Adam HaRishon from there, as well as to Moses, and to all who were worthy of it. This is an extensive matter and not every mind can bear it.

This is why it is said in *The Zohar* that as they unite in one above, she unites in one below, since the level of the great *Zivug* of the end of correction—as it is written, "The Lord will be one and His name One"—this level has already come out above—all the souls and all the deeds in the world, which will be created through the end of correction, in relation to His eternity, for the future is as the present to Him. It follows that this pillar of light—which shines from the end of the world through its end, which will shine at the end of correction—is already standing in the upper Garden of Eden and shines before Him as it will appear to us at the end of correction.

It says there, "One opposite one," since the Creator is one. This is so because at the end of correction, the two levels will shine one opposite the other, and then "The Lord will be one and His name One." And it was written, "Those matters make a line from the dwellers above and from the dwellers below," a line that shines from the dwellers above and from the dwellers below, one opposite the other.

This is so because that level shines from the dwellers above—which are the souls who are all in the upper Garden of Eden—and shines from the dwellers below—which are all the souls once they have actually been dressed in a body in this world and arrived at the end of correction. In other words, those two levels shine at the end of correction together, and then the unification of "The Lord is one and His name One" appears.

156) **When the Creator wished to create man,** He summoned sects of the upper angels, sat them down before Him, and said, "I wish to create man." They replied, "What is man, that You should remember him?" That is, "What is the nature of this man?" He told them, "Man was created in our image; his wisdom will be greater than your wisdom, since man's soul comprises

all the angels and upper degrees, just as his body comprises all the creations of this world. For this reason, upon the creation of man's soul, He called upon all the upper angels to include themselves in man's soul, as it is written, "Let us make man in our image, after our likeness." In other words, He incorporated all the angels so they would be included in man's *Tzelem* [image] and likeness. They asked the Creator, "What is the nature of this man?" meaning, "What will we gain from him, by our inclusion in him?"

P!!He replied, "Man was created in our image; his wisdom will be greater than your wisdom." He promised them that this man, who was to be comprised of our image, his wisdom would be greater than your wisdom. By that, you, too, will gain that great attainment that you are now lacking.

In the future, Israel's merit will be greater than that of the angels. Thus, they all partook and were incorporated in man's image.

163) **Whereby the engagement in Torah and Mitzvot Lishma** [for Her name], Israel are rewarded with actually adhering unto Him, and His Divinity dresses in them until they perform the same deeds as the Creator: reviving dead,

bringing down rains, and sustaining heaven and earth. In that respect, they are completely like Him, as it is written, "By Your actions we know You." However, they attain all that only by complete and whole faith, and they do not even contemplate attaining Him with their wisdom, as do the sages of the !nations.

175) By the breaking of the *Kelim* of *Kedusha* and their falling into the separated *BYA*, sparks of *Kedusha* fell into the *Klipot*. From them, all sorts of pleasures and fancies come into the domain of the *Klipot*, for the sparks transfer them into man's reception and for his pleasure. By that, they cause all kinds of transgressions, such as theft, robbery, and murder.

However, we were also given Torah and *Mitzvot*. Thus, even if one begins to engage in them in *Lo Lishma*, for one's own delight, to satisfy one's base desires, according to the powers of the breaking of the vessels, he will eventually come to *Lishma* through them and will be rewarded with the purpose of creation—to receive all the delight and pleasure in the thought of creation in order to bestow contentment upon Him.

175) One should always engage in Torah and *Mitzvot*, even *Lo Lishma* [not for Her name]

because from *Lo Lishma* he comes to *Lishma* [for Her name]. This is so because for man's lowness, he cannot engage in *Mitzvot* in order to bestow contentment upon his Maker right from the start. Rather, by his nature he can make any movement only if it is for his own benefit. For this reason, first he must engage in *Mitzvot Lo Lishma*, out of his own benefit. And yet, during the act of *Mitzvot*, he extends abundance of *Kedusha* [holiness/sanctity], and through the abundance that he extends, he will eventually come to engage in *Mitzvot Lishma*, in order to bring contentment to his Maker.

183) **The prayer that we pray is the correction of the Holy Divinity**, to extend abundance to her, to satisfy all her deficiencies. Hence, all the requests are in plural form, such as "And grant us knowledge from You," or "Bring us back, our Father, into Your law."

This is so because the prayer is for the whole of Israel, since all that there is in the holy Divinity exists in the whole of Israel. And what is lacking in her is lacking in the whole of Israel. It follows that when we pray for the whole of Israel, we pray for the Holy Divinity, since they are the same. Thus, before the prayer, we must look into the deficiencies in Divinity, to know what needs to be corrected and filled in her.

184) **Abraham is the root of *Hesed* in the souls of Israel,** since he is the one who corrected the holy Divinity into a receptacle for the light of *Hesed*. She received the *Hassadim* for all the souls of Israel in their fullest. Had it remained so, all of Israel would have been adhered to the Creator permanently, and the holy Divinity would be the house of *Malchut*, filled with every delight and pleasure, and not a single person would wish to part from her for even a minute.

However, Abraham's entire correction consisted of making a complete receptacle for the light of *Hassadim*, without any possibility of a flaw. In other words, he elevated the holy Divinity into bestowal and contentment upon our Maker, and to not receive anything for our own delight, for this is the quality and the receptacle of the light of *Hesed*. It is written about it, "Anyone who says 'What is mine is yours and what is yours is yours— a *Hassid* [from the word *Hesed*],' for he does not demand anything for his own pleasure.

And since all the restrictions and the whole of the grip of the *Sitra Achra* are only in reception for oneself, it follows that by that, he entirely removed the scum of the *Klipot* and the *Sitra Achra*, and Divinity has been established in complete purity. However, that still did not complete the thought of creation, since the essence of the thought of creation was to delight His creatures, and the measure of pleasure depends and is measured only by the amount of the desire to receive, where by the amount of the desire to receive, so is the measure of pleasure from reception.

Hence, once Divinity has been corrected only in a vessel of bestowal, without any reception for oneself at all, which is the departure from reception for the Creator and giving only to Him, still no correction has come from that to the basic thought of creation, which comes only by the greatness of the desire to receive.

This is the meaning of Abraham's begetting of Isaac. Once Isaac found Divinity in utter wholeness and fulfillment with the light of *Hesed* through Abraham's corrections, he felt the deficiency in her, that she was still unfit for reception of all that is included in the thought of creation. For this reason, he went and corrected her into a receptacle so she will be fit to receive that desired fullness in the thought of creation. He evoked the desire to receive from the Creator, too, but only in reception in order to bestow. This means that he has a great desire to receive, but only because the Giver wishes it. Had the Giver not wished for it, there would have been no desire in him to receive anything from Him.

It is known that reception in order to bestow is regarded as actual bestowal. Thus, the *Sitra Achra* still has no grip there, in this will to receive. For this reason, the holy Divinity was established by him in the last, great wholeness, for now she was fit to receive all the pleasantness and softness from all that the Creator contemplated to delight His creatures when they arose in the mind to create them.

For this reason, now the holy Divinity is called "His holy Temple," for now the King is in her with all his grandeur and splendor, like a king in his palace.

185) **Rabbi Pinhas was usually before Rabbi Rehumai, by the shore of the Sea of Galilee.** A great and elderly man was Rabbi Rehumai, and his eyes grew weak. He said to Rabbi Pinhas, "Indeed, I heard that Yochai, our friend, has a gem, a good stone, a son. I looked in the light of that gem and it is as the illumination of the sun from its sheath, illuminating the entire world."

Explanation: *Malchut* in all her corrections is called "a good stone," and she is called "a gem." He says, "Yochai, our friend, has a gem, a good stone, a son," meaning he has already been rewarded with *Malchut*, with all her corrections and adornments. He looked in the spirit of holiness, in the light of the gem, that it was as illuminating as the light of the sun upon its exit from its sheath, which is the correction of *Malchut's* future, so the light of the moon will be as the light of the sun, that then she illuminates the entire world.

And behold, after the light of *Malchut* became the light of the sun and her peak rose to heaven, she illuminated from the heaven to the earth in another pillar of light, to the entire world. He was illuminating and going until it was enough for Rabbi Shimon to properly correct the throne of *Atik Yomin*. The intimation is that he was already rewarded with the two disclosures at the end of correction. These are the six verses from the verse, "The heavens tell," to "The law of the Lord is whole," and the six names that are written from the verse, "And there is nothing hidden from its heat," through the end of the psalm. This is so because the light standing from the heaven to the earth and illuminating the entire world implies to the six verses, and until *Atik Yomin* comes and properly sits on the throne, it indicates those six names.

188) It said, "Rabbi Shimon Bar Yochai has come out of the cave with his son, Rabbi Elazar." Rabbi Pinhas went to him and found that he has changed. His body was filled with holes and sores from sitting in the cave. He wept over him and said, "Woe that I have seen you so." Rabbi Shimon told him, "Happy I am that you have seen me so, for had you not seen me so, I would not be so." Rabbi Shimon started with the *Mitzvot* of the Torah and said, "All the *Mitzvot* of the Torah that the Creator gave to Israel are written in the Torah in a general way."

Commentary: For all the years that he had to dwell in a cave, he had to sit there inside the sand to cover his nakedness and engage in Torah, and his flesh was punctured and with sores because of it. Rabbi Pinhas wept over him and said, "Woe unto me that I have seen you so." Rabbi Shimon replied to him, "Happy I am that you have seen me so, for had you not seen me so, I would not be so," meaning I would not have been rewarded with the revelations of the secrets of the Torah, for he was awarded all the great sublimity of his wisdom during those 13 years of hiding in the cave.

189) **"In the beginning God created."** This is the very first *Mitzva* [commandment]. This *Mitzva* is called "the fear of God," and it is called *Resheet* [beginning/head], as in "The fear of the Lord is the *Resheet* [beginning] of wisdom." It is also written, "The fear of the Lord is the *Resheet* [beginning] of knowledge," since fear is called *Resheet*. Also, it is the gate by which to enter faith, and the whole world exists on this *Mitzva*.

Why is it written that fear is the beginning of wisdom and that it is the beginning of knowledge? It is because fear is the beginning of each and every *Sefira*, for no *Sefira* can be obtained if not by first obtaining fear.

This is why he says that it is the gate by which to enter faith, as it is impossible to obtain whole faith if not out of fear of God. And by the measure of fear is the measure of the installment of faith. For this reason, the whole world exists on this *Mitzva*, for the world exists only on Torah and *Mitzvot*, as it is written, "If not My covenant day and night, I would not put the ordinances of heaven and earth."

And since fear is the beginning and the gate of every *Mitzva*, as it is the gate of faith, it follows that the whole world exists on fear, as it is written, "In the beginning God created the heaven and the earth." With fear, which is called *Resheet*, in which all the *Mitzvot* are included, God created the heaven and the earth. And were it not for fear, God would not create a thing.

191) There are three manners in the fear of God, only one of which is considered real fear:

When fearing punishments of Hell, as well.

1. Fear of the Creator and keeping His *Mitzvot* so that his sons may live and he will be kept from bodily punishment or a punishment to one's money. This is a fear of punishments in this world.

2. All my perception occurs within my soul. My soul is my world and the world outside of me is so abstract that I can't even say for sure if it exists or not.

Those two are not real fear, for he does not keep the fear because of the commandment of the Creator, but because of his own benefit. It follows that his own benefit is the root, and fear is a derived branch of his own benefit.

3. Fear, which is the most important, when one fears one's Master because He is great and rules over everything, the essence and the root of all the worlds, and everything is considered nothing compared to Him, for He is the root from which all the worlds expand. Also, His glory appears over all His deeds, and He rules over everything because all the worlds He has created, upper and lower, are considered nothing compared to Him, for they add nothing to His essence.

It was said, "And he will place his will in that place, which is called 'fear,'" meaning he will place his heart and desires in that place, which is called "fear." He will cling to the fear of the Creator willingly and voluntarily, as is befitting and proper with the King's commandment.

198) **The second commandment is a commandment to which the commandment of fear clings** and which it never leaves: it is love— that one should love one's Master with whole love. And what is whole love? It is great love, as it is written, "Walk before Me and be whole." "Whole" means whole with love.

When it is written, "And God said, 'Let there be light,'" it is whole love, which is called "great love." And here it is a commandment for one to love one's Master properly.

This is so because there is conditioned love, which comes because of the good that the Creator has given to him, by which his soul clings to Him with heart and soul. And although he is completely adhered to the Creator, it is still considered incomplete love, as it is written, "Noah walked with God." This means that Noah needed support to assist him because he was supported by all the good that the Creator had bestowed upon him.

Abraham, however, did not need support, as it is written, "Walk before Me and be whole." "Walk before Me" means without support, but "Before Me," even though you do not know if I will come after you to support you. This is whole love, great love, where although I am not giving you anything, your love will still be whole, to adhere to Me with all your heart and soul.

200-201) **The love for the Creator is interpreted on both sides:** There is one who loves Him so as to have wealth, long life, sons around him, rule over his enemies, his ways are firm, and thus, he loves Him. And if it were to the contrary, and the Creator would reverse the fortune upon him with harsh judgment, he would hate Him and not love Him at all. For this reason, this love is not love that has a foundation.

Complete love is love on both sides, whether in *Din*, or in *Hesed* and successful ways. He will love the Creator even if He takes His soul away from Him. This love is complete, for it is on both sides, in *Hesed* and in *Din*. Hence, the light of the act of creation came out, and was then concealed. When it became concealed, the harsh *Din* came out and the two sides, *Hesed* and *Din*, were included together, becoming whole...This is so because now it became possible to disclose the wholeness of His love even while He takes one's soul away from him. Thus, room was given to complement the love in a way that had it not been hidden and the harsh *Din* had not been revealed, this great love would have been devoid of the righteous, and it never would have been possible for it to become disclosed.

204) **The third commandment is to know that there is a great and ruling God in the world, and to properly unify Him each day, in the upper six edges,** HGT NHY *de* ZA, **make them one**

unification in the six words of "Hear O Israel," and aim the desire with them upward. For this reason, the word "One" should be extended to the measure of six words.

The Zohar says two things: 1) We must know that there is a great and ruling God in the world. 2) Properly unify Him each day. This is so because first we must know those two sides in love—upper *AVI* and *YESHSUT*. That there is a great God, upper *AVI*, who is great in *Hassadim*, and that He is ruling in the world, *YESHSUT*, who is called "ruler," which implies to the *Dinim* that come out of them, that the light was concealed from them and the harsh *Din* comes out, since the name ruling and governing indicates *Dinim*.

The meaning is that we should know those two sides of love, and include fear in each of them, and he will receive the love of the Creator, both in *Hesed* and success of his ways, and in *Din*, since then it is regarded as complete love.

Afterwards, each day, a proper unification must be made in the six upper edges, to raise *MAN* to *ZON*, and *ZON* to *YESHSUT*. At that time, *YESHSUT* and *ZON* rise and unite as one with *AVI*, who are called six upper edges, as they clothe *VAK de AA*, where by this unification, *YESHSUT* rise in the place of *AVI*, above *Parsa de AA*, where there is upper water, and the light is not hidden from them. And when *YESHSUT* are filled with light, they give to ZON, ZON give to all the worlds, and the *Hassadim* appear in the worlds. This is the meaning of the reading of *Shema*.

211) **Yet, we should know that *Elokim* is *HaVaYaH* and it is one without separation. *HaVaYaH* is the *Elokim* ["The Lord He is the God], and when a person knows that it is all one, and does not place separation, even the other side will depart from the world and will not be drawn down.**

...This is so because if a person intensifies the raising of *MAN* and elevating the ZON to unite them in the place of *AVI*, as it should be, not only will the *Sitra Achra* not grip to the abundance, but it will cause the removal of the *Sitra Achra* so that she cannot govern the world.

217) **It is impossible to cling to the Creator and keep His *Mitzvot* properly before one believes in the names of the Creator, that He is good and does good to all, that He is merciful and gracious.** Those who have not been rewarded

with a *Nefesh* of *Kedusha* are still governed by the *Sitra Achra*. Hence, they go and roam the world and cannot find a place to rest.

When their thoughts roam the world and they see the Creator's guidance in people, they believe it is not as good as it should be, judging by His holy names. Thus, they blemish the holy names and find no place to rest where they can believe in the names of the Creator, to connect to Him. For this reason, they are defiled in the side of *Tuma'a* [impurity], meaning they come to deny the Creator. All that is because he did not enter the *Kedusha* and was not included in her, since he was not rewarded with a *Nefesh* of *Kedusha* and does not take actions to be included in *Kedusha*.

However, those who engage in Torah and extend a holy *Nefesh*, their body turns to be as angels and they are rewarded with preceding hearing to doing, as they do. This is why it is written about them, "And let fowl fly above the earth," meaning that the Creator will make wings for them, like eagles, and they will roam throughout the world, as they roam in their thoughts throughout the world and see the Creator's guidance.

And yet, not only are they not failing to the side of *Tuma'a*, they even receive strength to raise MAN and always increase their power. And "Those who wait for the Lord will gain new strength; they will mount up with wings like eagles," for thus they mount up wings like eagles to roam in all the people's incidents. Also, they always regain strength and raise MAN through the power of their faith in the Creator's uniqueness, and always extend the spirit of *Kedusha* from above.

BERESHEET

[GENESIS]

BERESHEET ALEPH [GENESIS 1]

1) "Before the emanations were emanated and the creatures were created, the upper simple light had filled the whole reality. And there was no vacancy" for the existence of the emanated and the created. "And there was no such part as *Rosh* or *Sof*, but all was simple light, equal in one similitude, and it is called "the light of *Ein Sof*." And when upon His simple will came the desire to create the worlds and emanate the emanations," the harsh spark came out, the force of *Din* that was disclosed in *Malchut*, emerging from *Ein Sof*, and carved a carving in the upper light. Thus, the light was restricted and departed from within the *Kli* of *Malchut* and around her. That departure of light is called "carving the upper light," for a space devoid of light was made there. And in that empty space, all the worlds and all that is in them subsequently emerged.

3) **And therefore, once people in this world raise MAN through *Mitzvot* and good deeds,** they extend a new illumination from above, which lowers the *Malchut* and the place of the *Zivug* back to her place, below *Tifferet*, and a complete degree comes out, *NRNHY*, received in

the *Sefirot Bina* and *Tifferet* that were previously included in *Malchut*, and which are fit for reception of upper light. Then the souls of the righteous, too, receive the upper *Mochin* from ZON *de Atzilut* because they are included in the upper *Malchut*.

Thus, all the *Mochin* are only because of *Malchut* that rose to *Bina*, making a new *Sium* there, called a "firmament." Were it not for the firmament, ZON would not be able to receive any of the upper light. This is why the text calls those *Mochin* "The brightness of the firmament," meaning the light that appears at the end of the association of *Rachamim* with *Din*. It is written, "And the educated," meaning ZON and the souls of the righteous, "Will shine as the brightness of the firmament," receive *Mochin* that illuminate like the brightness of the firmament, since all of their *Mochin* comes from the brightness of the firmament.

82) A man is male and female, and only they are called "man." *Malchut* in and of herself, when she is not in a *Zivug* with ZA, is not called "man," since she is without a male. Only when she mates with ZA are both of them called "man," as it is written, "He created them male and female,

and blessed them, and called their name Adam [man], on the day when they were created." Thus, both together are called "man," but each one for himself is like half a body, and he is not called "man."

110) **Happy are those who observe their desires, matters of the sublime secrets, to walk in the path of truth,** to be rewarded in this world and to illuminate for them for the next world. It is written about them, "And the enlightened ones will shine like the brightness of the firmament, and those who justify the many, like the stars forever and ever" are happy in this world and in the next world.

Those who cling to the Creator in truth, their desire guides them to advance in their work as it is established above, in the upper worlds, as it is written, "And Abram went as the Lord had commanded him." Hence, later, when they observe their desire, they know the sublime secrets, for they look into the tendencies in their own desire and know how the sublime secrets are determined above. (*New Zohar, Beresheet,* item 110)

121) Man is called "a small world" because all the details of the world are included in him.

159) In the verse, "And God said, 'Let us make man,'" there is a secret revealed only to those who fear Him. That elder of the elders started and said, "Shimon, Shimon, who is it who said, 'Let us make man,' and of whom is it written, 'And God said'? Who is that name 'God' here?" As Rabbi Shimon heard that he was calling him Shimon and not Rabbi Shimon, he said to his friends, "This must be the Creator, of whom it is written, 'And the ancient of days [*Atik Yomin*] is sitting.' Therefore, now is the time to disclose that secret, for there is a secret here that was not permitted to be disclosed, and now it means that permission to disclose has been given."

It is known that the secrets that were revealed to the sages of *The Zohar* were by attainment of the lights of the upper degrees by instilling. There are *Panim* and *Achoraim* [anterior and posterior respectively] in them, meaning concealment and disclosure. According to the extent of the *Panim* of the degree, so is the extent of its *Achoraim*. The instilling of the *Achoraim* is a calling and an invitation to instill the *Panim*. This is why by the measure of the concealment of the *Achoraim* that they attained, they knew the measure of disclosure that they were about to attain.

As Rabbi Shimon heard, he was calling him Shimon and not Rabbi Shimon. This means that the instilling of the *Achoraim*, which is a calling, was so strong that he lost all his degrees and became a simple person, Shimon from the market. By that, he recognized that it was a calling and an invitation for very high attainment of *Panim*.

This is why he promptly said to his friends, "This must be the Creator, of whom it is written, 'And the ancient of days [*Atik Yomin*] is sitting,'" of whose degree there is no higher. And he said, "And now it means that permission to disclose has been given," meaning that now it was seen that he obtained permission to disclose that high secret.

169) The verse, "Let us make man" certainly relates to two, for each lower one said to the superior above it, "Let us make man." The lower one does not do anything without receiving permission and saying of that *Partzuf* that is above it. Likewise, its superior does not do anything until it receives an advice from his friend above him, so that each and every *Partzuf* from the *Partzufim* of *Atzilut* said, "Let us make man" to his superior, and the superior to the superior of the superior, for every novelty and emanation comes from *Ein Sof* and cascades through the

degrees until it comes to its place. The cascading is considered here that each lower one says, "Let us make man" to his superior when he receives from him the soul of man, to pass it on to the ones below him.

175) The words, "I, I am He" apply to the Creator and His Divinity, ZA and his *Nukva*. "I" is Divinity. "He" is the Creator. In the future, at the end of correction, the *Nukva* will say, "See that I," *Vav-Hey-Vav* are one, as it is written, "And the light of the moon shall be as the light of the sun," meaning that the *Nukva* is equal to ZA.

"And there is no God with Me" refers to other gods, SAM and the serpent, for then it will be revealed that SAM and the serpent never separated between the Creator and His Divinity, as it is written, "By the mouth of two witnesses ... shall he that is to die be put to death," relating to SAM, who was dead from his beginning and was but a servant to hurry the redemption of our souls.

This is the meaning of "I will put to death and make alive." I will put to death with My Divinity the one who is guilty, and I will make alive with my Divinity the one who is innocent. The Creator's guidance from the beginning will appear throughout the world, and then, as it is written, "Sinners will cease from the earth, and the wicked shall be no more." That is, unlike what it seems to us during the 6,000 years, that there is a governance that objects to *Kedusha*, which are *SAM* and the serpent, as it is written, "When man rules over man it is to his harm," then it will appear to all—"I will put to death and make alive" with My Divinity, and there is none else besides Him.

180-181) The friends replied to him: "Why then is all that? Meaning, if the whole reason for the creation of man is that he can repent and correct his corruption, then what is all that for? It would have been better not to create the darkness in the *Nukva*, and the man would not sin to begin with."

Rabbi Shimon replied to the friends: "Were it not so, that the Creator created the good inclination and the evil inclination, which are light and darkness, there would not be *Mitzvot* and transgressions for Adam *de Beria*. But Adam [the man] was created from both, from light and darkness, which is why the writing says, "See, I have set before you this day life and good, and death and evil," meaning this is why there are

Mitzvot and transgressions in man, and the choice has been prepared for him, to choose between good and evil."

They replied to him: "What is all that for? It would be better if the darkness were not created and there would not be reward or punishment for man, rather than being created, sinning, and causing all those many corruptions that he has caused by his sin."

He said to them, "It was right to create him in light and in darkness because the Torah was created for the man, for punishment to the wicked and reward for the righteous are written in it, and there cannot be reward and punishment unless in Adam *de Beria*, who consists of light and darkness, as it is written, 'He created it not a waste, He formed it to be inhabited.' That is, the world was not created to be in chaos, in darkness, for the wicked. Rather, 'He formed it to be inhabited,' to give a good reward to the righteous.

"The reward is the attainment of the Torah, as it is written, 'For the earth shall be full of the knowledge of the Lord,' since the Torah and the Creator are one. And if the man were not created in light and darkness, in which choice between good and bad and reward and punishment are possible, it would not be possible for that good reward that is received in the Torah, and for which it was created, to be revealed to the righteous."

The friends told him: "Indeed, we heard now what we have not heard thus far. Now it is clear that the Creator did not create something that He does not need."

198) Sons, life, and nourishments extend to the lower ones only from the middle pillar, called "My son, My firstborn, Israel." He is called "the tree of life," meaning that the middle pillar, Israel, bestows upon Divinity for the lower ones. Bestowals of life to Divinity are the lower children of Israel who extend their lives from Divinity, and the giving of the secrets of Torah for the lower ones is considered Divinity's nourishments. The prayer, which is her *Zivug* with ZA, extends sons, who are souls, for the lower ones. It is about her that he says, "Give me sons."

200) Rabbi Shimon started and said, "Listen, O upper ones, and gather, O lower ones, dwellers of the seminary of above and of below. Elijah, I adjure you, take permission from the Creator and come down here, for a great war has come to

you. Hanoch, Matat, come down here, you and all the dwellers of the seminary under you, for it is not for my own glory that I did this, but for the glory of Divinity."

Those righteous ones, the authors of *The Zohar*, and especially Rabbi Shimon, their thoughts and words were in actual deeds, for according to the quality of the innovations in the Torah that they discovered, the upper degrees were promptly set up and arranged after them in actual fact, for the righteous build worlds with their innovations in the Torah. And Rabbi Shimon prepared himself here to fight with the primordial serpent and subdue him through the unification of the sling-stone, and to open a door for the people of the world, so they too would know how to subdue the serpent.

It is known that one cannot correct in a place where he is not present. Thus, Rabbi Shimon had to be at that time in the place where the serpent was so he would be able to subdue him. To be certain that he would not be at risk in that lowly place, he asked for assistance from Elijah, Matat, dwellers of the upper seminary and the lower one.

201) The prayer should be raised to that certain place. Like a sling-stone hurled toward a certain

target, and one is careful not to miss the target so he should raise his thought and aim in the prayer.

218) It is written, "Let the waters under the heavens gather." "Let the waters ... gather" is the Torah, called "water." "Unto one place" is Israel. It is so because the souls of Israel extend from that place, of which it was said, "Blessed be the glory of the Lord from His place." "The glory of the Lord" means the lower Divinity, *Malchut*. "From His place" means the upper Divinity, *Bina*. Thus, *Bina* is called "a place," and because their souls are from *Bina*, who is called "a place," the name *HaVaYaH* is indeed on them. It is said about them, "For the portion of the Lord is His people," as it is written, "Let the waters gather unto one place," where water means Torah, and "One place" means Israel, the receivers of the Torah. To elicit the nations of the world, who did not wish to receive the Torah, and for which the land remained desolate and dry.

255) The Torah is called water, as it is written, "There is no water but the Torah." The origin of the Torah is the two tablets of the testimony, which are *Bina* and *Malchut*. This is why they are called "Two stone tablets," as they spring water, the Torah. Israel received the first tablets in

full, as it will be at the end of correction, as it is written, "'It is *Harut* [engraved] on the tablets,' do not pronounce it *Harut*, but *Herut* [freedom], that they will be freed from the angel of death," as it will be at the end of correction. Yet, through the sin of the calf, they corrupted the correction, and the dominion of the angel of death returned over them, the tablets broke, and they were given second tablets—of life and death.

The whole correction is only by extending the light of Torah, since through the *MAN* that Israel raise by keeping the *Mitzvot* and good deeds, they cause upper *Zivugim* that gradually reveal the light of Torah to Israel until they are rewarded by it with the end of correction.

255) At the end of correction, when *SAM* is revoked, it will appear to all that *SAM* never lived. Rather, unification was always the governor, as it is written, "There is none else besides Him."

260) As with *Adam HaRishon* whom He elevated in *Gadlut* from the separated *BYA* to the Garden of Eden of *Atzilut*, so will the Creator do to a person who repents and engages in Torah.

280) It is known that the Emanator initiated creation and established it in a way that the

children of Israel could finish it, as it is written, "You are in partnership with Me," I began creation and you finish it.

The Emanator corrected *Malchut* only in the first nine in her, and He gave the correction of *Malchut de Malchut* to Israel, so that they would correct her through work and keeping of the upper nine. Therefore, the whole of the work of Israel prior to the end of correction is only in *Malchut's* first nine, regarded as sorting of 288 sparks that were corrected through the Emanator.

The two Temples were built above in that respect—first *Hey* and bottom *Hey*—and likewise below. For this reason, they are considered to have been built by people, through the work of people who were appointed to complete creation. And because the last 32 sparks that belong to *Malchut de Malchut* were still not corrected, the *Sitra Achra* and the mixed multitude are among them, making Israel sin. This is why the two Temples were ruined.

However, after the children of Israel sort all 288 sparks due to the breaking of the vessels, the Creator Himself will sort the last 32 sparks from *Malchut de Malchut*, which are called "The stony heart," as it is written, "And I will remove the stony heart from your flesh." Then *Malchut de Malchut*, the last Temple, will be corrected, as it is written, "Unless the Lord builds the house," meaning prior to the end of correction, when the work was given to people and by which the two Temples were built, "They who build it labor in vain," for they were ruined. But after people complete the correction given to them, the Creator will lower the built Jerusalem, meaning *Malchut de Malchut*, as well as the built Temple, the internality of *Malchut de Malchut*, and then it will be an everlasting building for eternity.

294-295) Until the Creator created the world, His name was hidden in Him, and He and His hidden name within Him were one. His name is *Malchut*. Prior to creation, she was included and hidden in *Ein Sof* without any disclosure and recognition. At that time, He and His hidden name within Him were one, and nothing was revealed until He wished to create the world. He would inscribe and build worlds, but they were unsustainable and were ruined. The worlds that emerged from *Malchut* during *Tzimtzum Aleph* are called "worlds of *Tohu* [chaos]," and the breaking of the vessels was in them, which are the ruins of those worlds.

It was said about them, "In the beginning, the world was created in *Midat ha Din*," *Malchut de Tzimtzum Aleph*, called *Midat ha Din*. "He saw that the world could not exist," that they were ruined, "He associated *Midat ha Rachamim* with it," meaning that the Creator, *Bina*, wrapped in a wrapping of light and created the world, raising *Malchut* to her, and her light was diminished because of it to *VAK*, called "enveloped light." At that time *Midat ha Din*, *Malchut*, partook with *Midat ha Rachamim*, *Bina*, and by that the world existed.

He elicited the great high cedars out of that enveloped light, from that upper brightness, which afterwards extended *GAR* to the above mentioned enveloped light once more, and placed His *Merkava* on 22 inscribed letters. These are *ZON*, since the letters *ELEH de Bina*—which descend from her to *ZON* during *Katnut*, and during the *Gadlut* of *Bina*, she brings them back to her—are regarded as a *Merkava* [chariot/assembly] that journeys to and fro. He placed His *Merkava* on 22 letters, meaning *ZON* in *Katnut*, and later, in *Gadlut*, *ZON* were carved in ten utterances, which mean *Mochin de GAR*. Then they settled and were properly corrected.

309) The *Nukva* is nourished by the male, since the *Nukva* has nothing of her own, and receives from the male the nourishments, the abundance for her sustenance, as well as the begetting of the souls.

348) "And God said, 'Let there be light.'" This is the light that the Creator created in the beginning, the light of the eyes, the light that the Creator showed *Adam HaRishon*, in which he saw from the end of the world to its end. It is the light that the Creator showed to David, which he would praise and say, "How plentiful is Your goodness, which You have hidden for those who fear You." It is also the light that the Creator showed to Moses, and in which he saw from Gilad to Dan, the whole of the land of Israel.

424) The awakening always begins from the lower to the upper, and then everything is completed. Above, too, each lower degree raises MAN to its adjacent superior, and the superior to the super-superior, all raising MAN, first up to the highest of all, and then the abundance pours from *Ein Sof* from above downward, descending from degree to degree, from each superior to its inferior until they arrive at the bottom. Thus, with respect to the MAN, each lower one precedes its upper one.

And with respect to MAD—the *Mochin* poured down from above—each upper one precedes its lower one. If the Assembly of Israel, the *Nukva*, were not initially awakened, ZA would not have awakened above opposite her. By the craving below, it is completed above.

424) As long as the *Nukva* does not raise MAN to ZA, ZA has no need to extend *Mochin* from AA. But after *Nukva* raises MAN he extends the *Mochin* of illumination of *Hochma* from AA for her and they obtain the *Mochin* of PBP [face-to-face].

472-473) A book was lowered to *Adam HaRishon*. In it, he knew and attained the supernal wisdom. The writing says about it, "This is the book of the generations of Adam." This book comes to the children of God, the sages of the generation. Anyone who is rewarded with looking in it knows the supernal wisdom in it, and they look in it and attain in it. The one with the secrets, Angel Raziel, lowered it to *Adam HaRishon* in the Garden of Eden, and three appointed angels before him were guarding the book lest the outer ones grip it.

When Adam left the Garden of Eden he was still holding that book. When he went outside, the book left him. He prayed and cried before his Master and He returned it to him as before so the wisdom would not be forgotten from people and they would engage in order to know their Master.

482) The Creator is destined to correct the world and correct the spirit of life in people in a way that they live forever, as it is written, "He shall swallow up death forever."

New Zohar, Beresheet Aleph [Genesis 1]

110) Those who cling to the Creator in truth, their desire guides them to advance in their work as it is established above, in the upper worlds, as it is written, "And Abram went as the Lord had commanded him." Hence, later, when they observe their desire, they know the sublime secrets, for they look into the tendencies in their own desire and know how the sublime secrets are determined above.

327) Rabbi Akiva wept. He told him, "Why are you crying?" He replied, "Woe unto a generation that will be orphaned of you."

He told him, "Do not say this, but rather, 'Woe unto a generation that will be orphaned without a father, without a sage teacher or a contemplating disciple.' Days will come when the whole generation is impudent and insolent, the Torah is forgotten, and no one demands or seeks, and one whose heart awakens in the Torah is despised and considered worthless. Woe unto that generation when that generation comes."

771) Happy are the righteous, who are called "Life for the next world." Is it because the soul remains existing that the righteous are considered living? But does the body decay in the earth even though it is complete and righteous? The soul always exists. Death and life do not apply to it. Only in the body are there death and life.

2-3) The Creator crowned *Adam HaRishon* with high crowns, with *Mochin de GAR*, and created him in the six edges of the world, in *Mochin de VAK*, so he would be complete in everything. All the animals dreaded and feared him because when *Adam HaRishon* was created, he was created in the high form, and the people would look at that form and dread and fear him.

Afterwards, the Creator admitted him into the Garden of Eden to be refined there in sublime delights. High angels surrounded him, served him, and informed him the secrets of their Master. When the Creator admitted him into the Garden of Eden, he saw and beheld from there all the high secrets and all the wisdom so he would be able to know and to behold the glory of his Master. All of it came to *Adam HaRishon* because he was created in the upper form, that of *Bina*.

7) Those who attain the *Malchut* in the palaces are the righteous who did not replace the glory of their Master with other gods, who attain the *Malchut*, as it is written, "A virtuous woman is the crown of her husband." It is so because the

power of *Malchut's* faith is that one who attains it is rewarded with *Dvekut* [adhesion] with his Maker, with always fearing Him, and never straying to the right or to the left.

24) The palace of the Hassidim [pious] whose quality is "What's mine is yours and what's yours is yours," meaning to bestow and not to receive.

That palace is superior to all the palaces because the degree of *Hesed* is the highest of the six *Sefirot HGT NHY*. It is a palace that stands above all the palaces. It is impossible to be rewarded with that palace unless one has been completed in all the degrees in the palaces below. It is considered as though he was relying and standing over their degrees. It is the palace of the right because the degree of *Hesed* is considered the right line and there is no one to attain it except for those holy Hassidim and all those who love their Master with great love. At the palace door stand all those who unified for their Maker each day, who extend each day the disclosure of the unity of the Creator from *Ein Sof* to the *Sefirot* and to all the worlds. They are the first to rise from there to higher palaces.

60) Rabbi Shimon says, "I have found in the books of the ancients the order by which to tie

the degrees, which are the secrets of secrets, in one connection, meaning the explanations of the seven palaces."

A connection means unification of two degrees or more in one another so they illuminate together in a joint illumination to the lower ones. Sometimes, the prayer must be ordered properly and unify unifications to mitigate and appease his Master properly, to tear the firmaments and to open the gates and the doors, and there will be no one to protest against him, meaning that the slanderers will not be able to slander him.

Firmaments mean ends of *Tzimtzum Bet* that halve the degrees and leave them in *VAK* without *GAR*. The three worlds *BYA* came out of *Atzilut* and became the worlds of separation, as well as the constant, except when the righteous raise *MAN* through work and good deeds, extending illumination of *Tzimtzum Aleph* from above, from *Tabur de AK*. At that time that illumination lowers the firmament from the place of *Bina* back to the place of *Malchut*, as she is in *Tzimtzum Aleph*, and *Bina* and *TM de Kelim* return to their degree, complementing the ten *Sefirot de Kelim* and *GAR* of lights. Likewise, the three worlds *BYA* become *Atzilut* once more.

Thus, through their work, the righteous cancel the boundaries of *Katnut*, called "firmaments," and extend the *Mochin de Gadlut*. That matter is considered that they tear the firmaments, as it was said, "To tear the firmaments," meaning they tear and cancel the boundaries of *Katnut*, which elicit the three worlds *BYA* to separation from *Atzilut* and return them to *Atzilut*.

96-97) All the degrees need each other to complement one another and illuminate in one another until they all rise to the place that requires wholeness.

First, they rise from below to complement the upper place, then they come down from above downward to complement the lower ones, then wholeness is made from all sides, and all are completed as it should be.

One who knows these secrets and makes the wholeness above and below clings to his Master and revokes all the harsh decrees. He crowns his Master, extending *GAR* to *ZA*, and extends blessings to the world. This is the man who is called "righteous," "the pillar of the world." That is, the world stands and exists because of him. His prayer is not returned empty; he is answered in all his prayers, his portion is in the next world, and he is counted among those with faith. That is, he is counted among those with faith who are in the world.

103) It is written, "There was no joy before Him as on the day when heaven and earth were created." This means that all the people of the world are in utter wholeness, to such an extent that there has never been such joy before Him. However, a person cannot take part in that great joy unless he has made complete repentance from love. Before that, he will not rejoice at all with himself or with the people of the world. On the contrary, he feels before him a world full of sorrow and pain, and all of that came to him because he is going against the nature of creation, since the world was created only in bestowal, to engage in Torah and good deeds in order to bestow contentment to one's Maker, and not for one's own pleasure. It is written, "All the works of the Creator are for Him," so that people would bestow contentment upon Him. But in the beginning, "A man is born a wild ass' colt," whose sole interest is his own delight and who has none of the desire to bestow. He argues, "All the works of the Creator are for me, for my own delight," since he wishes to devour the entire world for his own good and benefit.

Hence, the Creator imprinted bitter and harsh afflictions in self-reception, instilled in man from the moment of his birth—bodily pains and emotional pains—so that if he engages in Torah and *Mitzvot* even for his own pleasure, through the light in it he will still feel the lowliness and the terrible corruptness in the nature of receiving for self. At that time he will resolve to retire from that nature of reception and will become completely devoted to working only in order to bestow contentment upon his Maker. Then the Creator will open his eyes and he will see before him a world filled with utter perfection in which there are no deficiencies whatsoever. Then he partakes in the joy of the Creator as at the time of the creation of the world it was said, "If he is rewarded, he sentences himself and the entire world favorably," for wherever he casts his eyes, he sees only good and only perfection, and he does not see any faults at all in the works of the Creator, only merits.

103) There are two ways in the corporeal and spiritual afflictions that a man suffers before he repents:

1. All that the Creator does, He does for the best. He sees that were it not

for the terrible pains that he suffered for being immersed in the nature of reception for himself, he would never have been rewarded with repentance. Therefore, he blesses for the bad as he blesses for the good, since without the bad he would not be rewarded with the good, as well. It follows that all are causing good.

2. That, too, is for the best. Not only did the evils that were done cause good, but even the evils themselves have turned into good through very great lights that the Creator illuminates through all those evils until they are inverted into goods—both the bodily afflictions and the emotional afflictions, which are the transgressions. Thus, the demerits have been inverted and have taken on the form of merits.

124-125) The sixth palace is the spirit, called "the scarlet thread."

The spirit is the will that all those lower spirits chase in order to obtain and cling to it with a kiss of love. That palace is the palace of desire, since it is the desire of all, the one who ties ties, who unifies unifications and raises the lower palaces to that palace. It is he who yields good will from the Creator with love.

140) One who knows how to tie that unification is happy. He is loved above and loved below; the Creator sentences and he revokes.

Is it conceivable that the righteous would slander his Master's will, that he would revoke the will of the Creator? It is not. Rather, when the righteous ties ties and knows how to unify unifications, all the faces illuminate and all the wholeness is found, and everything is blessed properly, all the *Dinim* are removed and cancelled, and there is no *Din* in the world. Happy is he in this world and in the next world. It follows that the meaning of the Creator sentencing and the righteous revoking is through many lights that the righteous extends through the unifications that he makes, and those lights cancel the decrees and *Dinim* from the world. Everything we said about the righteous is what he does below in this world. This is why it is written about him, "A righteous is the foundation of the•world," since the righteous is the existence of the world.

141-143) The priests extend right and the Levites extend left. One without the other is incomplete.

A palace enters a palace, spirit in spirit, until all bond in their rightful places, organ to organ, rising to *Atzilut*, to ZON, and each *Behina* of ZA bonds with its corresponding *Behina* in the palaces, and they complement one another through *Zivug de Yesodot*. They unite in one another until they become one through *Zivug de Neshikin* [a coupling of kissing] and illuminate in one another through the embrace.

Then the highest soul of all comes from above and illuminates upon them, and all the candles, the *Sefirot*, shine in full as it should be, until that upper light awakens and all the palaces enter the holy of holies, the seventh palace, in a *Zivug* of seventh in seventh. The seventh palace is blessed and filled like a well of springing waters that do not stop, and all the palaces are blessed above and below.

Here is the secret of secrets, a light that is not known and does not enter the count of the ten *Sefirot*, the desire that is never captured, meaning the light of *Yechida*. It is so because the ten *Sefirot* begin with *Hochma*, *HBD HGT NHYM*, mitigated completely, and that desire is neither known nor perceived even in the thought to know it. Then all the degrees unite and become one desire through *Ein Sof*, since when the light of *Yechida* mitigates and fully clothes the degrees, all the degrees unite in its illumination and become one desire, united, through *Ein Sof*, and all is in completeness from above and from below, from the very inside, until all become one.

151) "And there was evening and there was morning." "And there was evening" extends from the side of darkness, the *Nukva*. "And there was morning" extends from the side of light, ZA. Since ZA and *Nukva* partake together in a *Zivug*, it is written about them, "One day," indicating that the evening and morning are as one body, and both make the day, meaning that the light of day comes from the *Zivug* of ZA and *Nukva* together.

Each day it is written, "And there was evening and there was morning," since it indicates *Zivug* ZON, that the light of day comes out of both. Thus, after the text notified it on the first day, what is the point that on each day, it is written, "And there was evening and there was morning"?

The text announces it to us repeatedly each day to indicate that it is impossible that it will ever happen that there will be light of day without prior darkness of the night. And likewise, there will not be darkness of the night that does not bring after it the light of day, since they never part from one another.

174) "And God saw all that He had done." Did He not see what He had done before? But it is written, "And God saw all that He had done," which means that He saw only after He had done. However, the Creator saw everything—both what He had already done, and before it was done. But the verse comes to add that He saw all the future generations and all that was to be innovated in the world in each generation, even before they would come to the world. The verse, "That He had done" means the whole work of creation because in the work of creation, the foundation and root of all that would come and be innovated in the world was created. This is why the Creator saw even before it came to be, and placed everything in the work of creation, since the work of creation is the foundation and root of all that would be. For this reason, the Creator included in them seeing all the future that would come to the world throughout the generations.

Our sages said about the verse, "And to say unto Zion, 'You are My people,'" with Me in partnership; I began the worlds and you finish them, since the Creator established the whole of reality in a way that people could complete the correction. And since the end of correction was left for people, they are partners in creation.

This is why there are two discernments in heaven and earth: 1) That which the Emanator has already corrected. This is called "the work of creation." 2) The new heaven and earth, which are to appear after the end of correction, as it is written, "The new heaven and the new earth."

176-177) The Creator created the man in the world and corrected them so he would be whole in his work and correct his ways so he would be rewarded with the upper light that the Creator had concealed for the righteous. It is written about it, "Neither has the eye seen a God besides You," meaning the hidden light, "Will do for the one who awaits Him," meaning the righteous.

By what will the man be rewarded with that hidden light? He will be rewarded with it through engagement in Torah, since anyone who engages in Torah each day will be rewarded with a part in the next world. It will be considered for him as though he built worlds, since the world was built and perfected with the Torah, as it is written, "The Lord established the earth with wisdom, set up the heaven with intelligence," the wisdom and intelligence of the Torah. It is also written, "And I was with Him as a master craftsman," meaning that the Torah was His craftsman to create the world. The Creator made the world with spirit, and the world persists with spirit, by the spirit of those who study the Torah.

189-190) In the *Shema* reading, a person should unify his Master and tie ties of faith in the heart's desire. When he reaches *Ehad* [one], he should aim in the *Aleph* of *Ehad*, which is hidden and more ancient than all, the *Sefira Keter de* ZA. In the *Het* of *Ehad* he should aim with the eight upper degrees, which are from upper *Hochma* through *Tzadik* [righteous], *Yesod*. In the big *Dalet* of *Ehad*, he should aim to cling to the Assembly of Israel, *Malchut*, David's portion, who is called "poor and meager," when *Malchut* is not attached to ZA, when she is now attached to those upper degrees implied in the *Aleph-Het* of *Ehad*, which are from *Keter* through *Yesod de* ZA. At that time *Malchut* is great, and this is implied by the big *Dalet* in *Ehad*, and the whole world nurses from her. And the breasts are as towers because the whole world nurses from them when Divinity says, "I am a wall and my breasts are as towers. Then I was in His eyes as one who has found peace."

When the Assembly of Israel, *Malchut*, is in exile with her sons among the nations of the world, she is called "small," as it is written, "We have a little sister." When Israel cling to the Torah and walk on the path of truth, *Malchut* is filled with abundance, peace, *Yesod* bonds with *Malchut*, and she replies and says, "I am a wall and my breasts are as towers," meaning they are big and full of bounty for the world. At that time, when He bonds with me, then, "And peace." He interprets the *Aleph* of *Az* [then] as the most holy *Atik*. *Keter*, the *Zayin* of *Az*, is seven degrees from *Hochma* to *Hod*, and "peace" is called *Tzadik*, *Yesod*. Because those degrees bond with me, I was in His eyes as one who has found peace. The eyes are seven degrees, ZAT *de Hochma*, called "eyes of the Lord," "Face of the Lord," and then there is peace to the world and *Hesed de Atik* is in the place of male and female, ZA and *Malchut*. This is why Moses commanded in the Torah and said, "Hear O Israel, the Lord our God, the Lord is one," tying all the ties of faith.

205) "He who marries his daughter." As long as she did not enter her husband, her father and mother fix her and give her everything she needs. Once she has connected with her husband, the

husband nourishes her and gives her what she needs. In the beginning, it is written, "And the Lord built," when AVI established her. Then it is written "And brought her to the man," to connect with one another and so the husband would give her what she needs.

217-219) "And the man said, 'This time.'" These are words of sweetness, to extend love with her and draw her to his will, to evoke love in her. See how pleasant these words are, how they evoke love. These words—"A bone of my bones, flesh of my flesh"—to show her that they are one and there is no separation whatsoever between them.

Now he began to praise her, "She shall be called 'a woman,' for there are none other like her, the glory of the house. All the women compared to her are as a monkey before a man, but she shall be called 'a woman,' she and none other." The name "woman" indicates the fire of the Lord, the wholeness of illumination of the left, called "fire," which is connected to the letter *Hey*, the *Nukva*. This is why he praised her, "She shall be called 'a woman,'" for because of the illumination of *Hochma* that illuminates in her after she has been included in her husband's *Hassadim*, she is given the name "woman," which is illumination of *Hochma*, called "fire," as it is written, "And the light of the Lord shall become fire."

It was said, "Woman" because fire is connected to *Hey* [*Esh* (fire) + *Hey* make up *Isha* (woman)]. It is her, and there are none other like her, since the illumination of *Hochma* is not revealed at any degree except hers.

"Therefore shall a man leave his father and his mother, and shall cleave unto his wife, and they shall be one flesh," to extend her with love and to cling to her, since he has been awakened toward her with all those things.

226) When he comes to his home, he should make his wife happy because it is his wife who caused him that upper *Zivug*. This is so because through the road-prayer that he prayed while still at his home, when he was in wholeness because he was in male and female, he was rewarded with the high *Zivug* on the road. Thus, his wife caused him the high *Zivug* on the road—the instilling of Divinity. When he comes to her, he should make her happy for two reasons: because of the joy of the *Zivug*, for that *Zivug* is a joy of *Mitzva*, and the joy of *Mitzva* is the joy of Divinity.

229) Disciples of the wise depart from their wives all the days of the week so they would not idle away from engagement in the Torah. The high *Zivug* mates in them and Divinity does not part from them so they would be male and female. When the Sabbath begins, the disciples of the wise must make their wives happy for the glory of the upper *Zivug*, for they cause a high *Zivug* for imparting of souls and must aim their hearts with the will of their Master.

230) Come and see. When a person is in his home, the essence of the house is his wife, since Divinity is in the house thanks to his wife.

259-266) The secret of the wisdom in the holy unification—the bottom *Hey* of the holy name, the *Nukva*—is the light of azure and black that connects in *Yod-Hey-Vav*, ZA, the illuminating white light.

Sometimes the azure light is *Dalet*, sometimes it is *Hey*. When Israel do not adhere to her below, to light her and connect her with the white light, she is regarded as the letter *Dalet*. When Israel awaken her, raising MAN to bond with the white light, she is called *Hey*.

It is written, "If there be a virgin damsel," but it writes "damsel" without a *Hey* since she did not connect to the male, and wherever there are no male and female, there is no *Hey* there. This is why it is written "damsel" without a *Hey*, and the *Hey* went up from there, leaving the *Nukva* in the letter *Dalet*, indicating meagerness and poverty.

When she unites with the illuminating white light, she is called *Hey*, since then everything is connected as one—the *Nukva* clings to the white light, and Israel cling to her, standing below her to light her through the *MAN* that *ELEH* raise. Then, everything is one because ZA and *Nukva* conjoined and Israel raise *MAN* to the *Nukva* to light her and to connect her with ZA, for without their *MAN* she would not connect. Then they bond with them as well because all the measure that the lower one causes in the upper one, it is rewarded with it, as well, and then the Creator, His Divinity, and Israel become one.

This is the offering, the smoke that rises from the fire, evoking the azure light to be lit up. When it lights, it connects to the white light. The candle, Divinity, is lit in one unification, clinging to the white light and to smoke, and the three of them become one.

And because it is the conduct of this azure light to consume and to burn all that clings below it, when there is a time of good will and the candle burns in one unification, it is written, "Then the fire of the Lord fell and consumed the burnt-offering." And then, when everything burned beneath it, it is known that the candle, Divinity, burns in one bonding and one unification, since the azure light clung to the white light, and it is one. How are they one? The azure light, the *Nukva*, connected with the white light, ZA, and both became one. Likewise, the azure light burns and consumes beneath it fats and offerings. This means that it does not consume and burn under it, but rather rises to the white light. It follows that everything—the smoke and the azure light—were connected and bonded with the white light, and then peace extended through all the worlds, and everything was connected in one unification.

And once the azure light completed burning and consuming everything beneath it, priests and Levites and Israelites come and cling to it with joy of songs—the poet Levites—with the aim of the heart—the priests—and with prayer—Israel. And the candle, Divinity, burns over them and illuminates, the lights cling as one, the worlds illuminate, and the upper and lower are blessed.

Then it is said about Israel, "And you who cleave to the Lord your God are alive everyone of you this day."

318) Where a person walks, and in that way to which he has clung, so he extends on himself an appointed force that walks opposite him. If he walks in a good way, he extends upon him an appointed force from the side of *Kedusha* that assists him. If he walks in a bad way, he extends upon him an evil force from the side of *Tuma'a* that harms him.

326-327) When a man walks on the path of truth, he goes to the right and extends upon himself the upper spirit of holiness from above. That spirit becomes for him a holy desire to unite above and to cling to the upper *Kedusha* so it will never cease from him. When a person walks on the bad way and his ways lean from the straight path, he extends upon him the spirit of *Tuma'a* on the left, which defiles him and he is defiled in it, as it is written, "And you shall not make yourselves impure with them and you were defiled in them." He who comes to defile is defiled.

368-369) "He created them male and female." This means that any form in which there are no male and female is not a high form as it should be. Wherever you do not find a male and a female together, the Creator's abode is not there. There are blessings only in a place where there are male and female, as it is written, "And He blessed them and called their name 'man' on the day when they were created." It is not written, "And He blessed him and called his name 'man,'" teaching you that he is not called even by the name "man" unless a male and a female are together.

445-446) Any man who fears the Creator, faith is with him properly because that man is complete in the work of his Master. One in whom there is no fear of his Master, faith is not in him and he is not worthy of having a portion for the next world.

Happy are the righteous in this world and in the next world because the Creator desires their glory. "The path of the righteous is as the light of dawn." What is "As the light of dawn"? It is as that light that illuminates, which the Creator created in the work of creation. It is the light that the Creator hid for the righteous for the next world. It shines stronger and stronger because it always rises in its light and is never deficient.

New Zohar, Beresheet Bet [Genesis 2]

5) It is written, "How plentiful is Your goodness, which You have hidden for those who fear You." This is the first light that the Creator hid for the righteous, for those who fear sin, as it is written, "And there was evening," on the part of darkness, "And there was morning," on the part of light. And when they conjoin, "One day."

Although the first light was concealed through the middle line, He still did not intend to hide it altogether. On the contrary, He intended that by concealing, that light could illuminate to the righteous who fear sin. Since they are careful to receive that light from below upward—for there is wholeness only by the illumination of *Hassadim* on the right together with the *Hochma* on the left—then the joy of all is in the middle line that unites them. This is why it ends, "And there was evening," on the part of darkness, the left line, "And there was morning," on the part of light, the right line, and when they conjoin through the middle line, it is written, "One day," which is all the wholeness and unity.

21) When the Creator crowns in His crowns, He crowns from above and from below. From above is from the deepest place, which is *AVI*. He also crowns from below, from the souls of the righteous. Then life is added from above and from below, the place of the Temple is included with all the sides, the pit is filled, the sea completed, and He gives life to all.

63) If a person comes to be purified he is aided with a holy soul, he is purified and sanctified, and he is called "holy." If he is not rewarded and does not come to be purified, only two degrees open for him, *Nefesh* and *Ruach*, but he has no holy soul [*Neshama*]. Moreover, if he comes to defile he is defiled and the upper aid is removed from him. Henceforth, each according to his ways. If he repents and comes to be purified, he is aided once again.

110) **There is an allegory about a king who invited his loved one for a meal that he was having on a certain day, so the one who loved the king would know that the king favors him.** The king said, "Now I want to rejoice alone with

the one who loves me, yet I fear that when I am at the meal with the one who loves me, all those appointed officers will come and sit with us at the table to join the meal of joy together with the one who loves me."

What did the lover do? First, he made stews, vegetables, and ox meat, and gave it to those appointed officers to eat, and then the king sat with his lover alone for that sublime meal with all the delicacies in the world. And while he was alone with the king, he asks him for all his needs, and he gives it to him, and the king rejoices alone with the one who loves him, and no foreigners will interfere between them. So are Israel with the Creator.

123) As the soul is given clothing, which is the body, to exist in this world, the soul is also given the clothing of the upper brightness in which to exist in the next world, and to look inside the illuminating mirror, which is ZA, from the land of the living, the *Nukva de* ZA.

138) How obtuse are people, for they do not know and do not notice the words of Torah, but look at worldly matters and the spirit of wisdom is forgotten from them.

295) Rabbi Shimon said, "If I were in the world when the Creator placed the book of Enoch [Hanoch] and the book of Adam in the world, I would exert that they would not be among people because at the time, all the sages were not fearful of looking in them, erred—misinterpreting the literal meaning of the words as other things—and brought them out of the domain of the upper one of *Kedusha* into another domain, which is not holy. But now, all the sages of the world know things and hide them, not revealing the secrets, and grow stronger in the work of their Master. This is why now it is permitted to engage in the secrets."

304-306) Happy are the righteous because the Creator desires their glory and has revealed to them the high secrets of the wisdom.

"The Lord is my God; I will extol You; I will thank Your name for You have done wonders, counsels from afar, steadfast faith." People should indeed regard the glory of the Creator and praise His glory because anyone who knows how to properly praise his Master, the Creator does his wish. Moreover, He multiplies blessings above and below.

For this reason, one who knows how to praise his Master and unify His name is favored above and coveted below, and the Creator is praised by him. It is written about him, "And will say unto me, 'you are My servant, Israel, in whom I am glorified.'"

368) "And the Lord said, 'Behold, they are one people,'" since they were all as one, in unity, they will do and succeed in their works.

386-388) Because they were in one will and in one heart, and spoke in the holy tongue, it is written, "Nothing which they purpose to do will be impossible for them"; the upper *Din* could not rule over them.

We, or the friends who engage in Torah, are of one heart and of one will. It is even more so that nothing which we purpose to do will be impossible for us. This means that all who dispute have no persistence, for as long as the people of the world were of one will and one heart, even though they rebelled against the Creator, the upper *Din* did not govern them as it happened during the generation of separation [generation of Babel]. And when they were divided, it was immediately written about them, "And the Lord scattered them abroad from there." Thus, those who dispute have no persistence.

This means that everything depends on the words of the mouth, for because their language was confused, promptly, "And the Lord scattered them from there." But in the future, it is written, "For then will I turn to the peoples a pure language, that they may all call upon the name of the Lord, to serve Him with one consent," and the Lord will be king over all.

New Zohar, Noah

1) Happy are Israel whom the Creator desires and to whom He has given the holy Torah, and warned them, and given them counsel to beware the slanderers above and the harm-doers below so that only the Creator would rule over them. They know how to repel from them all the slanderers and saboteurs so they are a part of His lot and inheritance, as it is written, "For the portion of the Lord is His people, Jacob, the lot of His inheritance."

24) It is written about man, "It is not good that the man is alone; I will make him a help made against him." This is the soul, which is a help within him to guide him through the ways of

his Maker. That is, he who comes to be purified is aided. When a person walks in the ways of his Maker, many help him: his soul helps him, the ministering angels help him, the Creator's Divinity helps him, and all declare about him and say, "When you walk, your step will not be straitened; and if you run, you will not stumble." The souls of righteous help him.

46) "And Noah begot three sons." These are the three governances in a man. The governance of the soul is to be an assistance for him in the work of his Maker. This is called Shem. The governance of lust and the evil inclination, which guides and stuns the body with transgressions is called Ham. And the guidance of the good inclination, which guides the man with great abundance, to beautify his works in the Torah and the fear of God, is called Yafet. That guidance will lead the man to guide him through the path of life.

152) Michael said, "Lord of the world, You should have been merciful toward them because You are merciful, and so You are called." He told him, "I have sworn an oath on that day when the sentence was given before Me to not redeem them until they repent. If the Assembly of Israel

begin to repent even as an eye of a needle, I will open for them great gates."

153-155) All the exiles that the Assembly of Israel exiled, the Creator gave her time and end, and she always awoke in repentance. The last exile has no end or time. Rather, everything depends on repentance, as it was said, "And you shall return unto the Lord your God, and you shall obey His voice." It is also written, "If your outcast is at the end of the heaven, from there the Lord your God will gather you, and from there He will take you."

Thus, how will it happen that they all awaken in repentance together? One who is at the end of the heaven and one who is at the end of the earth, how will they conjoin to make repentance? If the heads of the synagogue repent, or a single synagogue, the whole exile will gather thanks to them, since the Creator always waits for when they repent, that He may do good to them, as it is written, "And therefore will the Lord wait, to pardon you." He always waits for the time when they repent.

Lech Lecha [Go Forth]

4) People should observe the work of the Creator. After all, all the people do not know and do not consider what the world stands on and what they themselves stand on.

4-5) Everything stands on Torah, since when Israel engage in Torah, when they raise **MAN** to **ZON** and extend the middle line, which is the Torah, the world exists.

When midnight awakens and the Creator enters the Garden of Eden to play with the righteous, all the trees in the Garden of Eden sing and praise before Him, as it is written, "Then shall all the trees of the wood sing for joy before the Lord, for He has come." The night is the *Nukva* with respect to her own dominion. She is essentially the illumination of the left line, from the illumination of *Hochma* that extends from the point of *Shuruk* in *Ima*. Also, *Hochma* shines only from the *Chazeh* down because the *Man'ula* [lock] governs from the *Chazeh* and above of each *Partzuf*, and the illumination of *Hochma* cannot appear there. This is the division of the night into two halves, since the point of midnight is the point of *Chazeh*.

At midnight, the *Nukva*, awakens to receive the mitigation of *Bina*, to shine from the *Chazeh* down in her, which is the Garden of Eden, the Creator enters the Garden of Eden to play with the righteous. In other words, the righteous raise MAN and extend illumination of the middle line there, which is the Creator who shines in the Garden of Eden.

All the trees in the Garden of Eden sing and praise before Him, as it is written, "Then shall all the trees of the wood sing for joy." "The trees of the wood" are infertile trees, which do not bear fruit. Before the coming of the Creator, the *Sefirot* of *Nukva* were regarded as the trees of the wood, which have no fruits to them. After the illumination of the Creator enters there through the righteous, "The trees of the wood sing for joy before the Lord, for He has come," and bear fruit.

9) The existence of all the people is on the middle line, which is extended only by engagement in the Torah. Were it not for the middle line, they would have no existence whatsoever.

18-19) Anyone who comes to be purified is aided...Thus, one who comes and awakens himself from below is aided from above. But

without the awakening from below, there is no awakening from above.

Nothing above awakens if the thing upon which the thing from above is placed does not awaken below first. This is the meaning of the black light in the candle, the *Nukva*, who does not grip the white light in the candle, ZA, before she awakens first. When she awakens first, the white light immediately comes over her because the lower one must awaken first.

116) **Woe unto the wicked of the world who do not know and do not look to understand that all that there is in the world is from the Creator,** that He alone did, does, and will do all the deeds in the world. He knows in advance all that will unfold in the end, as it is written, "Declaring the end from the beginning." And He watches and does things in the beginning in order to repeat them and to do them perfectly after some time.

129) **"And a river came out of Eden to water the garden,"** *Yesod de* ZA, which comes out of *Bina* that returned to *Hochma*, who is called "Eden." This is the pillar upon which the world stands, and this is the one who waters the garden, the *Nukva*, and the garden is watered by it and makes fruits from it, which are souls of people. All the

fruits blossom in the world, *Nukva*, and they are the persistence of the world and the keeping of the Torah. These fruits are the souls of the righteous, which are the fruits of the deeds of the Creator.

131) **The upper world needed awakening from the lower world.** When the souls of the righteous depart from this world and rise to the Garden of Eden, they all clothe the upper light in a precious way. The Creator plays with them and yearns for them, for they are the fruit of His deeds. This is the reason why Israel are called "The sons of the Creator," since they have holy souls, as it is written, "You are the sons of the Lord your God," since souls are sons, the fruit of the Creator's actions.

144) **Had Abram not gone down to Egypt and had not been purified there first, he would have had no share and lot in the Creator**. It was likewise with his sons when the Creator wished to make them one nation, a whole nation, and to bring them closer to Him. Had they not gone down to Egypt first and had they not been purified there, they would not have been His one nation. Similarly, had the land of holiness not been given to Canaan first, and

had they not ruled it, the land would not have been the share and lot of the Creator, and it is all one.

163) **All the friends came and kissed Rabbi Shimon's hands. They wept, "Woe, when you depart from the world, who will light the light of Torah?" Happy are the friends who heard these words of Torah from your mouth.**

209-210) **The Creator said to the Assembly of Israel, Divinity,** "From Me is your fruit found." It does not say, "Is My fruit found," but "Your fruit," indicating to that craving of the female, who makes the female of the soul, which is included in the strength of the male. Also, the soul of the female is included in the soul of the male and they become one, mingled in one another. Afterwards, they are separated in the world.

Indeed, by the force of the male is the fruit of the female present in the world. The words, "Your fruit" point to the fruits of the female, to the soul that extends by her craving. The text tells us that even the soul of the female is not from her self, but from her mingling with the soul of the male. This is why he says, "From Me is your fruit found."

"From Me is your fruit found." This is so because by the craving of the female herself, from which the female of the soul comes, the fruit of the male is found. Had it not been for the craving of the female for the male, there would be no fruits in the world, meaning there would be no offspring.

225-227) When the Creator created the world, the world did not stand, but collapsed to this side and to that side. The Creator said to the world, "Why are you falling?" It told Him, "Dear Lord, I cannot stand because I have no foundation [*Yesod*] on which to stand."

The Creator told it, "Thus, I will place a righteous one within you, Abraham, who will love Me." And the world immediately stood and existed. It is written, "These are the generations of the heaven and the earth when they were created." Do not read it, *BeHibar'am* [when they were created], but *BeAvraham* [in Abraham, same letters in Hebrew], since the world existed in Abraham.

The world replied to the Creator, "Abraham is destined to beget sons who will destroy the Temple and burn the Torah." The Creator told it, "One man will come out of him, Jacob, and twelve tribes will come out of him, all of which are righteous." Promptly, the world existed for him.

231) **The awakening of the upper one is only through the awakening of the lower one because the awakening of the upper one depends on the craving of the lower one.**

268-269) **It is written, "I am my beloved's, and his desire is for me."** In the beginning, "I am my beloved's," and afterwards, "And his desire is for me." "I am my beloved's" is to first set up a place for him with an awakening from below, and then, "And his desire is for me."

Divinity is not present with the wicked. When a person comes to purify and bring himself closer to the Creator, Divinity is over him. It is written about it, "I am my beloved's," first, and then, "And his desire is for me," since when one comes to purify, he is purified.

278-279) **When the Creator created the world**, it was on the condition that if Israel came and received the Torah, they would exist. And if not, then I will turn you back to chaos. Indeed, the world did not exist until Israel stood at Mount Sinai and accepted the Torah, and then the world existed.

From that day forth, the Creator creates worlds. And who are they? They are the *Zivugim* [plural of *Zivug*] of people.

310) **"When the Creator, Bina, wished to create the world, ZON, which are called "heaven and earth,"** He looked into the thought—*Hochma*, the Torah—inscribed inscriptions, and extended the light of *Hochma* to ZON, to heaven and earth. But the world could not stand because they could not receive the light due to the force of *Tzimtzum* [restriction] and *Din* that was in *Malchut*.

Then He created penance, the hidden inner and high *Heichal* [palace]. "Until He created penance" means until He elevated *Malchut* to *Bina*, at which time *Bina* is called "penance," for *Bina* was diminished into a point in the *Heichal*. By that, *Midat ha Din* [quality of judgment] in *Malchut* was mitigated in *Bina* and became fit for reception of the light of *Hochma*.

315-317) **"Bless the Lord, you His angels... hearing unto the voice of His word."** Happier are Israel than all the other nations of the world, for the Creator has chosen them from among all nations, and has made them His share and His lot. Hence, He has given them the holy Torah, since they were all in one desire at Mount Sinai and preceded doing to hearing, as they said, "We shall do and we shall hear."

And since they preceded doing to hearing, the Creator called upon the angels and told them: "Thus far, you were the only ones before Me in the world. Henceforth, My children on the earth are your friends in every way. You have no permission to sanctify My name until Israel bond with you in the earth, and all of you together will join to sanctify My name, since they preceded doing to hearing, as the high angels do in the firmament," as it is written, "Bless the Lord, you His angels ... They do His word," first. And then it is written, "Hearing the voice of His word."

"Bless the Lord, you His angels" are the righteous in the land. They are as important before the Creator as the high angels in the firmament, since they are mighty and powerful, for they overcome their inclination like a hero who triumphs over his enemies. "Hearing the voice of His word" means being rewarded hearing a voice from above every day and at any time they need.

327-328) **King David said, "For who is God, save the Lord? And who is a Rock, save our God?"** "Who is God" means who is the ruler or the appointee who can do anything, besides the Creator? Rather, they do what they were commanded by the Creator because none of them is in his own authority and they cannot do anything. "And who is a rock" means who is strong and can make his own assertion and might, "Save our God"? Rather, they are all in the hands of the Creator and they cannot do anything except with His permission.

"For who is God, save the Lord?" Everything is in the permission of the Creator. It is not as it seems in the stars and fortunes, which show something and the Creator changes it into another way. "And who is a Rock, save our God?" means that there is no such painter as the Creator. He is the perfect painter, who makes and paints a form within a form, a fetus in its mother's insides, and completes that picture in all its corrections, and instills a high soul within it, which is similar to the upper correction.

330) **How great are the deeds of the Creator? The art and painting of a man are like the artisanship and the depiction of the world.** In other words, man comprises the entire deed of the world, and he is called "a small world." Each and every day, the Creator creates a world

that makes *Zivugim* for everyone as he should, and this is considered creating worlds. And He depicted the shape of each of them before they came to the world.

356) **"The law of the Lord is perfect" because it contains everything**. Happy are those who engage in the Torah and do not part from it, for anyone who is separated from the Torah for even an hour, it is as though he has parted from life in the world. And it is written, "For it is your life and the length of your days," and it is written, "For length of days, and years of life, and peace, will they add to you."

363-367) **At midnight, when the roosters awaken**, the north side awakens in *Ruach* [wind], meaning the left line in illumination of *Shuruk*, meaning illumination of *Hochma* with absence of *Hassadim*, GAR de *Ruach*. The scepter, the south side—right line, *Hassadim*—rises and mingles with that *Ruach* of the left line, and they mingle with one another. At that time, the *Dinim* of the left line rest and it is mitigated in *Hassadim*. Then the Creator awakens in His custom to play with the righteous in the Garden of Eden.

At that time, happy is a man who rises to play in the Torah, since the Creator and all the righteous in the Garden of Eden listen to his voice, as it is written, "You who dwells in the gardens, the friends are listening to your voice; let me hear it."

Moreover, the Creator draws upon him a thread of grace, to keep him in the world so that the upper ones and lower ones will guard him, as it is written, "By day the Lord will command His grace; and in the night, His song is with me."

Anyone who engages in Torah at that time will certainly have a permanent part in the next world. What is permanent? These *Mochin* extend from *YESHSUT*, whose *Zivug* is intermittent and not permanent. But each midnight, when the Creator awakens in the Garden of Eden, all those plantings—the *Sefirot* in the Garden of Eden, the *Nukva*—will be watered abundantly from that stream, which is called "a primordial stream," "a stream of delights," "upper *AVI*," whose waters never stop, meaning that the *Zivug* of *AVI* never stops. And one who rises and engages in the Torah, it is as though that stream pours down on his head and waters him inside the plantings in the Garden of Eden. Hence, he has a permanent share in the *Mochin* of the next world, too, meaning *YESHSUT*, since the *Mochin de AVI* contain the *Mochin de YESHSUT* within them, too.

Moreover, since all the righteous in the Garden of Eden listen to him, they put a share for him in that potion of the stream, which are the *Mochin* of upper *AVI*. It turns out that he has a perpetual part for the next world, which are included in *Mochin de AVI*.

445) He said about Rashbi and his disciples: "Happy are you in this world and in the next world. You are all holy; you are all sons of the Holy God…Each of you is tied and connected to the High and Holy King."

New Zohar, Lech Lecha [Go Forth]

1) Oh how one should qualify his works before his Creator and engage in His Torah [law] day and night, for the virtue of the Torah is above all virtues.

5-6) All the souls of the righteous were cut off from under the throne to lead the body as a father leads the son, for without the soul, the body cannot be led, nor know or do its Creator's will. The soul is a teacher, teaching the man and educating him in every upright path.

When the Creator sends her from the place of holiness, He blesses her with seven blessings, as it is written, "And the Lord said to Abram." This is the soul, called *Av Ram* [high father], for she is a father in teaching the body, and higher than it, for she comes from a high and supernal place.

61) Oh how fond is the Creator of the Torah, for which man is rewarded with the life of the next world, and for anyone who teaches others Torah—more than everyone.

61-62) They who teach others and infants Torah are rewarded doubly. One who teaches children Torah, his abode is with Divinity. When Rabbi Shimon came to see the children in the seminary, he would say, "I am going to meet the face of Divinity."

VaYera [The Lord Appeared]

1-3) **It is written, "The buds appear on the earth."** When the Creator created the world, He placed in the earth all the power it deserves, but it did not bear fruit until man was created. When man was created, everything appeared in the world and the land revealed the fruits and forces that were deposited in it. And then it was said, "The buds appear on the earth."

Similarly, the heaven did not endow the earth with force until man came, as it is written, "No shrub of the field was yet in the earth... for the Lord God had not sent rain upon the earth." Thus, all these offshoots were not revealed in it and the heavens halted and did not pour rain upon the earth since man was absent, for he has not yet been found and created. Thus, everything was delayed from appearing because of him. When man appeared, the buds immediately appeared in the land and the hidden forces appeared and were placed in it.

"The time for singing [in Hebrew it also means pruning] has arrived," for the midnight correction has been corrected, of song and praises, to sing before the Creator. This did not exist prior to man's creation. "And the voice of the turtledove was heard in our land." This is the speaking of the Creator, who was not present in the world prior to man's creation. When man was present, everything was present.

76-78) **"Who shall ascend into the mountain of the Lord, and who shall stand in His holy place?"** All the people in the world do not see why they are in the world. They do not observe so as to know for what purpose they are living in the world, and the days go by and never return. And all those days that people live in this world rise and stand before the Creator, for they were all created and they are real.

When a person in this world does not watch and does not consider why he is alive, but considers each day as walking in a void, when the soul departs this world, she does not know which way it is being lifted. This is so because the way up to where the illuminations of the high souls shine—the Garden of Eden—is not given to all the souls. Rather, as one draws upon himself in this world, the soul continues to walk after she departs him.

79) **If that person follows the Creator and desires Him in this world,** later, when he passes

away from this world, he follows the Creator, too, and is given a way to rise to the place where the souls shine due to the craving that his desire followed everyday in this world.

81-82) **"According to the direction of a person's desire in this world,** he draws upon himself the spirit from above, similar to the desire that had become attached to him. If his desire aims for a sublime and holy thing, he extends upon himself that same thing from above downwards.

"And if his desire is to cling to the *Sitra Achra*, and he aims for it, he extends that thing upon himself from above downwards." And they said that extending something from above depends primarily upon the speech, the act, and the desire to adhere. This draws from above that same side that had clung to him."

84-87) **Similarly, when one wishes to adhere to the holy spirit above, it depends on the act, the speech, and on aiming the heart to that thing, so one will be able to draw it from above downwards and to adhere to it.**

And they said that a person is pulled out when he leaves this world by what attracts him in this world; and he is attached and attracted in the world of truth to what he had been attached and attracted to in this world. If it is holiness—holiness; and if it is impurity—impurity.

If it is holiness, he is pulled to the side of holiness. It clings to him above and he becomes appointed as a servant, to serve before the Creator among all the angels. Also, he adheres above and stands among those holy ones, as it is written, "And I will grant you access among those who are standing here."

Similarly, if he clings to impurity in this world, he is pulled to the side of impurity and becomes as one of them, adhering to them. These are called, "damagers to people," and when one passes away from this world, he is taken and submerged in hell, that same place where the impure ones who have defiled themselves and their spirits and then clung to them are judged. And he becomes a damager, as one of those damagers of the world.

114) When *Adam ha Rishon* sinned, he sinned with the tree of knowledge of good and evil, as it is written, "but of the tree of the knowledge." And he sinned in it and caused death to the whole world. It is written, "And now, he might reach out his hand and take from the tree of life, as well, and eat, and live forever." And when

Abraham came, he corrected the world with the other tree, the tree of life, and announced the faith to all the people in the world.

151-154) "Her husband is known in the gates." The Creator rose in His honor, since He is hidden and concealed in great transcendence. There is no one, nor was there ever anyone in the world who could perceive His wisdom. Hence, none can perceive His wisdom because he is hidden and concealed and is transcended above and beyond. And all the upper ones and lower ones cannot attain Him until they all say, "Blessed be the glory of the Lord in His place."

The lower ones say that Divinity is above, as it is written, "His glory is above the heavens." And the upper ones say that Divinity is below, as it is written, "Your glory is above all the earth." Until all the upper and lower ones say, "Blessed be the glory of the Lord in His place" because He is unknown and there has never been anyone who could perceive Him. And you will say, "Her husband is known in the gates."

"Her husband is known in the gates" is the Creator, who is known and attained by what each assumes in his heart, to the extent that he can attain by the spirit of the wisdom. Thus, according to that which one assumes in one's heart, He is known in his heart. This is why it is written, "Known in the gates," in those measures [the same word as "gates" in Hebrew] that each assumes in his heart. But it should be properly known that there is no one who can attain and know Him.

"Her husband is known in the gates." What are gates? It is written, "Lift up your heads, O gates." By these gates, which are high degrees, by them is the Creator known. Were it not for these gates, they would not be able to attain in Him.

155) **There is no one who can know man's soul, except by these organs of the body and those degrees of the body that disclose the actions of the soul.** For this reason, the soul is known and unknown—known through the organs of the body, and unknown in its own essence. Similarly, the Creator is known and unknown, as He is a soul to a soul, a spirit to spirit, hidden and concealed from all. But one who is rewarded with these gates, the upper degrees that are doors to the soul, to him the Creator is known. Thus, He is known through the upper degrees, which are His actions, and is unknown in His own essence.

156-158) There is a door to a door and a degree to a degree, and from them is the glory of the Creator known. And the door of the tent is the door of *Tzedek* [justice], which is *Malchut*, as it is written, "Open to me the gates of justice." This is the first door by which to enter in attainment. Through this door, all the other upper doors are seen, and one who is rewarded with this door is rewarded with attaining it and all the other doors with it, since they are all on it.

And now that the bottom door, called "The tent door" and the "door of justice," is unknown because Israel is in exile, all the doors depart it and they cannot know and attain. But when Israel come out of exile, all the upper degrees will be on the door of *Tzedek* as they should.

And then the world will know the sublime and precious wisdom that they have never known before, as it is written, "And the spirit of the Lord shall rest upon him, the spirit of *Hochma* [wisdom] and *Bina* [understanding]." They are all destined to be on that bottom door, which is the tent door, *Malchut*, and they are all destined to be on the Messiah King to sentence the world, as it is written, "But with justice shall he judge the poor."

169) **One who is rewarded with righteousness with people when there is *Din* in the world,** the Creator remembers that righteousness that he performed because at any time when a person is rewarded, it is registered so for him above. Hence, even while there is *Din* in the world, the Creator remembers the good that he had done and was rewarded with people, as it is written, "Righteousness delivers from death."

230) **People should consider the deeds of the Creator and engage in Torah day and night.** Anyone who engages in Torah, the Creator is praised by him above and praised by him below, for the Torah is a tree of life for all who engage in it, to give them life in this world and to give them life in the next world.

239) **"And these are the nations which the Lord left, to test Israel by them."** I was looking at that eternal world, and the world stood only on those righteous that reign their hearts' desire. It is said, "He appointed it in Joseph for a testimony." Why was Joseph rewarded with that virtue and kingship? For he had conquered his inclination. This is because we learned that all who reign their inclination, the kingdom of heaven awaits them.

296-297) **"He turns for reasons in His tactics that they may do."** The Creator causes reasons in the world and brings destructive lights to do His deeds, and then turns them around and makes them in a different way. It is the conduct of the Creator to first bring destructive lights that destruct, and then turn them around and correct them.

How does He turn them? The Creator executes tactics and causes reasons to turn them until they are not as the previous ones. "That they may do" means according to what people may do. He turns those actions according to the deeds that they do. Thus, people's actions induce turning those deeds in all that the Creator commands them on the earth, that they receive all kinds of forms in the world by the merit of people's actions.

304) **The Creator caused the reasons and deeds in the world so that everything will be done properly, and everything comes out and extends below in the world from the essence and the root above.**

430) **As long as one engages in Torah, Divinity comes and joins.** It is all the more so when traveling along the way—Divinity comes and puts

herself ahead, walking before the people who have been rewarded with the faith of the Creator.

453) **Man is created in utter wickedness and lowliness,** as it is written, "When a wild ass's foal is born a man." And all the vessels in one's body—the senses and the qualities, and especially the thought—serve him only wickedness and nothingness all day. And for one who is rewarded with adhering unto Him, the Creator does not create other tools instead, to be worthy and suitable for reception of the eternal spiritual abundance intended for him. Rather, the same lowly vessels that have thus far been used in a filthy and loathsome way are inverted to become vessels of reception of all the pleasantness and eternal gentleness.

Moreover, each *Kli* whose deficiencies had been the greatest has now become the most important. In other words, the measure that they reveal is the greatest. It is so much so that if he had a *Kli* in his body that had no deficiencies, it has now become seemingly redundant, for it does not serve him in any way. It is like a vessel of wood or clay: the greater its deficiency, meaning its carving, the greater its capacity and the greater its importance.

453) And this applies in the upper worlds, as well, since no revelation is dispensed upon the worlds except through concealed discernments. And by the measure of concealment in a degree, so is the measure of revelations in it, which is given to the world. If there is no concealment in it, it cannot bestow a thing.

460) When the days of the Messiah draw near, even infants in the world will find the secrets of the wisdom, to know in them the ends and the calculations of redemption. At that time it will be revealed to all.

New Zohar, VaYera [The Lord Appeared]

1-4) "And Abraham was and will be." "Will be" is 30 in *Gematria*. One day, Rabbi Shimon went out and saw the world dark and murky with its light hidden. He said to Rabbi Elazar, "Come let us see what the Creator wants."

They went and found an angel who was like a big mountain, emitting 30 flames of fire from his mouth. Rabbi Shimon said to him, "What do you wish to do?" He replied, "I want to destroy the world because there aren't 30 righteous in the generation, for so the Creator decreed about Abraham, 'And Abraham was and will be,' and

'Will be' is 30 in *Gematria*." Rabbi Shimon said to him, "Please go to the Creator and tell Him, 'Rabbi Shimon is in the world, whose merit is as great as 30 righteous.'" The angel went to the Creator and told Him, "Lord of the world, it is revealed before You what Rabbi Shimon said to me." The Creator replied to him, "Go, destroy the world, and do not look at Rabbi Shimon."

When he came, Rabbi Shimon saw the angel. He told him, "If you do not go to the Creator on my behalf, I will sentence that you will not enter the heaven and you will be in the place of Aza and Azael, whom the Creator dropped from heaven to earth. When you come before the Creator, tell Him, 'And if there aren't thirty righteous in the world, there will be twenty,' for so it is written, 'I will not destroy it for the twenty's sake.' And if there aren't twenty, there will be ten, for afterwards it is written, 'I will not destroy it for the ten's sake.' And if there aren't ten, there will be two, who are me and my son, for so it is written, 'By the mouth of two witnesses ... shall a matter be established,' and there is no matter but the world, as it is written, 'By the word of the Lord were the heavens made.' And if there aren't two then there is one, and I am he, as it is written, 'And a righteous is the foundation of the world.'" At that time, a voice came forth from heaven and said, "Happy are you Rabbi Shimon that the Creator sentences above and you revoke below. It is written about you, "He will do the will of those who fear Him."

CHAYEI SARAH [THE LIFE OF SARAH]

40) **The shape of Adam ha Rishon and his beauty were as the brightness of the upper firmament over all the firmaments, and as that light that the Creator had concealed for the righteous for the next world.**

94) Happy are the righteous in the next world, for the Torah in their hearts is as a great fountain—even when it is blocked, the abundance of water breaks through and opens springs to all directions.

119-120) **Abraham was drawn near to the Creator.** All his days, this was his wish—to draw near Him. Abraham did not draw near on one day or at one time, but his good deeds drew him near every single day, from degree to degree, until he ascended in his degree.

When he was old, he properly entered the high degrees, as it is written, "And Abraham was old." Then he was "Advanced in days," in those high days, those days that are known as faith. "And the Lord had blessed Abraham in everything," meaning *Yesod* of upper *AVI*, called "everything," from which all the blessings and good emerges, for its abundance never ceases.

121-122) Happy are the penitents, for in one hour, in one day, in one moment, they draw near to the Creator. This was not so even for complete righteous, for they drew near to the Creator over several years. Abraham did not enter those high days until he was old. And so was David, as it is written, "Now King David was old and advanced in days." But a penitent immediately enters and adheres to the Creator.

Where penitents stand, in that world, the complete righteous have no permission to stand, since they are closer to the King than anyone and they draw the abundance from above with more intention in the heart and with greater force to draw near to the King.

123) The Creator has several corrected places in that world, and in all of them there are abodes for the righteous, to each according to his appropriate degree.

136-137) Happy are the righteous, for much good awaits them in that world. And there is not a more intrinsic place for all those righteous as those who know their Master and know how to adhere to Him every day.

And those who are remote from perceiving a word of wisdom and wait for it, to understand the heart of the matter and to know their Master, those are the ones in whom the Creator is praised everyday. They are the ones who come among the upper holy ones, and they are the ones who enter all the upper gates, and there is no one to protest against them. Happy are they in this world and in the next.

171) **Anyone who knows his true name knows that He is one and His name one.** He is the Creator, and "His name one" refers to Divinity, as it is written, "In that day shall the Lord be One, and His name one," meaning the name, Divinity, and He, ZA, are one.

188) **When the sages of truth clarify the secrets of the writings, the very degrees that the writings speak of come to those sages at that time and present themselves so as to be made revealed. Had it not been for their assistance, they would not have had the power to reveal any secret.**

212) **When the Creator revives the dead,** all those souls that will awaken before Him will all stand before Him, shapes upon shapes, in the very same shape they had had in this world. And the Creator will call them by names, as it is written, "He calls them all by name," and each

soul will come in to its place in the body and they will be revived in the world as they should be. Then the world will be complete.

219) **"Open my eyes, that I may see wonders from Your law."** How foolish are people, for they do not know and do not consider engaging in the Torah. But the Torah is the whole of life, and every freedom and every goodness in this world and in the next world. Life in this world is to be rewarded with all their days in this world, as it is written, "The number of thy days I will fulfill." And he will be rewarded with long days in the next world, for it is the perfect life, a life of joy, life without sadness, life that is life—freedom in this world and liberation from everything—for anyone who engages in Torah, all the nations of the world cannot rule over him.

270) **And when the Creator visits His nation to deliver them from exile,** the Assembly of Israel, Divinity, will return from the exile first, and will go to the Temple, since first, the Temple will be built for the gathering of the nations, where there is the presence of Divinity. This is why Divinity comes out of exile first. And the Creator will tell her, "Rise up from the dust." And Divinity will reply, "Where will

I go? My house is ruined, my palace burned by fire." And the Creator will build the Temple from the start. He will erect the palace and will build the city of Jerusalem, and then He will raise Divinity from the dust.

TOLDOT [GENERATIONS]

1-2) **When the Creator wished to create the world, He gazed in the Torah and created it. And in each act by which the Creator created the world, He would look in the Torah and create it, as it is written, "Then I was beside Him, as a cadet, and I was daily His delight." Do not read it as *Amon* [apprentice], but as *Oman* [master craftsman], for it was his tool of craftsmanship.**

When He wished to create man, the Torah said to Him, "If man is created and later sins, and You will sentence him, why should Your deeds be in vain? After all, he will never be able to tolerate Your judgments." The Creator told her, "But I have created repentance before I created the world. If he sins, he will be able to repent and I will forgive him."

The Creator said to the world when He created it and created man, "World, you and your nature persist only by the Torah. This is why I have created man within you, to engage in Torah. If he does not engage in Torah, I will revert you back to chaos." Thus, all is for man, and the Torah stands and calls before people to engage and exert in the Torah, but no one lends an ear.

3-4) **Anyone who engages in Torah sustains the world and sustains each and every operation in the world in its proper way. Also, there is not an organ in a man's body that does not have a corresponding creation in the world.**

This is so because as man's body divides into organs and they all stand degree over degree, established one atop the other and are all one body, similarly, the world, meaning all creations in the world are many organs standing one atop the other, and they are all one body. And when they are all corrected they will actually be one body. And everything, man and the world will be like the Torah because the whole of Torah is organs and joints standing one atop the other. And when the world is corrected they will become one body.

The Torah holds all the hidden, sublime, and unattainable secrets. The Torah holds all the sublime, revealed, and unrevealed matters, that is, that for their profoundness, they appear to the eye of the one who observes them and soon after disappear. Then they briefly reappear and disappear, and so on and so forth before those who scrutinize them. The Torah holds all the things that are above in the Upper World and that are below. And everything in this world and everything in the next world is in the Torah.

14) Bless the Lord all the servants of the Lord. Who are they who are worthy of blessing the Creator? All of the Creator's servants. Even though all the people in the world are from Israel, they are all worthy of blessing the Creator.

But blessings for which upper and lower are blessed, who are they who bless Him? It is the servants of the Creator. And who are they whose blessing is a blessing? It is them who stand in the house of God at night, those who rise at midnight and awaken to read in the Torah. They are the ones who stand in the house of God at night. And they need both: to be servants of the Creator, as well as to rise at midnight, for then the Creator comes to entertain with the righteous in the Garden of Eden.

21) For twenty years, Isaac waited on his wife and she did not deliver, until he prayed his prayer. This was so because the Creator desires the prayer of the righteous, when they ask before Him for their needs. And what is the reason? It is so that an ointment of holiness would grow and proliferate through the prayer of the righteous for anyone in need, for the righteous open the upper hose with their prayer, and then even those who are unworthy of being granted are granted.

40) On that day when the Lord rejoices with His deeds, the righteous are destined to attain the Creator in their hearts. Then, wisdom will increase in their hearts as though they were seeing it with their eyes.

44-45) The meal of the righteous in the future will consist of wild bull and whale.

Our sages said to the majority of the world that they are invited to that meal. They are destined to eat and rejoice in a great feast that the Creator will do for them. Hence, the majority of the world suffers the exile for that feast.

57) The evil inclination is needed in the world like the rain is needed in the world. Without the evil inclination there would be no joy of studying in the world.

86-87) The Creator does not judge a person according to his bad deeds, which he always does. If He had done so, the world would not be able to exist. Rather, the Creator is patient with the righteous and with the wicked. He is even more patient with the wicked than with the righteous, so they will return in complete repentance and exist in this world and in the next world. This is so because when a wicked returns from his way, he lives in this world and in the next world, and this is why He is always patient with them. Or, because a good stem will emerge in the world from them, as Abraham emerged from Terah, who educed a good stem and root in the world.

However, the Creator is always meticulous with the righteous in everything that they do because He knows that they will not stray to the right or to the left, and therefore He tries them. But the Creator does not try them for Himself, since He knows their inclination and the power of their faith, and does not need to try them. Rather, He tries them so as to raise their heads through the tries.

124) **However, one should not trust and say, "The Creator will save me" or "The Creator will do this and that to me."** Rather, one should place one's trust in the Creator to help him, as it should be when he exerts in the *Mitzvot* of the Torah and tries to walk in the path of truth. And when man comes to purify, he is certainly assisted. In that, he should trust the Creator—that He will help him. He should place his trust in Him and trust none other than Him. One should establish one's heart properly, so no alien

thought will come in it. Rather, his heart will be as that rail that is built to pass through it to every place that is needed, to the right and to the left. This means that whether the Creator does him good or to the contrary, his heart will be ready and corrected to never question the Creator under any circumstances.

147) **It is known that because of the breaking of the vessels,** 320 sparks fell from holiness to the *Klipot* [shells], and that afterwards the Emanator corrected some of them. And because of the sin of the tree of knowledge, they fell into the *Klipot* once more, and our whole work in Torah and *Mitzvot* is to take those 320 sparks out of the *Klipot* and bring them back to holiness. They are the MAN that we raise, which draw all the *Mochin* during the 6,000 years of the existence of the world. And when all 320 sparks are sorted through the *Mochin* that extend from them, the end of correction will come.

170-171) **"When a man's ways please the Lord, He makes even his enemies be at peace with him."** There are two angels for a person, emissaries from above to unite with him, one to the right and one to the left. And they testify to a person, and they are present in everything he does. Their names are "the good inclination" and "the evil inclination."

When a man comes to be purified and to exert in the Mitzvot of the Torah, that good inclination that has become connected to him has already prevailed over the evil inclination and reconciled with it, and the evil inclination has become a servant to the good inclination. And when a person comes to be defiled, that evil inclination intensifies and overcomes the good inclination.

When that person comes to be purified, he needs to overcome several intensifications. And when the good inclination prevails, his enemies, too, make peace with him, since the evil inclination, which is his enemy, surrenders before the good inclination. When a person goes by the Mitzvot of the Torah, his enemies make peace with him, meaning the evil inclination and all who come from his side make peace with him.

189) Everything that the Creator does in the land is with wisdom, and it is all in order to teach people the upper wisdom, so they will learn the secrets of the wisdom from those deeds. And everything is as it should be, and all His deeds are the ways of the Torah, since the ways of the

Torah are the ways of the Creator, and there is no small thing that does not have several ways and routes and secrets of the upper wisdom.

190) There are several secrets of the Torah in each and every action that is written in the Torah, and there is wisdom and true law in every single word. Hence, the words of the Torah are holy words, to show wonders from them, as it is written, "Open my eyes, that I may behold wonderful things from Your law."

VaYetze [And Jacob Went Out]

109) Happy are they that keep justice" means happy are Israel that the Creator gave them a true law [Torah] to engage in day and night, for anyone who engages in the Torah is liberated from everything. He is freed from death for it cannot govern him. This is so because anyone who engages in Torah and clings to it, clings to the tree of life. And if he lets himself go of the tree of life, the tree of death will be on him and will cling to him.

111) **When a person clings to the ways of Torah,** he is loved above and loved below, and he becomes the Creator's loved one. He is loved by the Creator and the Creator loves him. But when a person strays from the ways of Torah, the power of *Koh*, Divinity, lessens and she becomes his foe and enemy, and he becomes her enemy. Then, that evil, the evil inclination, governs him until it slanders him in this world and in the next world.

118) "Happy are they that keep justice," who keep the faith of the Creator. The Creator is called "Justice," and man must keep himself

from straying to another way, but keep the justice, since the Creator is justice, for all His ways are just.

The name, "Justice," indicates to deciding about matters. This comes after hearing two opposite sides. It is like a judge: once he has thoroughly listened to the arguments of the two sides in dispute, he gives his sentence and says, "So and so, you are innocent. And so and so, you are guilty." This sentence is called "justice," and this is the middle line, which decides between the two lines—right and left—which are opposite from one another in a way that both shine to the side of holiness. Because of this sentencing of His, He is called "Justice."

119) **"That do righteousness at all times."** But can man do righteousness at all times? One who walks in the ways of Torah and does righteousness with those who need righteousness is regarded as one who does righteousness at all times, since anyone who does righteousness with the poor increases righteousness, the *Nukva*, above and below, meaning causes a *Zivug* of ZON above, and plentiful blessings below.

139) **But *The Zohar* speaks nothing of corporeal incidents, but of the upper worlds, where there**

is no sequence of times as it is in corporeality. Spiritual time is elucidated by change of forms and degrees that are above time and place.

167) **"I will give thanks to the Lord with my whole heart,** in the council of the upright, and in the congregation." David, the upper of the Holy Name, *HaVaYaH*, wished to thank the Creator. "I will give thanks to the Lord with my whole heart" means with the good inclination and with the evil inclination, which are two hearts, in the two inclinations that reside within the heart, on the two sides, right and left.

176-177) **Children of the upper one, high holy ones,** blessed of the world with a hazel brain, gather to know that a bird comes down each day and awakens in the garden with a flame of fire in its wings. In its hand are three rakes and shovels as sharp as a sword, and the keys to the treasures are in its right hand.

She calls out loud to the righteous in the Garden of Eden, "Whomever among you whose face shines (who has been rewarded with wisdom [*Hochma*], as it is said, 'Man's wisdom makes his face shine'), who came in and came out and grew strong in the tree of life (who has been rewarded with three lines), entered (in the right line) and came out (in the left line), and grew strong in the tree of life (the middle line), who has reached his branches (HGT NHY de ZA, which are the tree of life and its branches), and has clung to his roots (GAR de ZA), who eats of its fruits that are sweeter than honey (the illumination of *Hochma* in *Nukva de* ZA, which is its sweet fruit), who gives life to the soul and healing to himself (to his body), she declares and says, 'Who is the one who is rewarded with all that?' It is one who is kept from bad thoughts, from a thought that is deceitful in the tree of life, from a thought that defiles the river and the stream, the source of Israel, from a source that gives death to the soul and shattering to himself; he has no existence whatsoever."

181-182) **A good thought that rises above** clings to the tree of life, the middle line, holds onto its branches, and eats of its fruits. All the sanctities and all the blessings come from him, and he inherits life for his soul and healing for himself. It is said about him, "For he shall be as a tree planted by the waters, and ... by the river."

All the words of the world follow the thought and the contemplation. It is written, "Sanctify yourselves and be holy." This is so because He brings out and extends all the sanctities in the world with a good thought.

189) "If He set His heart upon man, He will gather his spirit and his breath unto Himself." The will and the thought draw the extension and does the deed with everything that is needed. This is why in prayer, a desire and a thought to aim in are required. Similarly, in all the works of the Creator, the thought and the contemplation does the deed and draws extension to all that is needed.

276) But in the Torah, even two who sit and engage in Torah give greatness, strength, and the glory of Torah to the Creator.

284-285) Wherever a person prays his prayer, he should incorporate himself in the public, in the manifold public, as it is written about Shunammite when Elisha told her, "Would you be spoken for to the king or to the captain of the army?" "Would you be spoken for to the king," since that day was the festival of the first day of the year, and the day when *Malchut* of the firmament rules and sentences the world. At that time, the Creator is called "The king of the sentence," and this is why he told her, "Would you be spoken for to the king," since he called the Creator "King."

And she said, "I dwell among my own people." In other words, she said, "I have no wish to be mentioned above, but to put my head among the masses and not leave the public. Similarly, man should be included in the public and not stand out as unique, so the slanderers will not look at him and mention his sins.

340) **It is written about the *Nukva*, "And it repented the Lord ... and it grieved Him,"** since *Dinim* and sadness are in this place. However, in everything that is above, in *Bina*, it is all in light and life to all directions, and there is no sadness before the place, which indicates to the inner one, *Bina*, who is the only one in whom there is no sadness. But the external one, the *Nukva*, there is sadness in her. This is why it is written, "Serve the Lord with gladness; come before His presence with singing." "Serve the Lord with gladness" corresponds to the upper world. "Come before His presence with singing" corresponds to the lower world.

341-343) **Woe unto the wicked of the world who do not know and do not look at words of Torah.** And when they do look at it, because there is no wisdom in them, the words of Torah seem to them as though they were empty and useless words. It is all because they are devoid of knowledge and wisdom, since all the words in the Torah are sublime and precious words, and each and every word that is written there is more precious than pearls, and no object can compare to it.

When all the fools whose heart is blocked see the words of Torah, not only do they not know, but they even say that the words are spoiled, useless words, woe unto them. When the Creator seeks them out for the disgrace of the Torah, they will be punished with a punishment fit for one who rebels against one's Master.

It is written in the Torah, "For it is no vain thing." And if it is vain, it is only vain for you, since the Torah is filled with every good stone and precious gem, from all the abundance in the world.

344) King Solomon said, "If you are wise, you are wise for yourself." This is so because when one grows wise in the Torah, it is to his benefit, not for the Torah, since he cannot add even a single letter to the Torah. "And if you scorn, you alone shall bear it," for nothing shall be subtracted from the praise of Torah because of that. His scorn is his alone and he will remain in it, to annihilate him from this world and from the next world.

350-352) King David always attached himself to the Creator. He did not worry about anything else in the world except to cling unto Him with his soul and his will, as it is written, "My soul cleaves unto You." And since he clung to the Creator, He supported him and He did not leave him, as it is written, "Your right hand holds me fast." We learn from this that when a person comes to cling to the Creator, the Creator holds him fast and does not leave him.

"My soul cleaves unto You," so that his degree would be crowned above. This is so because when his degree clings to the upper degrees, to rise after them, the right side, *Hassadim*, holds him so as to elevate him and connect him with the right in one bonding, as it should be. It is written about it, "Your right hand would hold me," and it is written, "And his right hand embrace me." This is why "Your right hand holds me fast."

When he grips to the Creator, it is written, "Let his left hand be under my head, and his right hand embrace me." This is one unification and one bonding with the Creator. And when it is one bonding with Him, his degree is filled and blessed.

361) **Divinity connects with those who walk on ways, to keep them.** Anyone who engages in words of Torah and exerts in it is rewarded with extending it, meaning ZA, who is the Torah. Then ZA and *Nukva*, meaning Divinity, will be connected in them in one unification.

New Zohar, VaYetze
[And Jacob Went Out]

25) Happy are Israel, to whom the Creator has given the Torah, to disclose to them high secrets.

One who grips the Torah, the Torah grips and supports him on her thighs, *Netzah* and *Hod*, so he does not stray right or left, but in the middle line, which is the Torah. Happy are Israel, to whom the Creator has given the Torah, to disclose to them high secrets. It is written about them, "And you who cleave unto the Lord your God are alive every one of you this day."

40) Rabbi says, "All things will perish, but the Torah will not perish. Nothing is as favorable to the Creator as the Torah and they who learn

it. Anyone who engages in Torah each day, the secrets of above will be renewed for him."

42-43) The secrets of Torah were given to sages, to those who always engage in Torah.

Anyone who engages in Torah sufficiently, his soul is elevated while he sleeps and he is taught from the depths of the Torah. And from it, his lips utter and whisper during the day, as it is written, "Moving gently the lips of those who are asleep." When one who engages in Torah Lishma [for Her sake] sleeps at night, his soul rises and is shown those things that are to be in the world.

44-47) Rabbi Aba and Rabbi Yosi sat and engaged in Torah until midnight. Rabbi Aba fell asleep, and Rabbi Yosi was sitting. He saw that Rabbi Aba's face was turning red and he was laughing, and he saw a great light in the house. Rabbi Yosi said, "This means that Divinity is here." He lowered his eyes, sat there until the dawn rose in the morning and the light was illuminating in the house. While he was raising his eyes, he saw the dawn and the house was darkened.

Rabbi Aba awoke, his face was glowing, and his eyes laughing. Rabbi Yosi held him. Rabbi

Aba said, "I know what you want. Indeed, I saw high secrets. When Matat, minister of the face was holding my soul, he elevated her to great and high rooms, and I saw the souls of the rest of the righteous go up there. The minister of the face told them, 'Happy are you, O righteous, because thanks to you I am built in a holy building of the honorable Name, to whom the lights of the holy Name are extended, to answer and to bestow upon the hosts of the high King.' I have seen my Torah that I had taught laid there in piles over piles, like a big tower, and this is why I was delighted with my lot and my eyes were laughing."

VaYishlach [And Jacob Sent]

1-2) When a person arrives in the world, the evil inclination immediately comes along with him and always complains about him, as it is written, "sin crouches at the door." Sin crouches—this is the evil inclination. "At the door"—the door of the womb, meaning as soon as one is born.

David called the evil inclination by the name, "sin," as it is written, "and my sin is ever before me," because it makes man sin before his Master every day. And this evil inclination does not leave man from the day he is born and for all time. And the good inclination comes to a person from the time he comes to be purified.

17) One who does not follow the evil inclination and is not proud at all, who lowers his spirit, his heart, and his will toward the Creator, the evil inclination overturns and becomes his slave, since it cannot control him. On the contrary, that man controls it, as it is written, "and thou may rule over it."

45) A prayer of many rises before the Creator and the Creator crowns Himself with that prayer, since it rises in several ways. This is because one asks for *Hassadim*, the other for *Gevurot*, and a third for *Rachamim*. And it consists of several sides: the right side, the left, and the middle. This is so because *Hassadim* extend from the right side, *Gevurot* from the left side, and *Rachamim* from the middle side. And because it consists of several ways and sides, it becomes a crown over the head of the Righteous One That Lives Forever, *Yesod*, which imparts all the salvations to the *Nukva*, and from her to the whole public.

But a prayer of one does not comprise all the sides; it is only on one way. Either one asks for *Hassadim* or *Gevurot* or *Rachamim*. Hence, a prayer of one is not erected to be received like the prayer of many, as it does not include all three lines like the prayer of many.

46) Happy are Israel, for the Creator desires them and gave them the true law, to be rewarded by it with everlasting life. The Creator draws the upper life upon anyone who engages in Torah, and brings him to the life of the next world, as it is written, "for He is your life, and the length of your days."

65) **Every man's prayer is a prayer. But the prayer of the poor is the prayer that stands before the**

Creator, for it shatters gates and doors, and enters and is admitted before Him. "...and pours out his complaint before the Lord."

69) One should first praise his Master and then pray his prayer.

90-91) **When the Creator erects Israel and delivers them from exile**, a very small and thin vent of light shall open to them. And then another, a little bigger opening will open for them, until the Creator opens for them the upper gates that are open to the four directions of the world. It is so that their salvation will not appear at once, but like the dawn, which shines gradually brighter until the day is set.

And all that the Creator does to Israel and to the righteous among them, when He delivers them bit by bit and not all at once, is like a person who is in the dark and has always been in the dark. When you want to give him light, you first need to light a small light, like the eye of a needle, and then a little bigger. Thus, every time some more until all the light properly shines for him.

121) There are sublime secrets in the words of Torah, which are different from one another, but are all one.

126) **For everything in the world depends upon Up High:** when they are first decided above, so they are decided below. And also, there is no government below until the government is given from above. And also, everything depends on each other, for all that is done in this world depends on what is done above.

164) **How favored are Israel before the Creator,** for you have not a nation or a tongue among all the idol worshipping nations in the world that has gods that will answer their prayers as the Creator is destined to answer the prayers and pleas of Israel any time they need the prayer answered. This is so because they pray only for their degree, which is Divinity. That is, each time they pray, it is for the correction of Divinity.

250-253) **The Creator placed all the idol worshipping nations in the world under certain appointed ministers,** and they all follow their gods. All shed blood and make war, steal, commit adultery, mingle among all who act to harm, and always increase their strength to harm.

Israel do not have the strength and might to defeat them, except with their mouths, with prayer, like a worm, whose only strength and might is in its mouth. But with the mouth, it breaks everything, and this is why Israel are called "a worm."

"Fear not, thou worm of Jacob." No other creature in the world is like that silk-weaving worm, from which all the garments of honor come, the attire of kings. And after weaving, she seeds and dies. Afterwards, from that very seed, she is revived as before and lives again. Such are Israel. Like that worm, even when they die, they come back and live in the world as before.

It is also said, "as clay in the hands of the potter, so you, the house of Israel, are in My hands." The material is that glass; even though it breaks, it is corrected and can be corrected as before. Such are Israel: even though they die, they relive.

254) Israel is the tree of life, ZA. And because the children of Israel clung to the tree of life, they will have life, and they will rise from the dust and live in the world, and they will become one nation, serving the Creator.

VaYeshev [And Jacob Sat]

1-2) **How many slanderers are there to a person from the day the Creator gives him a soul in this world?** And because he came into the world, the evil inclination immediately appears to partake with him, as it is written, "Sin crouches at the door," for then the evil inclination partakes with him.

A beast watches over itself from the day it is born, and runs from fire and from any bad place. When man is born, he immediately comes to throw himself into the fire, since the evil inclination is within him and promptly incites him to the evil way.

10-11) **A righteous man** is a person who did not believe that crafty wicked, the evil inclination, since he made his arguments before the arrival of his friend, the good inclination. Rather, he keeps the other one, and his friend came and questioned him. It is in this that people fail from being rewarded with the next world.

But a righteous one, who fears his Master, how much evil does he suffer in this world so as to not believe and partake with the evil inclination?

But the Creator saves him from all of them, as it is written, "Many are the ills of the righteous, but the Lord delivers him from them all." The text [in Hebrew] does not say, "Many are the ills of the righteous," but "Many ills, righteous." Thus, one who suffers many ills is righteous because the Creator wants him. This is so because the ills he suffers remove him from the evil inclination, and for this reason the Creator wants that person and delivers him from them all. And he is happy in this world and in the next world.

26-28) **When there is judgment over man, and he is righteous, it is because of the Creator's love for him.** It is as we have learned, that when the Creator is merciful to man with love, to bring him closer to Him, He breaks the body so as to ordain the soul. And then man comes closer to Him with love, as it should be—the soul governs man and the body weakens.

Man needs a weak body and a strong soul, one that prevails with strength. And then the Creator loves him. The Creator gives sorrow to the righteous in this world in order to purify him for the next world.

And when the soul is weak and the body is strong, he is an enemy of the Creator, for

He does not desire him and does not give him sorrow in this world. Instead, his path is straight and he is in complete wholeness. This is because if he acts justly or his deeds are good, the Creator pays his reward in this world, and he will have no share in the next world. For this reason, the righteous who is always broken is loved by the Creator. These words apply only if one has tested and has not found within him a sin for which to be punished.

29) Divinity does not dwell in a place of sadness, but in a place of joy. And if one has no joy, Divinity will not be in that place.

38) **This is so because once the body breaks** through the flaw and the *Katnut* of the soul, by which the *Kli* to receive the *Gadlut* of the soul was created, then the Creator wants them. But before the body breaks due to the flaw in the soul, the Creator does not want them because they are unfit to receive the light of *Neshama*.

60) **Each of the souls in the world,** which existed in this world and tried to know their Maker with the sublime wisdom, rises and exists in a higher degree than all those souls that did not attain and did not know. And they will be revived first.

And this is the question that that servant was about to ask and to know, "What was that soul engaged in, in this world?" to see if she is worthy of being revived first.

120) **"The law of the Lord is perfect, restoring the soul."** People should delve in the Torah abundantly, for anyone who delves in the Torah will have life in this world and in the next world, and he will be rewarded with both worlds. And even one who delves in it, but does not delve in it properly, he is still imparted a good reward in this world and is not judged in the world of truth.

155) **How foolish are people, for they do not know and do not observe the ways of the Creator. They are all asleep, lest sleep will depart the holes of their eyes.**

156) **The Creator made man as it is above, all in wisdom.** And there is not an organ in a man that does not stand in sublime wisdom, for each organ implies a unique degree. And after the whole body is properly corrected in its organs, the Creator partakes with it, and instills a holy soul within it, to teach man the ways of Torah and to keep His commandments so that man will be corrected appropriately, as it is written, "the soul of man shall teach him."

157) One should increase the similarity to the Upper King in the world. This is why the waters of that river that extends and flows out (which is the upper *Yesod*) never stop. Hence, man, too, should not stop the river and his source in this world, but should bear sons.

223-224) When one sees that bad thoughts come upon him, he should engage in Torah, and they will go away. When that evil inclination comes to tempt a person, he should draw it unto the Torah, and it will depart him.

We learned that when this evil side stands before the Creator to accuse the world for the bad deeds that they had done, the Creator has mercy on the world and advises people how to be saved from it so it may not control them or their deeds. And what is the advice? It is to delve in the Torah, and they will be saved from it, as it is written, "For the commandment is a candle and the teaching is light," "To keep you from the evil woman." Thus, the Torah keeps one from the evil inclination.

228) Happy are Israel, for they adhere to the Creator as it should be, and He gives them the counsel by which to be saved from all the other sides in the world, since they are a holy nation for His share and for His lot. Hence, He gives them advice on every single thing. Happy are they in this world and in the next.

252) **And one who delves in Torah and good deeds** causes the Assembly of Israel, Divinity, to raise her head while in exile. Happy are those who delve in the Torah at daytime and at night.

New Zohar, VaYeshev [And Jacob Sat]

9) When a person approaches the Torah, who is called "good," he approaches the Creator, who is called "good." Then he comes closer to being righteous, who is called "good." And when he is righteous, Divinity is upon him, teaching him the high secrets of the Torah because Divinity mates only with the good, who is righteous. And the righteous and justice [Tzadik and Tzedek respectively], who is Divinity, go together.

11-12) "The eyes of all await You," awaiting the high anointing oil that flows from the Moach that is more hidden than all who are hidden, from AA, illumination of GAR, to all, Yesod. And then "You give them their food in its time," in Malchut, called "Its time," since when "all," Yesod, awakens the bride, the Assembly of Israel–Malchut, called "The whole of the

Lord"—then He has pity on the world and all the worlds are in gladness and play from the illumination of GAR.

Then it is written, "You open Your hand and satisfy the will of every living thing." This is the desire of desires, which comes down from *Mocha Stimaa de AA* to all, *Yesod*. And when all is blessed, all the worlds are blessed, as it is written, "The Lord is righteous in all," "The Lord is near to all."

MIKETZ [AT THE END]

3-6) See how people should consider the work of the Creator and delve in the Torah day and night, so as to know and to observe His work, for the Torah declares before man every day and says, "Whoever is naive, let him turn in here."

And when a person engages in the Torah and clings to it, he is rewarded with strengthening in the tree of life, ZA. And when a person is strengthened in the tree of life in this world, he strengthens in it for the next world. And when the souls depart this world, the degrees of the next world will be corrected for them.

The tree of life divides into several degrees, and they are all one. This is so because there are degrees in the tree of life, one atop the other—branches, leaves, shells, trunk, roots, and it is all the tree. Similarly, one who delves in the Torah is corrected and strengthens in the tree of life, the trunk of the tree.

And all the children of Israel are strengthened by the tree of life; they all literally cling to the tree but some to its trunk, some to the branches, some to the leaves, and some to the roots. It turns out that they all cling to the tree of life, and all those who engage in the Torah cling to the trunk of the tree. For this reason, one who engages in the Torah clings to the whole tree, for the trunk of the tree contains all of it.

10) **When the Creator created the upper world,** *Bina*, He established everything as it should be and elicited upper lights that shine from all sides, which are the three lines, and all are one. He created the heavens above, ZA, and the earth above, the *Nukva*, so they would all be established as one, *Bina* and ZON, in favor of the lower ones.

32) **"The Lord favors those who fear Him."** Oh how the Creator desires the righteous, since the righteous make peace above, in *AVI*, and make peace below, in ZON, and bring the bride to her husband. And for this reason, the Creator desires those who fear Him and do His will. Through the MAN that they raise to ZON, ZON, too, raise MAN to AVI, and a *Zivug* occurs above, in AVI, and below, in ZON. And they bring the bride, *Nukva*, to her husband, ZA, to mate. For this reason, the Creator, ZA, desires only them, for without them there would be no peace, which is a *Zivug*, neither above in AVI nor below in ZON.

51) **All the deeds in the world depend on a few appointees,** for you do not have a blade of grass below that does not have an appointee above, which strikes and tells it, "Grow." And all the people in the world do not know and do not watch over their root—the reason why they are in the world.

52) **Happy are those who engage in Torah and know how to observe the spirit of wisdom.** "He has made every thing beautiful in its time," meaning in all the deeds that the Creator has done in the world, there is a degree that is appointed over that deed in the world, both for better and for worse.

53) **For the whole world and all the deeds in the world are connected to holiness only by the desire of the heart, when it comes into man's will.** It is written, "Know this day, and lay it to thy heart." Happy are the righteous who draw good deeds by the will of their hearts, to do good to themselves and to the entire world. They know how to adhere at a time of peace, when there is a *Zivug* of the upper one, called "peace."

55) **Why should one rejoice with the bad?** If the deed he has done harmed him because of the

degree that was appointed over it from the left, he should be happy and thankful for this bad that has come to him, for he caused that himself, since he went without knowledge, like a trapped bird. And now, since he has obtained knowledge through the punishment, he will know how to do good in his life. Hence, he should be happy and thankful for the punishment.

56) **Happy are those who engage in Torah, who know the ways and trails of the law of the High King, to walk in it on the path of truth.**

57) **One should never open one's mouth for evil, for he does not know who receives the word. And when a person does not know, he fails in it. And when the righteous open their mouths, it is all peace.**

177-178) **There is not a word in the Torah that does not possess sublime and holy secrets, and ways for people to strengthen themselves.**

The Creator made it for man to strengthen himself in the Torah and to walk on the path of truth and toward the right side, and not to the left side. And because people need to walk to the right side, they should increase the love between each other. This is because love is considered "right," and there will not be hatred between each other, which is considered left, so as to not weaken the right—the place to which Israel cling.

179) **This is why there is a good inclination and an evil inclination. And Israel need to make the good inclination prevail over the evil inclination through good deeds.** If a person leans to the left, the evil inclination overcomes the good inclination. And in one who is flawed, the evil inclination complements his sin, since this villain is complemented only through people's sins.

180) For this reason, man must be wary so the evil inclination will not be complemented by his sins. And he should always be watchful, for the good inclination must be complemented with continuous wholeness, and not the evil inclination. Hence, "Do not say, 'I will repay evil,'" since through hatred you will intensify the left and complement the evil inclination. Rather, "Hope for the Lord and you will be salvaged."

195) **One should always anger the good inclination over the evil inclination and exert**

after it. If it parts with him, good. If not, let him engage in Torah, since nothing breaks the evil inclination except the Torah.

209) When one prays to the Creator, he should not look whether his salvation came or not, for when he looks, several litigants come to look at his actions.

266) **The Creator made the right, and He made the left, to lead the world.** One is called "good," "right," and one is called "evil," "left." Man includes both and approaches the Creator with everything, as it is written, "In both of your inclinations—the good inclination and the evil inclination."

VaYigash
[Then Judah Approached]

10-11) When the Creator created the world, He made the lower world as the upper world. He did everything one opposite the other, where each detail in the lower world has a corresponding root in the upper world, and this is His glory above and below.

And He created man over everything, to contain and complement all the details of creation.

11) Since man is the purpose of the whole world and its perfection.

16-17) And these three degrees—*Nefesh, Ruach, Neshama*—are included in those who have been rewarded with the work of their Master. This is so because first, one has *Nefesh*. This is a holy correction for people to be corrected in. Since man comes to be purified in that degree, he is corrected to be crowned with *Ruach*. This is a holy degree that is on the *Nefesh*, for that man who has been rewarded to crown himself with it.

When he ascends in *Nefesh* and *Ruach* and comes to be corrected in the work of his Master properly, then *Neshama* is upon him, a superior, holy degree that governs everything, so he would be crowned in a degree of sublime holiness. And then he will be whole in everything, whole from every side, rewarded with the next world and the Creator's loved one, as it is written, "To endow those who love me with substance." "Those who love me" are those with a holy *Neshama* in them.

27) Here, faith is *Nukva* because when the desire is revealed and the unification is crowned in ZON as one, the two worlds, ZON, connect together and are assembled together. ZA is to open the treasure and bestow, and the *Nukva* gathers and collects the abundance into her.

41) "By wisdom did the Lord establish the earth." When the Creator created the world, He saw that it could not exist because the world was created under the domination of the left line, *Hochma* without *Hassadim*, and *Hochma* does not shine without *Hassadim*. Hence, it could not exist until He created the Torah, the middle line. ZA is called "Torah"; it includes the two lines—right and left—in one another, so *Hochma* was included in *Hassadim* and then *Hochma* illuminated.

From it, from the middle line, arrive all the upper and lower conducts, in which the upper and lower persist. This is why it is written that *HaVaYaH*, meaning ZA, middle line, establish the earth by wisdom, meaning He established the earth with wisdom because He clothed the *Hochma* in *Hassadim* and the illumination of *Hochma* could exist in the world. Every existence in the world exists in *Hochma* and everything stems from it, as it is written, "In wisdom have You made them all."

61) **Happy are the righteous, whose closeness to each other brings peace to the world** because they know how to unite the unification and to make nearness, to increase peace in the world. As long as Joseph and Judah were not close to one another, there was no peace. When Joseph and Judah drew close together, peace increased in the world and joy was added above and below while Joseph and Judah were brought closer.

62-63) **The Creator created the world and made man its ruler, to be king over everything.**

And from this man, several kinds part in the world—some are righteous, some wicked, some are fools, and some are wise. All four kinds exist in the world, rich and poor, so they will be purified and do good to one another. The righteous will do good to the wicked and reform them; the wise will do good to the fools and teach them wisdom; and the rich will do good to the poor and fulfill their needs. It is so because by that, man is rewarded with everlasting life and connects to the tree of life.

VaYechi [Jacob Lived]

22) "From afar the Lord appeared unto me; 'I have loved you with an everlasting love.'" "From afar" means in exile. This was because of the great love that appears only through exile. Exile is the correction; when the children of Israel are liberated from the exile, the Creator's love for us will be revealed.

58) Rabbi Shimon said, "Once I rose and descended to illuminate in the place of the streams." In other words, he raised MAN and brought down MAD to the *Malchut* from the source of the streams, *Bina*. It is written, "All the streams go unto the sea, but the sea is not full." All the ministers in the world were created from the light of *Bina*, and all the streams in the world stem from His light, meaning that "All the streams go unto the sea, but the sea is not full."

"The sea is not full" is *Malchut* in this exile, since the darkness and gloom in the exile were made by the love of *Ima*, *Bina*. If the darkness had not been made, the stream that shines to the daughter, *Malchut*, would not have been made. Also, the sea will not be full and complete until the other side comes, that which was not in exile, the right side, which no *Klipa* governs, and then the sea, *Malchut*, will fill.

116-117) Divinity is present only in a whole place, and not in a deficient place or a flawed place or a place of sadness, but in a proper place—a place of joy.

"Serve the Lord with gladness; come before Him with singing." There is no service of the Creator unless out of joy.

120) Since the day Rabbi Shimon came out of the cave, nothing was hidden from the friends. They looked at the high secrets and were revealed in them as though they were given at that time at Mount Sinai. After Rabbi Shimon died, the fountains of the deep and the windows of heaven were closed. The fountains of wisdom were stopped. The friends were contemplating matters, but they did not stand in them, to know their meaning.

156) We have no attainment in GAR, even the GAR of the ten *Sefirot* of the world of *Assiya*, but only in ZAT. In ZAT, a chosen few can attain even in ZAT de GAR of the world of *Atzilut*. Rabbi Yitzhak's father tells us that Rabbi Shimon held the ZAT of all the *Partzufim* of *Atzilut*, even the ZAT de GAR de Atzilut.

157) **How much longer is one given to live in this world?** There is no permission to inform this, and one is not informed of this. But Rabbi Shimon was in great joy on the day of his demise, and there was great joy in all the worlds because of the many secrets he had revealed then.

210) **How important are the works of the Holy King.** In the deeds that are done below, they tie them with the high things above, in their root, since anything below in this world has its root above in the upper worlds. And when they are taken down and worked with, the act above awakens corresponding to them, in the roots in the upper worlds.

212) **"Every one that is called by My name ... for My glory,"** so that I will be respected. **"Whom I have created,"** to unify Me. **"I have formed him"** to do good deeds unto Me, and **"I have made him"** to evoke the upper force through it.

237) **People do not look, do not know, and do not observe** that when the Creator created man and cherished him with the upper *Mochin*, He asked of him to adhere to Him so he would be unique

and would have one heart, and would adhere to a single place of *Dvekut* [adhesion], which does not change—in ZA. It was said about it, "I the Lord do not change," and never invert, and everything ties to it in a knot of unification.

295) **"The deaf heard and the blind looked, so as to see."** "The deaf heard" are those people who do not listen to the words of Torah and do not open their ears to hear the commandments of their Master. "The blind" are those who do not look to know what they are living for because each day, a herald comes out and calls, and there is no one to notice him.

408) **When the blessings extend from above**, from this depth, *Bina*, all of heaven receive them, meaning ZA, and from him, they extend below until they reach the righteous, *Tzadik* and *Tzedek*, everlasting covenant, the *Nukva*, and from her, all the armies and all the camps, which are the lower ones in *BYA*, are blessed.

414) **Anyone who comes to serve the Creator should serve the Creator in the morning and in the evening.**

426) **When a man goes out to the road,** he should set up his prayer before his Master, to

extend the light of Divinity on himself, and then set out. It turns out that the *Zivug* of Divinity is to redeem him on the way and to save him however is needed.

495) Women are blessed only by males, when they are blessed first. And they are blessed from this blessing of the males. They do not need a special blessing of their own. Then why does the verse say, "Will bless the house of Israel," if the women do not need a special blessing? Indeed, the Creator gives an additional blessing to a male who is married to a woman so that his wife will be blessed from him.

Similarly, in all places, the Creator gives additional blessing to a male who has married a woman so she will be blessed by this addition. And since a man marries a woman, He gives him two shares, one for himself and one for his wife. And he receives everything, his own share and his wife's. This is why a special blessing is written for the women, "Will bless the house of Israel," for this is their share. However, the males receive their share, as well, and give it to them later.

497-498) **All those souls that have been since the day the world was created** stand before the Creator before they come down to the world in the very same form that they will later be seen in the world. In the same appearance as a body of a man who is standing in this world, so he stands above.

When the soul is ready to come down to the world, she stands before the Creator in the exact same form that she stands in this world, and the Creator adjures her to keep the *Mitzvot* [commandments] of the Torah and to not breach the laws of Torah.

507) **The sound of the rolling wheel rolls from below upwards. Hidden *Merkavot* [structures/ chariots] go and roll. The sound of melodies rises and falls, and wanders and roams the world; the sound of the *Shofar* [ram's horn] stretches through the depth of the degrees and orbits around the wheel.**

513-515) **"He has regarded the prayer of the destitute and has not despised their prayer."** It should have said, "listened" or "heard," but what is "regarded"?

Indeed, all the prayers in the world, prayers of many, are prayers. But a solitary prayer does not enter before the Holy King, unless with great force. This is so because before the prayer enters to be crowned in its place, the Creator watches it, observes it, and observes the sins and merits of that person, which He does not do with a prayer of many, where several of the prayers are not from righteous, and they all enter before the Creator and He does not notice their iniquities.

"He has regarded the prayer of the destitute." He turns the prayer and examines it from all sides, and considers with which desire the prayer was made, who is the person who prayed that prayer, and what are his deeds. Hence, one should pray one's prayer in the collective, since He does not despise their prayer, even though they are not all with intent and the will of heart, as it is written, "He has regarded the prayer of the destitute." Thus, He only observes the prayer of an individual, but with a prayer of many, He does not despise their prayer, even though they are unworthy.

678) **It is man's obligation to unite the holy Name, *Nukva*, with ZA, in mouth, heart, and soul**, and to connect wholly in ZON, to raise MAN to them as a flame tied to an ember. And in that unification that it does, it causes the King to be appeased about the queen and alerts the King of her love for Him. By the ascent of the

soul for MAN to ZA, she becomes a middle line between them, makes peace, and unites them with each other.

688) **Happy are the people in the world who engage in Torah,** because anyone who engages in Torah is loved above and loved below, and each day he inherits the inheritance of the next world, as it is written, "To endow those who love me with substance." The substance is the next world, *Bina*, whose waters—his abundance—never stop, since one who engages in Torah receives a good high reward, with which another person is not rewarded, meaning the substance, *Bina*. For this reason, this name, Issachar, who engaged in Torah, implies that *Yesh Sachar* [there is reward], and the reward of those who engage in Torah is substance, *Bina*.

713-714) **"One should always praise one's Master and then pray his prayer."** One whose heart is pure and wishes to pray his prayer, or is in trouble and cannot praise his Master, what is he?

Even though he cannot aim the heart and will, why should he diminish his Master's praise? Rather, he will praise his Master even though he cannot aim, and then he shall pray his prayer. It is written, "A prayer of David. Hear a just cause, O Lord, hear my singing, listen to my prayer." "Hear a just cause, O Lord," first, since he praised his Master. Afterwards, "Hear my singing, listen to my prayer." One who can praise his Master and does not do so, it is written about him, "Even if you pray profusely, I do not hear."

715) This is so because the lower ones in the world of *Assiya* cannot raise MAN directly to ZON *de Atzilut*, but only to the adjacent degree above. In turn, that degree raises higher, to the one adjacent to it from above, and so the MAN rises from degree to degree until the MAN reaches ZON *de Atzilut*. This is why it is said that upon the awakening below through the offering that the lower ones offer in the world of *Assiya*, above awakens, too, meaning that the degrees in the world of *Yetzira* awaken to raise the MAN that they received from *Assiya* to the world of *Beria*. And upon the awakening of the degrees of *Beria* above to the one above it, the world of *Atzilut*, its own adjacent superior awakens until the MAN reaches the *Nukva* and raises the MAN to ZA, and she shines from him. Lighting the candle means uniting the *Nukva*, who is called "a candle," in ZA, to receive light from it. This is considered that she is lit by it.

716) How is this done? The smoke of the offering begins to rise—those holy forms appointed over the world of *Assiya*. They are established to arise to raise MAN, and they awaken to degrees above them in the world of *Yetzira*, in high craving, as it is written, "The young lions roar for prey." Those in the world of *Yetzira* awaken to degrees above them in the world of *Beria* until the awakening reaches the place where they must light the candle, meaning until the king, ZA, wishes to unite with the queen, the *Nukva*.

717) What are MAN? In the craving below, lower waters rise, meaning MAN, to receive upper waters, MAD, from the degree atop them. This is so because lower waters, MAN, spring out only by an awakening of the desire of the lower one. At that time, the craving of the lower one and the upper one become attached, and lower waters spring out opposite the descending upper waters, the *Zivug* ends and the worlds are blessed, all the candles light up, and the upper ones and lower ones are in blessings.

717) **Each lower degree is considered a female with respect to the degree above it**. Thus, *Assiya* is considered a female with respect to the world

of *Yetzira*, and *Yetzira* is considered a female with respect to the world of *Beria*. Similarly, the upper degree is considered a male with respect to the one below it, such as *Yetzira* being considered a male with respect to the world of *Assiya* and *Beria* is considered a male with respect to the world of *Yetzira*. This is so because the rule is that the giver is a male and the receiver is a female.

And since a degree cannot receive anything from a degree that is more than one degree above it, and receives only from its adjacent higher degree, it follows that each upper degree that gives is a male, and each lower degree that receives from it is a female. And through the craving, when each lower one craves to receive abundance from the one above, it raises *MAN* to it in a way that each lower one raises *MAN* to the one above it, adjacent to it, until it reaches *Ein Sof*. At that time, *Ein Sof* brings down abundance, *MAD*, and each upper degree gives the abundance that it received to the adjacent degree below it, since the *MAD* cascades from one degree to the next, through the lower ones in the world of *Assiya*.

SHEMOT

[EXODUS]

SHEMOT [EXODUS]

1) "And the wise will glow as the brightness of the firmament." The wise are those who gaze at the wisdom, who have attained wisdom, since wisdom is called "the light of the eyes" and attaining it is called "looking."

60) **Woe unto people who do not know and are not careful with the work of their Creator.** This is so because each day, a voice comes out of Mount Horev and says, "Woe unto people, for they slight the works of their Creator. Woe unto people from desecrating the glory of the Torah."

Anyone who engages in Torah in this world and acquires good deeds inherits a whole world. And anyone who does not engage in Torah in this world and does not do good deeds, inherits neither this world nor the next world.

61) If people knew the love that the Creator loves Israel, they would roar as lions and chase Him in order to adhere to Him.

67-68) **"Happy are you who sow beside all waters, who send out freely the ox and the donkey."** Happy are Israel, whom the Creator desires more than all the nations and brought them close to Him, as it is written, "The Lord your God has chosen you." It is also written, "For the portion of the Lord is His people, Jacob the lot of His inheritance." And Israel adhere to the Creator, as it is written, "But you who cling unto the Lord your God."

They are righteous before Him because they sow beside all waters, they sow for righteousness, meaning they raise MAN to extend *Mochin* to *Malchut* so she will be called *Tzedakah* [righteousness], since without the *Mochin* she is called *Tzedek* [justice], without the *Hey* [in Hebrew]. And it is written of one who sows for righteousness, "For Your mercy is great above the heavens." "Above the heavens" is also called "Beside all waters." "Above the heavens" is the next world, *Bina*, which is above ZA, called "heavens." And Israel sow a seed and raise MAN beside all waters, *Bina*, to extend *Mochin* unto *Malchut* so she will be called *Tzedakah* [righteousness/almsgiving].

84) **Sages are more important than prophets at any time,** since prophets are sometimes imbued with the spirit of holiness and sometimes not. But the spirit of holiness is not removed from sages

for even a moment; they know what is above and below, and do not need to reveal...Were it not for sages, people would not know what is Torah and what are the *Mitzvot* [commandments] of the Creator, and there would be no difference between man's spirit and the spirit of a beast.

176) "My beloved is gone down into his garden, to the beds of spices." "His garden" is the Assembly of Israel, *Nukva*, because she is the bed of spices, for she consists of various spices and scents of the next world, *Bina*. When the Creator descends to that garden, the *Nukva*, meaning all the souls of the righteous are crowned there and receive *Mochin* and illuminations. They all emit scent, as it is written, "[How fair is] the smell of your ointments than all manner of spices," which are the souls of the righteous, called "spices." It is after them that the *Nukva* is called "the bed of spices." All those souls of the righteous who were in this world, and all those souls that are destined to come down to this world are standing here in this garden, in the *Nukva*.

185) Happy are the righteous whose will is to always adhere to the Creator. As they always adhere to Him, He is always adhered to them and never leaves them.

203-204) **All things in the world depend on repentance and on the prayer that a man prays to the Creator.** It is all the more so with one who sheds tears during his prayer, for there is no gate through which these tears do not come. It is written, "She opened it and saw the child." "Opened" is Divinity, who stands over Israel like a mother over her children, opening, always in favor of Israel.

When she opened and saw the child, a delightful child, Israel, who always sin before their King and promptly plea before the Creator, repent, and cry before Him as a son who cries before his father. It is written, "And behold a boy that wept." Since he wept, all the harsh decrees in the world were removed from him.

235-236) **"Hurry, my beloved, and be like a gazelle or a young hart."** Every yearning that Israel yearned for the Creator is the yearning of Israel that the Creator will not go and will not walk away, but run like a gazelle or a young hart.

No other animal in the world does what the gazelle or the hart does. When it runs, it turns its head slightly to the place from which it came. It always turns its head back. This is what Israel said, "God Almighty, if we cause You to depart from among us, may it be that You will run like the gazelle or the young hart." This is because it runs and turns its head to the place it had left, the place where it was before, which it left and fled from there.

This is the meaning of the words, "Yet in spite of this, when they are in the land of their enemies, I will not reject them, nor will I so abhor them as to destroy them, breaking My covenant with them." Another thing: The gazelle sleeps with one eye and is awake with the other eye. This is what Israel said to the Creator, "Do as the gazelle does, for "He who keeps Israel will neither slumber nor sleep."

241-242) **This is Rabbi Shimon. When he opens his mouth to begin to engage in Torah**, all the thrones, all the firmaments, all the *Merkavot*, and all those who praise their Master listen to his voice.

There is none to begin and say songs, and there is none to complete his singing. In other words, those who stand in the middle of the singing do not complete their song because they all become attentive to the voice of Rabbi Shimon, until an utterance of a mouth is heard through all the firmaments above and below.

When Rabbi Shimon concludes engaging in the Torah, who saw songs? Who saw joy of those who praise their Master? Who saw the voices that walk in all the firmaments? It is for Rabbi Shimon that all the souls and angels come and kneel and bow before their Master, and raise the fragrances of the perfumes in Eden—illumination of *Hochma*—all the way to *Atik Yomin*. All this is for Rabbi Shimon.

251-252) Rabbi Shimon sat, and Rabbi Elazar, his son, stood and interpreted the words of the secrets of the wisdom. His face was shining like the sun and the words were spreading and flying in the firmament. They sat for two days; they neither ate nor drank, and they did not know if it was day or night. When they came out, they knew that two days had passed without them eating a thing. Rabbi Shimon called out about it, "And he was there with the Lord forty days and forty nights; he neither ate bread." And what if we, who were rewarded with adhesion with the Creator, were so for one hour, having been in the light of the Creator for two days, not knowing where we are? Moses, the text testifies that he was there with the Creator forty days.

When Rabbi Hiya told the story to his father, Rabbi Shimon Ben Gamliel, he was bewildered and said, "Rabbi Shimon Bar-Yochai is a lion, and Rabbi Elazar, his son, is a lion. And Rabbi Shimon is not like all other lions. It is written about him, 'When a lion roars, who will not fear?' And if the worlds above shiver from him, we do even more. He is a man who never declared a fast for what he asked and prayed. Rather, he decides and the Creator keeps. The Creator decides and he revokes, as it is written, 'Ruler over men shall be the righteous, even he that rules in the fear of God,' meaning the Creator rules over man, and the righteous rules over the Creator; He sentences a decree, and the righteous revokes it."

288) **Israel were enslaved by all the nations so that the world would rise through them,** since they are opposite the whole world. It is written, "In that day shall the Lord be One, and His name one." And as the Creator is one, Israel are one, as it is written, "One nation in the land." As the name of the Creator is "One," and spreads in seventy names, Israel are one and spread into seventy.

354) **The cry is greater than all of them,** for the cry is in the heart. It is closer to the Creator than a prayer or a sigh, as it is written, "For if they cry unto Me, I will surely hear their cry."

356-357) **One who prays and cries and cries out** until he can no longer move his lips, this is a complete prayer that is in the heart. It is never returned empty, but is accepted. Great is the cry for it tears a man's sentence from all his days.

Great is the cry that governs the quality of *Din* above. Great is the cry that governs this world and the next world. For a cry, man inherits this world and the next world, as it is written, "Then they cried unto the Lord in their trouble, and He delivered them out of their distresses."

358-359) **When a thought came before the Creator to create His world,** all the worlds rose in one thought, and in that thought they were all created, as it is written, "In wisdom have You made them all." And in that thought, which is wisdom [*Hochma*], this world and the world above were created.

His right [side] leaned and He created the world above, ZA. His left [side] leaned and He created this world, *Malchut*, as it is written, "My hand has laid the foundation of the earth," *Malchut*, "And My right hand has spread out the heavens," ZA. "When I call unto them, they stand up together."

All were created in a single moment, and He made this world corresponding the world above, and all that there is above, its likeness appeared below. Thus, there is nothing below without a root in the upper worlds.

360) **It is written of man that He made man in the image of God. It is also written, "You have made him a little lower than God."** If people so cherish their deeds and they are lower than the dust of the well, for they are lowered by the *Klipot* that cling to the dust of *Malchut*, called "well," how will they come to pump out abundance from the well? He chose the upper ones, the angels, and He chose Israel. He did not call the upper ones, "sons," but called the lower ones, "sons," as it is written, "You are the children of the Lord your God." He called them "children," and they called Him "Father," as it is written, "For you are our father," and it is written, "My Beloved is mine and I am His," meaning He chose me and I chose Him.

371) "A Psalm of David. The Lord is my shepherd; I shall not want." "The Lord is my shepherd," my shepherd. As the shepherd leads the flock to a good grazing site, a lush grazing site, in a place of springs, and straightens their walk with righteousness and justice, so does the Creator, as it is written, "He makes me lie down in green pastures; He leads me beside the still waters, He restores my soul."

VaEra [And I Appeared]

1-2) **"Trust in the Lord forever and ever, for the Lord is God, an everlasting rock."** "Trust in the Lord" means that all the people in the world should strengthen themselves in the Creator and have confidence in Him.

Thus, what is "Forever and ever"? One's strength should be in a place of persistence and connection of everything, and this is called *Ad* [and ever], which is ZA. This "And ever" is a place that unites to this side and to that side, which is the middle line, which unites the right and the left in each other, to persist and to connect, so the two lines will persist and their illuminations would be permanently connected.

7) **"Trust in the Lord forever and ever."** In all of man's days, he needs to strengthen himself in the Creator. One who puts his trust and strength appropriately cannot be harmed by any person in the world, for anyone who places his strength in the Holy Name persists in the world.

15) **"A Psalm of David. The land is the Lord's, and all it contains; the world and those who dwell in it."** "The land" is the holy land of Israel,

which is destined to be watered by the Creator and to be blessed with Him first. And from it, the whole world will be watered. "The world and those who dwell in it" is the rest of the lands, which drink from it.

24) **"And the wise shall shine as the brightness of the firmament."** The wise are those sages that have observed sublime things of their own, of whom people cannot speak aloud for their great height. They are the ones called "wise."

31) **This is why the way of the righteous** is that it seems as though they speak to a person, but they raise their words to the Creator, to keep, "I have set the Lord always before me."

32) **How dense are people for not knowing and not observing why they are in the world. After all, when the Creator created the world, He made man in His image and established him with His corrections, to engage in Torah and to walk in His ways.**

61-63) **How do all the days of the year render healing to all the organs? After all, *Malchut*, the year, has nothing of herself? On the contrary, the organs, which are the general, are the 248 pipes of abundance of ZA, and they**

impart everything to Malchut. This is certainly so above, in ZA, and below, in man. The year and its days, which are its *Sefirot*, give healing to all the organs above, in ZA, and below, in man, since the organs impart abundance of blessings for the days of the year, which are the *Sefirot* of *Malchut*, the individual.

In each positive *Mitzva* that a person keeps, he extends abundance of blessings from an organ, a pipe of ZA, unto one of the days of the year, which is the individual. And then healing and life hang upon us from above until the organs are filled with all the perfection, imparting them upon the individual, which is the year. At that time, the *Mochin* of the individual appear.

Who caused the organs to be filled with all the perfection? The days of the year, since the organs came to complement it. If the year did not need correction, the organs—which are ZA's pipes of bounty—would not be filled with abundance. This is why it is regarded as though the days of the year gave healing and life to the organs.

And so it is below. When a person complements himself in these 248 positive *Mitzvot* in the Torah, there is not a day that does not come to be blessed by man. And when they are blessed by him, then life and healing hang over him from above, meaning they do not extend to *Malchut* before a person completes all 248 positive *Mitzvot* to the fullest. And until then, they hang over him from above.

Who caused the pipes above to be filled with healing and life? It is the days of the year. This is why it is regarded as though the days of the year gave them healing and life. As the days of the year are blessed from above, from man, which is ZA, they are blessed below, from the lower man, through the *Mitzvot* that he observes.

Happy are Israel in this world, in those *Mitzvot* that they keep, for this is why they are called "man," as it is written, "And you ... are men." This means that you are called "men," and the idol worshippers are not called "men." And because Israel are called "men," they should exert in the *Mitzvot* of the Torah, which are 613, corresponding to the 248 organs and 365 tendons in a man's body, which are all one body, man.

81) **In an awakening from below, when Israel awakened to the Creator and cried before Him**, it is written, "And I have remembered My covenant." Then the desire awakened to tie everything into one connection. Since the covenant, *Yesod de* ZA, awakened, the connection of all the *Sefirot*

to ZA awakened. "And I have remembered My covenant" means connecting him to *Malchut*. This is why it is written, "Therefore say unto the children of Israel, 'I am the Lord,'" that all the *Sefirot* connected in a single connection to redeem Israel from Egypt.

89-90) **"Know this day and take it to your heart that the Lord, He is God."** It should have said, "Know this day that the Lord, He is God," and in the end, "And take it to your heart," since knowing that the Lord is God qualifies him to respond so to the heart. And if he has already responded to his heart, it is especially so if he already has knowledge. Also, it should have said, "take it to your heart" [with one *Bet*] instead of "heart" [with a double *Bet*].

Heart with a double *Bet* means that the good inclination and the evil inclination, which reside in the heart, have mingled in one another and they are one. "And you shall love the Lord your God with all your heart" means with both your inclinations—the good inclination and the evil inclination, so the bad qualities of the evil inclination will become good, meaning he will serve the Lord with them and not sin through them. Then there will certainly be no difference between the good inclination and the evil inclination and they will be one.

Then you will find that the Lord [HaVaYaH] is God, that the quality of Din, called "God," is included in HaVaYaH, which is the quality of Rachamim [mercy], since they have been included in one another, as the evil inclination and the good inclination were included in the heart, and it is one. Thus, we can know that the Lord is God only by taking it to the heart. This is why the text places "Take it to your heart" first, to thus know the matter of the Lord being God.

176) When the friends are on the way, they should go with one heart. If there are wicked ones walking among them or people who are not from the King's palace, they should part them.

183) **"Her ways are ways of pleasantness, and all her paths are peace."** "Her ways are ways of pleasantness" are the ways of the Torah. Anyone who walks in the ways of Torah, the Creator brings upon him the pleasantness of Divinity, so it would never leave him. "And all her paths are peace" are the paths of the Torah, since all the paths of the Torah are peace—peace for him above, peace for him below, peace for him in this world, and peace for him in the next world.

Bo [Come unto Pharaoh]

98) **At midnight, Rabbi Hiya and Rabbi Yosi saw a deer walking passed them yelling and raising her voice.** They heard one voice declaring and saying, "Rise you youth, awaken those who are asleep. Worlds, prepare before your masters because your master is going to the Garden of Eden, *Malchut*, which is His palace, to entertain with the righteous."

100) When the Creator appears over the garden, the whole garden gathers, all the righteous in the garden, and it does not separate from Eden, *Hochma*. And springs, illumination of *Hochma*, come out of this Eden toward several ways and trails for the attainment of the righteous. And this garden is called, "The bundle of life," where the righteous are refined by the illumination of the next world.

126) **The Creator made Jerusalem below, *Malchut*, such as Jerusalem above, *Bina*. And He had made the walls of the city and its gates.** One who comes does not enter until the gates are opened to him, and one who climbs does not rise until the steps to the walls are fixed.

Who can open the gates of the holy city, and who fixes the high steps? It is Rabbi Shimon Bar-Yochai. He opens the gates to the secrets of the wisdom, and he fixes the high degrees.

235) **"All the rivers flow into the sea."** The rivers, which are the abundance from ZA, flow to *Malchut*, which is called, "a sea." And because she receives them from above, from *Bina*, she is called, "prayer," and she is sanctified by their holiness, and she is called, "holy," since *Mochin de Bina* is called, "holy," and it is called "prayer." Then, *Malchut* is called, "the complete kingdom of heaven."

241-242) **"The Lord our God, the Lord is One,"** since, "the Lord" is *Aba* and right line, and "our God" is *Ima* and left line. The Lord is ZA, middle line, which decides between *Aba* and *Ima*. And since they are three lines, they do not shine without each other, but rather all at once.

This is the voice, which one makes, as in unification, to implement one's aim on uniting all the degrees from *Ein Sof* to the end of all, in uniting this voice, which he does in these three lines, which are one. And this is the unification in each day, which appears in the spirit of holiness.

11) **"And she said, 'I dwell among my own people.'"** What is she saying? When the *Din* hangs in the world, one should not part from the collective by himself. He will not be mentioned above and he will not be known alone. This is so because when the *Din* hangs in the world, those who are known and are inscribed alone, though they are righteous, they are caught first. Hence, one must never retire from the people because the Creator's mercies are always on the whole people together. This is why she said, "I dwell among my own people," and I do not wish to part from them, as I have been doing thus far.

43) **How beloved is the Torah before the Creator. Anyone who engages in the Torah is loved above, loved below, and the Creator listens to his words, does not leave him in this world, and does not leave him to the next world.**

44) **One should engage in Torah day and night, as it is written, "You shall meditate upon it day and night,"** and as it is written, "If My covenant is not with you day and night." During the day, it is the time of work for all. But at night, the time

of rest, why is it necessary to engage in Torah? It is so that there will be a complete name in him. As there is no day without a night, and one is incomplete without the other, the Torah must be with the person day and night, and wholeness will be with man day and night.

Day is ZA and night is the *Nukva*. When one engages in the Torah day and night, he unites ZA and *Nukva*, and this is the entire wholeness, as it is written, "And there was evening and there was morning, one day."

45-47) **At midnight, the Creator comes to the Garden of Eden to play with the righteous who are there, and then one must rise and engage in Torah.**

The Creator and all the righteous in the Garden of Eden, all listen to His voice. It is written, "You who sit in the gardens, friends listen to your voice; let me hear it." "You who sit in the gardens" is the Assembly of Israel, *Malchut*. At night, she praises the Creator with the praise of the Torah. Happy is he who partakes with her in praising the Creator in the praise of the Torah.

When the morning comes, the Assembly of Israel, *Malchut*, comes and plays with the

Creator, and He gives her the scepter of *Hesed* [grace/mercy]. But not only to her, but to her and to all those who partake with her. One who engages in Torah at night, the Creator draws to him a thread of *Hesed* during the day. This is why *Malchut* is called "The morning star," for she praises the Creator at night with the praise of the Torah.

49-50) When half the night is through, the King begins to rise and the queen, *Malchut*, begins to sing. The King, ZA, comes and knocks on the palace's gate and says, "Open for me, my sister, my wife." And then He plays with the souls of the righteous.

Happy is he who has awakened at that time with words of Torah. For this reason, all the children of the queen's palace must rise at that time and praise the King. All praise before Him and the praise rises from this world, which is far from Him, and this is more favorable to the Creator than anything.

65-67) "And Pharaoh drew near"... We also learn that Pharaoh brought Israel closer to repentance. This is why it is written, "And Pharaoh drew near" and not "And Pharaoh brought closer."

It is written, "O Lord, they sought You in distress; they could only whisper a prayer, Your chastening was upon them." "They sought You in distress" means that Israel do not visit the Creator in times of contentment, but when they are in distress, and then they all visit Him. "They could only whisper a prayer" means that they are all praying with prayers and litanies, and pour out prayers before Him. When? "Your chastening before them," when the Creator visits them with His strap. Then the Creator stands over them in *Rachamim* [mercies] and welcomes their voice, to avenge their enemies, and He fills with mercy over them.

Israel were nearing the sea and saw the sea before them becoming stormier, its waves straightening upward. They were afraid. They raised their eyes and saw Pharaoh and his army, and slings and arrows, and they were terrified. "And the children of Israel cried out." Who caused Israel to draw near to their father in heaven? It was Pharaoh, as it is written, "And Pharaoh drew near."

125) **Happy is the man who has found wisdom. It is a man for whom the Creator has provided a treasure on the way: the face of Divinity. It is**

written about it, "But the path of the righteous is like the light of dawn."

138) **Through *Malchut's* ascent to *Bina*, all the degrees split in two.** *Keter* and *Hochma* remain in the degree, and *Bina* and *TM* fall off it, descend, and clothe the degree below it. At the time of *Gadlut*, the *Malchut* descends from *Bina* to her place, and *Bina* and *TM* in each degree rise from the lower one and return each to its own degree.

Along with their ascent from the lower one, they take the lower one with them and raise it to the place of the upper one. And because there is no absence in the spiritual they are always in the place of the lower one, even after they have risen to their degree. Thus, each lower one rises to its own superior, and this is why these *Bina* and *TM* are considered a pillar that exists in each degree, by which it rises to the degree above it.

"A pillar is stuck inside the sea." The sea is the *Nukva* from *Chazeh de ZA* downwards. And those *Bina* and *TM* of the degree of *Chazeh de ZA* upwards, which descend there, are considered the pillar through which all the discernments from *Chazeh de ZA* downwards rise to the degree of *Chazeh de ZA* upwards.

237) Adam knew the high wisdom more than the upper angels. He observed everything, and knew and recognized his Master more than all the people in the world.

245) **Man should love the Creator because there is no other work before the Creator but love. Anyone who loves Him and works with love, the Creator calls him, "Lover."**

251) **We should regard the words of the Torah.** We should regard everything because there is nothing in the Torah that is not implied in the high, holy Name, and there is nothing in the Torah that does not contain several secrets, reasons, roots, and branches.

252) **Anyone who wages a war in the Torah is rewarded with much peace at the end of his words.** All the wars in the world are strife and destruction, and all the wars of the Torah are peace and love... that there is no love and peace but that.

278-279) **Any person who seeks to unite the holy Name** and did not intend for it in heart, in desire, and in fear, so that upper and lower will be blessed in him, his prayer is thrown outside, everyone declares him bad, and the Creator calls upon him, "If you come to see My face."

"To see My face" means all those faces of the King, illumination of *Hochma*, as it is written, "A man's wisdom illuminates his face," hidden in the depth behind the dark, which are the *Dinim* in the left line. And all those who know how to properly unite the holy Name break all those walls of darkness and the King's face is seen and shines for all. And when it is seen and shines, all are blessed, upper and lower. Then there are blessings in all the worlds, and then it is written, "To see My face."

296-297) **When the Creator gave the Torah to Israel,** light came forth from that pleasantness, from *Bina*, and the Creator, ZA, was crowned in it, meaning received GAR from her, which are called "crown." From that pleasantness glowed the effulgence of all the worlds, firmaments, and crowns. It is written about that time, "Go forth, O daughters of Zion, and see King Solomon with the crown with which his mother has crowned him." King Solomon is ZA, his mother is *Bina*, and the crown is GAR.

When the Temple was built, the Creator was crowned in that crown and sat in His throne, *Malchut*, and was crowned in His crowns.

305-307) **There is nothing in the world that breaks the force of idol worshipping nations as**

when Israel engage in Torah. As long as Israel engage in Torah, the right strengthens and the power and courage of the idol worshipping nations breaks. This is why the Torah is called "strength," as it is written, "The Lord will give strength to His people."

When Israel do not engage in Torah, the left intensifies and the power of the idol worshipping nations grows. They suckle from the left, rule over Israel, and inflict upon them laws that they cannot endure. Because of that, Israel were exiled and scattered among the nations.

Why was the land lost? The Creator said, "For abandoning My law." As long as Israel engaged in Torah, the power and courage of all the idolaters was broken, as it is written, "Your right hand, O Lord, shatters the enemy." As long as the voice of Israel was heard in synagogues and seminaries, as it is written, "The voice is the voice of Jacob." And if not, "The hands are the hands of Esau."

367) It is written, "For the Lord hears the poor." Why does He hear the poor and not others? It is because they are closer to the King, as it is written, "A broken and a contrite heart, O God, You will not despise," and no heart in the world is broken as that of the poor. All the people in the world are seen before the Creator in body and in soul. But the poor appears before the Creator only in a soul, for his body is broken, and the Creator is nearer to the soul than to the body.

409-410) Anyone who prays his prayer before the holy King must ask his pleas and pray from the bottom of the heart so that his heart will be wholly with the Creator, and he will aim his heart and will, as it is written, "Out of the depths I have called You." But it is written, "With all my heart I have sought You." This verse is sufficient, to pray with all of one's heart, so why the need for "From the bottom"?

Every person who asks his request of the King must aim his mind and will to the Root of Roots, to extend blessings from the depth of the pit, so that blessings will pour from the fountain of all. The place from which that river comes out is the concealed *Hochma*.

New Zohar, BeShalach
[When Pharaoh Sent]

8-10) Israel were engaged in studying Torah that they learned from a bitter one, and that holy covenant, *Yesod*, bonded with them. The slant-serpent, the *Sitra Achra*, parted from that well of water, *Malchut*, for the serpent was making that water bitter—what their iniquities have caused thus far.

But once they returned to their Master in repentance and the Creator taught them the ways of the tree of life, *ZA*, as it is written, "And the Lord showed him a tree," which is the written Torah, *ZA*, "And he cast it into the water," which are the oral Torah, *Malchut*—"Cast" has the letters of "You have" [in Hebrew], "Have" is the next world, the *Hochma* in the next world, *Hochma de Bina*, as it is written, "To inherit substance upon those who love Me," "You is upper *Ima*, *Bina* in the next world, since "You" is 50 in *Gematria*, the 50 gates of *Bina* that cling to *ZA*—then the waters were sweetened and the upper dew came down from holy *Atik*, *Keter*, and the field of apples, *Malchut*, was filled.

Who caused all that? Elima, Israel's reply to their Master.

Yitro [Jethro]

23) **Rabbi Aba raised his hands on his head, wept, and said,** "Now the light of Torah rises to the height of the firmament of the uppermost throne. When my lord departs from the world, who will illuminate the light of Torah? Woe to a world that will be orphaned from you. But the words of my lord will illuminate in the world until the Messiah King arrives, and then it is written, 'And the earth shall be full of the knowledge of the Lord.'"

28) **"And Jethro ... heard." Can it be that Jethro heard and the rest of the people in the world did not hear?** Indeed, the whole world heard, but they did not break, hence their hearing is not hearing. He heard and was broken, surrendered before the Creator, and drew nearer to fearing Him, hence his hearing is hearing.

29-31) **Everything that the Creator does above and below is true, and His work is true. There is nothing in the world that one should reject or despise, since they are all true works, and everything is needed in the world.**

It is written, "If the serpent bites before being charmed." The serpent does not bite people until it is whispered to from above. It is told, "Go and kill this or that person."

Sometimes—as it does that—so it saves people from other things. Through it, the Creator works miracles to people; it all depends on the Creator; it is all the work of His hands. But the world needs them. If it did not need them, the Creator would not make them. Hence one need not be contemptuous toward things in the world, and certainly not toward the words and deeds of the Creator.

32) **"And God saw all that He had done, and behold, it was very good."** "And God saw" is the living God, *Bina*. "Saw" means that He looked, to illuminate for them and to watch over them. "All that He had done" means it is all included as one, above and below. "And behold, it was very good" is the right side. "Very" is the left side, "Good" is the angel of life. "Very" is the angel of death, and it is all one matter for those who observe the wisdom.

44) **Job was fearful with fear, and in that fear was the core of his power.** This is so because through a circumcision above—whether of *Kedusha* [holiness] or of the *Sitra Achra*—one cannot draw the spirit above to below and bring it near him

unless with fear, by aiming one's heart and will with fear and with breaking of the heart. Then he will extend downward the spirit that is above, as well as the required desire.

86) **This is a person who is always laughing, always joyful, and thinks positive thoughts. And the thoughts are not completed because he always elevates them from his will. He engages in mundane matters, and when he engages in heavenly matters he succeeds.**

98) **When a man walks on the path of truth, those who know their master look at him,** since that spirit within is corrected in it, and the form that includes everything bulges out. And that form is the face of a man. It is a more complete form than all the forms, and one who passes temporarily before the eyes of the wise-at-heart, when looking at his face outside, those faces that stand before him, the eyes of the heart love them.

123) **When the Creator created man,** He set up all the forms of the high secrets of the upper world—*Bina*—within him, as well as all the forms of the lower secrets of the bottom world, *Malchut*. They are all engraved in man, who is in the shade of God, since he is called "a

creation of the hand," a creation of the hand of the Creator.

126) When the man was created, it is written about him, "Clothe me with skin and flesh." And what is the man himself? Is man not merely skin, flesh, bones, and tendons? He is not, since indeed, man is only the soul [*Neshama*], while skin, flesh, bones, and tendons are only clothes. They are the man's *Kelim*, not the man himself. When the man passes away, he takes off those *Kelim* that he wore.

170) **Happy are those who sit before Rabbi Shimon and are rewarded with hearing the secrets of the Torah from his mouth.** Happy are they in this world and happy are they in the next world. Rabbi Shimon said, "Happy are you, friends, for no secret is hidden from you, and several high places await you in the next world."

223-224) **Intelligent people of the world, whose eyes are open, who are wise, who are with faith— which is Divinity—which was concealed in you.** Those of you who rose and came down, who received the lights that shine from below upward, which are called "ascent," and the lights that shine from above to below, which are called "descent," those in whom there is the spirit of the holy God should rise and know that when the white head–*Keter*–wished to create man, he imparted within one light, which is *Bina*, and the light imparted in the expansion of the light, ZA, which sentences and illuminates the two lines–right and left of *Bina*. And the expansion of the light brought forth the souls of human Similarly, he mated and imparted the expansion of the light, ZA, into one strong rock, the *Malchut*, and that rock elicited one flaming blaze, comprising several colors, which is the *Ibur* of the moon, which is full of *Dinim*. And that flame rises, receiving *Yenika*, meaning that the lights illuminate in it from below upwards. And descends, meaning that he receives GAR of *Ruach*, meaning that the lights illuminate from above to below but in *Dinim*, due to the deficiency in *Hassadim*. Finally, the expansion of the light, ZA, bestowed in him, imparted in him a middle line and *Hassadim*, and then he returns and sits in his place and becomes the spirit of life to *Adam HaRishon*.

257-258) **"And Moses went up to God."** Happy is Moses, who was awarded this honor, that the Torah testifies about him so. Come and see what is between Moses and the rest of the people in the world. When the rest of the people in the world rise, they rise to wealth, they rise to greatness, they rise to kingship. But when Moses rose, it is written, "Moses went up to God." Happy is he.

We learn from it that he who comes to be purified is aided, for it is written, "Moses went up to God," and after that, it is written, "And the Lord called to him," since he who wishes to draw close is brought closer.

259) **Happy is the man whom the Creator favors and whom He has brought to dwell inside the holy palace.** Anyone that He wishes to accept into His work, it is inscribed that he is inscribed above, to know that he was chosen before the high and holy King, to dwell in His abode. And anyone in whom there is that inscription passes through all the gates of above and no one stops him.

331-332) **There are several ways by which the Torah testifies that a person will not sin before his Master.** There are several ways by which it advises him so he will not stray to the right or to the left. There are several ways by which it advises him on how to repent before his Master and He will forgive him.

The Torah gives 613 counsels to a person on how to be whole with his Master, because his Master wishes to do good to him in this world and in the next world, especially in the next world.

333) **This world, compared to the next world, is only like an entry room before the hall.** When that righteous one is rewarded with his, it is written, "He shall have no inheritance among his brothers," since "The Lord is his inheritance." Happy is he who is rewarded with this superior inheritance. He is rewarded with it in this world, in the house of this world, and thus he is rewarded in the next world, in the upper, holy house, as it is written, "To them I will give in My house and within My walls a hand." Happy is that righteous, whose dwelling place is with the King, in His house.

405-406) **Happy are Israel, whom the Creator names "man," as it is written, "And you, My sheep, the sheep of My pasture, you are men."** It is also written, "When any man of you brings an offering." What is the reason that He calls them "men"? It is because it is written, "And you that cleave unto the Lord your God," meaning you, and not the rest of the idol-worshipping nations. This is the reason why you are men. You are called "man," and the idol-worshipping nations are not called "man."

When a person from Israel is circumcised, he enters the covenant that the Creator made with Abraham, as it is written, "And the Lord blessed Abraham in all." It is also written, "Mercy [*Hesed*] for Abraham." And he begins to enter in that place. When he has been rewarded with keeping the *Mitzvot* of the Torah, he comes into that man of the upper *Merkava* [chariot/assembly] and clings to the King's body, and then he is called "man."

421-422) "It is all one thing, and counts as a single degree. There are several faces within faces to the Creator. There are illuminating faces, faces that do not illuminate, lower faces, remote faces, near faces, faces within faces, faces without, faces of the right, and faces of the left."

Happy are Israel before the Creator, for they cling to the King's upper face, that face to which He and His name cling, and He and His name are one. The rest of the nations grip the remote faces, the lower faces. This is why they are remote from the King's body.

411) It is written, "For it is your life and the length of your days." One who has been rewarded with the Torah and did not part from it is rewarded with two lives: one in this world and one in the next world. It is written, "Your life" in plural tense [in Hebrew it can be perceived as plural], which are two. And anyone who parts from it, it is as though he parted from life. And one who parts from Rabbi Shimon, it is as though he parted from everything.

412) **Woe unto a generation from whom Rabbi Shimon departs, since when we stand before Rabbi Shimon, the fountains of the heart are open to all directions and everything is revealed. And when we part from him, we know nothing and all the fountains are hidden.**

413) **Like that candle from which several candles shine, yet it is complete, with none of it missing because the candles were lit from it. So is Rabbi Shimon Bar Yochai, owner of the candles. He shines for all and the light does not depart from him, and he remains whole.**

414-416) **All of Israel's prayers are prayer, and the prayer of the poor is the highest** because it rises up to the throne of the King and crowns itself in His head and the Creator is praised in this prayer. This is why the prayer of the poor is called "a prayer."

As for the rest of the people in the world, at times He listens and at times He does not listen, since the tabernacle of the Creator is in those broken *Kelim*, as it is written, "The Lord is near to those with a broken heart."

428) **One should be so careful with words of Torah,** and one should be so careful not to err in them and utter a word of Torah that he does not know, and which he did not receive from his teacher. Anyone who says words of Torah that he does not know or did not receive from his teacher, it is written about him, "You shall not make for yourself an idol or any likeness."

430) **The whole Torah is a holy name,** for there is nothing in the Torah that is not included in the holy name. Hence, we must be careful not to err in His holy name and not lie with it. One who lies with the upper King is not admitted into the King's palace and will be abolished from the next world.

478-479) **Woe to the people of the world whose ways are as beasts, who do not know and do not look. It is better for them if they were not born**. Woe to the world when Rabbi Shimon departs it: who will be able to reveal secrets, who will know them, and who will look in the ways of Torah?

Rabbi Shimon said to them, "The world is only for friends who engage in Torah and know the secrets of the Torah.

New Zohar, Yitro [Jethro]

13) There is not a creature in the upper ones or in the lower ones that is not inscribed in His name. Everyone is also inscribed in Divinity. The finest of all the creations that He has created is the man, who is a form comprised of the entire world, and of all the creations in the world. This is why He favors him more than all creations.

171-175) A thought was given to man, that man will contemplate the Creator of the worlds, to unify his name through *Ein Sof* and through eternity. He created everything in *Bina*, as it is written, "See who has created these." "Who" [MI] is *Bina*.

Speech was given to man to engage in the Torah with it, and to know from it the Maker of everything. It is said about Him, "Who makes light." It is so because the speech is *Yetzira*, *Tifferet*, and there is no light but the Torah, as it is written, "For a candle is a *Mitzva* and the Torah is light." It is He who is the Maker, who made in man a face, eyes, ears, nose, and mouth, to engage in the Torah in them and to know Him through her.

Likewise, He fashioned a mouth to speak of the Torah; He fashioned eyes to look in the light of Torah; He fashioned ears in him to hear with them the words of Torah. These are the six edges that *Tifferet* includes: two eyes, two ears, a mouth, and a tongue.

He fashioned the nose, and in it, "He breathed into his nostrils the breath [soul] of life," which man would contemplate in the unification of the Name, as it is written, "I am the Lord, maker of everything." This is the lower Divinity, *Malchut*, from whom the noetic soul was given to man, for the *Nefesh* [both *Nefesh* and *Neshama* are translated as "soul"] is from *Malchut*, to know with it all the works of Torah, the *Mitzvot* of the Torah, He who is called "Maker of all," which is *Malchut*, in whom there is making.

They are three ties that were placed in a person: noetic soul, by which to know the Maker of all the worlds, who says and does, speaks and keeps, who creates, makes, and does, and all are one. He is *Ein Sof*. He brings everything from potential to actual, He changes His deeds, and there is no change in Him.

73-74) On the part of the animate soul, man's days are short, few, and bad. All of man's days, which are in poverty, sorrow, and pressure, are not life, especially if the days are without Torah and *Mitzvot*, it is not a life.

If he repents—even if he is in a tail of a lamb or an ox, for in every sign on the part of the animate soul the Creator adds more spirit than the angels—and rises from the tail of the signs to be intermediate, in the middle of each star and sign, like the wind, if he is more rewarded with repenting in his thought, the Creator gives him a soul from the throne and he rises to be a head at the beginning of each star and sign like the soul [*Neshama*].

MISHPATIM [ORDINANCES]

11-13) When one is born, he is given *Nefesh* on the part of the beast, on the part of purity, on the part of those called "holy *Ofanim*," from the world of *Assiya*. If he is rewarded further, he is given *Ruach* on the part of holy animals from the world of *Yetzira*. If he is rewarded further, he is given *Neshama* on the part of the throne from the world of *Beria*. Those three are maid, man-servant, and maid-servant of the king's daughter, meaning *NRN* from the expansion of *Malchut* in *BYA*. Maid is *Neshama* in *Beria*, man-servant is *Ruach* in *Yetzira*, and maid-servant is *Nefesh* in *Assiya*.

If he is rewarded further, he is given *Nefesh*, as in *Atzilut*, on the part of the only daughter, who is called "the king's daughter," *Malchut de Atzilut*. If he is rewarded further, he is given *Ruach de Atzilut* on the part of the middle pillar, *ZA*, and he is called "a son of the Creator," as it is written, "You are the children of the Lord your God." If he is rewarded further, he is given *Neshama* on the part of *AVI*, *Bina*, as it is written, "And He breathed into his nostrils the breath of life." "Life" is *Yod-Hey*, *AVI*, of whom it is written, "The whole soul praises *Koh* [the Lord, *Yod-Hey*]," and the name *HaVaYaH* is completed in them because *Ruach* and *Nefesh de Atzilut* are *Vav-Hey*, and *Neshama de Atzilut* is *Yod-Hey*, and together, they are *HaVaYaH*.

If he is rewarded further, he is given *HaVaYaH* with a filling of letters such as this: *Yod-He-Vav-He*, who is Adam [man], 45 in *Gematria*, as in *Atzilut* above, meaning ZA, when clothing upper AVI, who are *Hochma*, the letters *Chaf-Het Mem-Hey* [forming the word *Hochma* in Hebrew]. He is named after the form of his master, and it is written about him, "And reign over the fish of the sea and the bird of the sky, and any animal that swarms over the earth." This is the one whose dominion is over all the firmaments, all the *Ofanim* and the *Serafim*, and the animals in all the hosts and powers above and below.

22) **How many are the words of wisdom that are hidden within each word in the Torah, and which are known to sages who know the ways of Torah?**

59-60) **How much should one be careful of deviating in his ways in this world?** If a person is rewarded in this world and properly watches over the soul, the Creator desires him and is praised with him each day in His company. He says, "See the holy son that I have in that world. He did so and so, and so and so are his deeds corrected."

When that soul comes out of this world pure, clean, and clear, the Creator illuminates for her with several lights. Each day, He declares about her, "This is the soul of My son, so and so. There will be keeping to that body that she left."

61-64) "**If he designates her for his son, he shall deal with her according to the custom of daughters.**" What is the custom of daughters? Within the strong rock, the world of *Beria*, in that high firmament which is there, is a palace of love that stands under the holy of holies of *Beria*. There are hidden treasures there, and all the kisses of the King's love are there, and souls that are loved by the King enter there.

When the King enters the palace, it is written, "And Jacob kissed Rachel," for there is *Zivug de Neshikin* [a coupling of kissing] there, and there the Creator finds that holy soul. He promptly greets her and kisses her, embracing her and elevating her with Him, and plays with her.

"He shall deal with her according to the custom of daughters." As the father does to his daughter, whom he loves, kissing her, embracing

253

her, and giving her gifts, the Creator does to the pure soul each day.

It is written, "Will do for the one who waits for Him." As the daughter, the soul, complements the *Assiya* in this world, the Creator complements another *Assiya* for her in the next world.

81) **Wherever words of Torah are said**, the Creator and the Assembly of Israel, *Malchut*, are there, and they are listened to. Then the good side prevails in the tree of good and evil, *Malchut*, and rises up, and the Creator and the Assembly of Israel are crowned in good.

93) **The Creator puts all the hidden things He does into the holy Torah and everything is in the Torah.** The Torah reveals a hidden thing and promptly dresses in another garment, hides there and does not appear. The sages are filled with eyes, and even though that thing hid in its garment, they see it from within the garment. When that thing is revealed, they cast an opening of eyes in it before it reenters its garment, and although it promptly disappears, it no longer disappears from their eyes.

97-99) **Many are the people in the world whose minds are confused and they do not**

see truthfully in the Torah. Each day, the Torah calls upon them with love for them, yet they do not wish to turn their heads back and listen to her.

In the Torah, a thing comes out of its sheath, appears briefly, and promptly hides. When it appears out of the sheath and promptly hides, the Torah does it only for those who know her and are known in her.

It is similar to a loved one, beautiful in appearance and shapely, who hides in her palace. She has a lover of whom people do not know. Rather, he hides. Out of the love that he loves her, that lover always passes by the gate to her house and looks in every direction. She knows that her lover always circles the gate to her house. She opens a small door in her palace and shows her face to her loved one, and promptly covers herself again.

All those who were with the lover neither saw nor looked, only the lover alone, whose guts and heart, and soul follow her. He knows that because of her love for him, she appears to him for only a moment, to evoke the love for him.

So is a word of Torah: it appears only to the one who loves her. The Torah knows that that wise of heart circles the gate to her house each day. What does she do? She shows her face from within the palace, gives him a hint, and promptly returns to her place and hides. All those from there neither know nor look, but he alone, whose guts and heart, and soul follow her. This is why the Torah appears and covers, and goes to her loved one with love, to awaken the love with him.

100-102) **When the path of Torah begins to appear to a person, it hints at him.** If he knows, fine. If he does not know, she sends to him and calls him a fool. The Torah said to the one whom she sent to him, "Tell that fool to come near here and I will speak with him." It is written about it, "Whoever is a fool, let him turn in here, and one who is heartless." The man approaches her and she begins to speak with him from behind a curtain, spreading matters his way according to his ways until he gradually observes. This is the interpretation.

Then she speaks with him in riddles from behind a thin sheet. And once he grows accustomed to her, she appears before him face-to-face and speaks with him of all the hidden secrets and all the hidden ways that have been hidden in her heart since the first days. Then he is a ruling man, possessing Torah, master of the house, since she revealed to him all of her secrets and did not keep away or hide anything from him.

The Torah says to him, "You have seen the hint that I hinted to you initially. So and so secrets were in it, so and so it is." Then he sees that those words in the Torah need not be added to or subtracted from, and then the literal meaning of the text is as it is—neither adding nor subtracting even a single letter. Hence, people should be careful and chase after the Torah, be among her lovers.

165) **It is written, "And God saw all that He has done, and behold, it was very good." "Good" is the good angel. "Very" is the angel of death. The Creator provides His corrections to all until even the angel of death returns to being very good.**

230) For this reason, even when there is transgression in a person and he flaws what he should not, but he repents, He accepts him and has mercy on him, since the Creator is full of mercy and is filled with mercy for all His works, as it is written, "His mercies are over all His works." His mercies reaches even beasts and

fowls. And if His mercy reaches them, it is all the more so with people, who know and are known for praising their Master. His mercies reach them and remain over them.

231) **If His mercies reach the wicked, it is even more so with righteous. After all, who needs healing? Those who are in pain.** And who are those in pain? They are the wicked. They are the ones who need healing and mercy, and the Creator is merciful toward them, so they will not be left away from Him. He does not depart from them and they shall return before Him in repentance.

When the Creator brings closer, He brings closer with the right. And when He repels, He repels with the left. When He repels, the right brings closer. He repels from one side and brings closer from the other. Thus, the Creator does not leave out His mercy from them.

232-234) **"And he went in mischief in the way of his heart."** Afterwards, it is written, **"I have seen his ways and I will heal him, and I will lead him and restore comfort to him and to his mourners."** Even though the wicked work maliciously, follow their hearts, and others warn them but they do not wish to listen to them, still, when they repent and take the good path of repentance, healing is provided for them.

Is the text speaking of the living or of the dead, since the beginning of the text is not its end and its end is not as its beginning? In the beginning of the text, it points to the living, "And he went in mischief." Its end indicates the dead when it says, "I will lead him and restore comfort to him and to his mourners." Rather, it speaks of while a person is alive, and so it is. "And he went in mischief in the way of his heart," since the evil inclination in him is strong and prevails in him, hence he goes in mischief and does not wish to repent.

The Creator sees his ways, that he is marching futilely in evil. The Creator says, "I must hold him by his hand." "I have seen his ways," that he is walking in the dark, I wish to give him a cure, "And I will heal him." The Creator brings into his heart the path of repentance and the healing for his soul. "I will lead him," as it is written, "Go now, lead the people." The Creator leads him in the upright path, as one who holds the hand of another and leads him out of the darkness.

367-369) "**Place me as a seal over your heart, as a seal on your arm,** for love is as strong as death, jealousy is as harsh as Sheol." "Place me as a seal." When the Assembly of Israel, *Malchut*, clung to her husband, ZA, she said, "Place me as a seal." Since I have clung unto you, my whole form will be engraved in you. And though I may roam to or fro, you will find my form engraved in you and you will remember me.

"As a seal on your arm," as it is written, "His left under my head and his right shall embrace me," so my form will be engraved there. By that I will forever be clung to you and will never be forgotten by you. "For love is as strong as death," with a strong *Gevura* such as that place in which there is death. Love is the place called "Eternal love."

"Jealousy is as harsh as Sheol," as it is with love, since the names, "Love" and "jealousy" come from the left side. "Its flashes are flashes of fire." "Flashes" are precious stones and gems that were born out of that fire, which are high degrees, from the flame that comes out from the upper world, from the left line of *Bina*, clinging to the Assembly of Israel, so all will be one unification. But the love and the flashes of the fire of the heart follow you, may our form be engraved in your heart as your form is engraved in ours.

460) Those who engage in Torah and *Mitzvot* for the Creator and His Divinity not in order to be rewarded, but as a son who must keep the glory of his father and mother, connect and register in the middle pillar—the Creator and His Divinity—as though they were one.

466) So it is, but in each *Mitzva* there was your effort to unite the Creator and His Divinity in all the camps above and below, the Creator in His Divinity, and all His camps above and below unite in your spirit in each *Mitzva* like a prince whose father and mother love him and kiss him. And for their love, they do not believe their camps but guard him themselves.

500) Happy are Israel, whom the Creator wishes to honor more than all the people in the world. In the beginning, He said to them, "And you will be unto Me, a kingdom of priests." The great love was not removed from them until He called them "A holy nation," which is more important. The love was not removed from them until He called them "For you are a holy nation." The love was not removed from them until He called them, "You shall be holy men unto Me," which is more important than anything.

510-511) **"And you shall be holy men unto Me."** It would be enough to say, "You shall be holy unto Me." It is holy men since Israel came out to freedom only from the *Yovel*, *Bina*. And after they went out to freedom, *Yovel* welcomed them with His wings and they are called "His men," "His sons." It is written about the *Yovel*, "*Yovel* shall be holy unto you." This is why it is written, "And you shall be holy men unto Me," actually His men.

The Creator said, "And you shall be holy men unto Me." This is why Israel were rewarded with being named "brothers of the Creator," as it is written, "For the sake of My brothers and friends," since Israel are sons of the *Yovel*, *Bina*, and ZA is also the son of *Bina*. It follows that they are brothers of ZA. Afterwards, they are actually called "holiness," as it is written, "Israel are holiness to the Lord, the first of His harvest.

543) The whole of the Torah is the name of the Creator. One who engages in it, it is as though he engages in the holy name, since the whole of the Torah is one holy name, a superior name, a name that includes all other names. And one who withdraws a single letter from it, it is as though

he put a blemish in the holy name. "And do not mention the name of other gods." Do not add to the Torah and do not withdraw from it, for he makes a flaw in the holy name and strengthens the other gods. The name "other gods" is one who engages in other books, which are not on the side of Torah. "Nor let them be heard from your mouth," meaning it is forbidden to even mention them and learn any reasoning from them, especially reasoning that regard the Torah.

Truma [Donation]

1) **How beloved are the children of Israel before the Creator,** who desires them, and who wishes to cling unto them and to bond with them, and who has made them a single nation in the world ... and they desired Him and bonded with Him ... And to the rest of the nations He has given ministers to rule over them, while He took Israel into His portion.

20) **"King Solomon has made him a sedan chair from the trees of Lebanon."** A sedan chair is the lower palace, *Malchut*, like the upper palace, *Bina*. The Creator called it "the Garden of Eden," and He planted it for His delight. His desire is to play in it with the souls of the righteous, where they all stand and are inscribed within it. These are the souls without bodies in this world; they all rise and become crowned there, and they have places to see, to be delighted in the sublime delight, called "the pleasantness of the Lord," and there they are filled with all the pleasures of the rivers of pure persimmon.

34) One who wishes to exert in a *Mitzva* [singular of *Mitzvot*] and exert in the Creator must not

exert in it futilely and for nothing. Rather, one should exert in it properly, according to one's strength. It is good for a person to accept the Creator's exertion.

39) When we see that man's will is to chase and to exert after the Creator with his heart, soul, and will, we know for certain that Divinity is present there. Then we need to buy that man for the full cost, bond with him and learn from him. We learn about that, "And buy yourself a friend." He should be bought for the full price to be rewarded with the Divinity that is in him.

41) Anyone who holds the hand of the wicked and exerts with him so he will leave the bad way rises in three ascensions, which no other man has risen. He causes the subjugation of the *Sitra Achra*, causes the Creator's glory to rise, and causes the keeping of the entire world in its existence above and below. It is written of such a person, "My covenant was with him, the life and the peace." He is rewarded with seeing sons to his sons, and he is rewarded in this world and rewarded with the next world. No litigator can sentence him in this world and in the next world, he enters through the twelve gates in the firmament, and there is none who can protest against him.

43-44) When Israel come to the synagogue and pray their prayer, when they come to redeem Israel and attach redemption to prayer, not stopping in the middle, by that they cause *Yesod*, which is called "redemption," to approach *Malchut*, which is called "prayer," that white color, *Netzah*, rises to the top of the chamber, *Malchut*, and becomes a *Keter* [crown] for it.

A herald comes out and says, "Happy are you, holy nation, for you do good, you cause the unification of *Yesod* (called 'good') before the Creator." It is written, "And I have done what is good in Your eyes," attaching redemption to prayer, for at that time, when reaching "Praises to God above," that color, *Netzah*, rises to the top of the chamber, that righteous, *Yesod de ZA*, awakens to bond in the place that is needed in love, in fondness, in gladness, and in good will. And all the organs, all the *Sefirot*, willingly conjoin with one another, upper ones in lower ones.

Then all the candles, all the degrees, illuminate and blaze, and they are all in a single bonding in this righteous who is called "good," as it is written, "Say, 'A righteous is good.'" This unites everyone in a single bonding, and then everything is in a whisper above and below, in kissing in good will, and the matter is in a bonding of the room, in an embrace.

46) **One who raised MAN in a *Masach de Hirik* and brought *Malchut* back, conjoining her with ZA,** by that he reformed the wicked from iniquity and extended for them *Nefashot de Kedusha*. He is worthy of being crowned with the crown of kingship on his head, since the lower one who causes lights to the upper one is himself rewarded with the same amount that he had caused to the upper one. And because the *Malchut* bonded with ZA and received GAR through his MAN, he is rewarded with GAR, as well. And because he caused the *Zivug* of the King and the queen, he is therefore worthy of being there, and the King and the queen ask about him and wish to impart upon him all that he had caused for them.

51) A poor man rewards people with several benefits, several upper treasures, and he is not as one who rewarded the wicked. What is the difference between them? One who exerts and does charity to the poor completes life for his soul and causes him to exist. By that, he is rewarded with several benefits in that world. One who exerts after the wicked, to reform them,

complements more, since he is making the other side of other gods surrender and not rule, and removes his governance from him. He makes the Creator rise on this throne of glory, and makes another soul for that wicked one, happy is he.

86) **If you make your requests before the King in prayer**, ask, pray, and ask your requests and return to your Master. "Come," as one who invites, greeting his sons and having mercy on them. So is the Creator. In the morning and also at night, He calls out and says, "Come." Happy are the holy nation whose Master seeks them and calls for them to bring them near Him.

111) **Happy is he who exerts to know his Master, happy is he in this world and happy is he in the next world.**

122) Happy is the man who places his will in that—to complement his Master each day.

125-126) **When Israel make the unification, "Hear O Israel," with a complete will,** a light comes out of the concealment of the upper world, upper AVI. This is the path of Aba. This light battered within the harsh spark, Yesod de Ima, and was divided into 70 lights, from which the Mochin of YESHSUT were emanated, meaning ZAT de AVI, HGT NHYM, where each consists of ten. These 70 lights illuminated in 70 branches of the tree of life, in HGT NHYM de ZA, where each comprises ten.

At that time, that tree, ZA, emits fragrances and perfumes, meaning illumination of *Hochma*, and all the trees in the Garden of Eden, *Malchut*, emit scents and praise their Master, ZA. It is so because then *Malchut* is established to enter the *Huppah* [wedding canopy] with her husband, ZA, and all the upper organs, meaning *Sefirot de* ZA, unite in one craving and in one desire to be one, without any separation. Then her husband, ZA, is set up toward the *Malchut*, to enter the *Huppah* in a single unification to be united in *Malchut*.

147) It is a *Mitzva* [commandment] to study Torah each day, as it is the upper faith to know the ways of the Creator, for all who engage in Torah are rewarded in this world and in the next world, and are saved from all the evil slanders. It is so because the Torah is the faith, and one who engages in it engages in the upper faith, and the Creator instills His Divinity within him so that she does not depart from him.

148-149) **One who knows a word of Torah should be chased and that matter should be**

learned from him, to keep the verse, "From every man whose heart moves him you shall take My donation." The Torah is the tree of life, to give life to all who strengthen in the Torah, who strengthen in the tree of life, as it is written, "She is a tree of life to they who hold her."

There are several high secrets in those who engage in Torah, who are rewarded with attachment with the upper Torah, ZA. They do not leave it in this world and do not leave it in the next world. Even in the grave, his lips utter Torah, as it is written, "Moving the lips of those who are asleep."

151-153) **Happy are the righteous who know how to aim their hearts' desire for the upper, holy King,** and all their hearts' desire is not for this world and for its idle lust, but they know and exert to aim their desire for clinging above, to extend their Master's will in them from above downward.

From which place do they take their Master's will to extend it to them? They take from a high and holy place, from which all are holy wills. This is "Every man," righteous, Yesod de ZA, who is called "every" [or "all"], as it is written, "The advantage of a land in everything," and as it is written, "Therefore I esteem right all Your precepts concerning everything." "Man," a righteous man, is righteous, the master of the house, *Yesod*, the master of *Malchut*, who is called "house." His will is always to the queen, *Malchut*, as a husband who always loves his wife. "His heart moves him" means that he loves her. His heart is his queen, *Malchut*, who is called "heart." "Moves him" means to cling to Him.

And even though they have great love for one another and they never part, still, "From every man," meaning *Yesod*, the master of the house, the queen's husband, "You shall raise My donation," *Malchut*. It is customary that if there is an attempt to take a woman from her husband, he is vigilant and does not leave her. But the Creator is not so, as it is written, "And this is the donation," meaning the Assembly of Israel, *Malchut*, that despite all her love for Him and His love for her, she is taken from Him to be among them, from a high place, where every love between a wife and her husband is present, *Yesod*. From there "You shall raise My donation." Happy are Israel and happy are all who are rewarded with it.

169-171) "Bless the blessed Lord." *Et* ["the"] implies *Malchut*, who is called *Et*. *Et* is the

Sabbath of the entering of the Sabbath, the Sabbath night, *Malchut*. "Blessed is the blessed Lord." "Blessed" is the origin of the blessings from the source of life, the place from which every potion to water everything comes out, meaning *Yesod* of *Bina*. Because it is the source that imparts in the letter of the covenant, *Yesod de ZA*, it is called "the blessed," which is the sprouting of the well. *Yesod* is the sprouting of *Malchut*, who is called "a well." And because the blessings reach *Yesod de ZA*, the well is certainly filled and its waters never stop. Also, *Hassadim* are called "water."

This is why we do not say, "Bless the blessed Lord," but "Bless the Lord," for had it not reached *Yesod de ZA*, the sprouting from the upper source, *Yesod de Bina*, the well would not have filled at all, meaning *Malchut*, since *Malchut* can receive only from *Yesod de ZA*. This is why we say, "The blessed," who is *Yesod de ZA*. "Blessed," since He always complements and waters. This is the Sabbath of the entering of the Sabbath, *Malchut*. We bring the blessings in a place that is called "Blessed," *Yesod de ZA*. And when they come there, they are all extended forever, meaning *Malchut*, to be blessed, be watered, and be whole as it should be, full on all sides.

"Blessed" is the upper source, *Yesod de Bina*, from which all the blessings emerge. When the moon is complete, we also call her "Blessed," in regard to the lower ones. However the "Blessed" here is the upper source, *HaVaYaH*, the middle in all the upper sides, ZA, the middle line. "Blessed" is peace at home, *Yesod de ZA*, who is called "peace," the springing of the well to complement and to water all. "Forever" is the lower world, which must be blessed, and the oil and the *Gadlut*, abundance, which extends in "Bless the blessed Lord," all for "forever," who is the *Malchut*.

184-189) **When the day illuminated on the Sabbath day, the ascent of joy rises through all the worlds in peace and joy.** Then it is written, "The heavens are telling the glory of God, and the firmament is declaring the work of His hands." "The heavens" is ZA, in which the name of the upper one, *Ima*, is seen, and in which the holy name, *Aba*, is inscribed. In other words, heavens is ZA, in which there are *Mochin de AVI*.

What is "Telling"? They illuminate and sparkle in the illumination of the upper light, and rise by a name, which is included in the illumination of the upper wholeness, in the name, *HaVaYaH*, in which there are *Yod-Hey*, the wholeness of the upper one, who are *AVI*.

What is telling, that the heavens tell? It is that they sparkle in illumination of the wholeness of the upper book, *Aba*, and that which extends from a book is called "a story." For this reason, they rise in a whole name, *HaVaYaH*, and illuminate in a complete light, in the right line, and sparkle in complete sparkling in the left line. They sparkle and illuminate by themselves from within the light of the sparkling of the upper book, sparkling and illuminating to each and every direction to which they cling. This is so because each and every ring illuminates from the sapphireness and the light, and sparkles in sparkling, meaning all the *Sefirot* in *Malchut* that are called "rings," for on this day the heavens, *ZA*, are crowned and rise in the holy name, *HaVaYaH*, more than on the rest of the days.

"The work of His hands" is the upper dew that illuminates from all the hidden sides, which are the works of the hands of *ZA*, and the correction in which he is corrected on that day more than in the rest of the days. The *Hassadim*, which are called "dew," appeared by raising MAN from *Masach de Hirik* that *ZA* raised, hence the dew is called "the works of His hands."

"The firmament is declaring." "Declaring" means it is pulling the dew and dripping down to *Yesod*, from the *Rosh* of the King, from His *GAR*, which are called *Rosh* of *ZA*, and is filled from all the sides. "The firmament" is a firmament that is the springing of the well, *Yesod*, which gives to the well, *Malchut*. This is a river that comes out of Eden, which pulls and drips down the pouring of the upper dew, illuminating and sparkling in a sparkling from all the sides. This firmament pulls it in an extension of love and craving to water the potion of joy for Sabbath night, the *Malchut*.

When it pulls and the crystal dew drips from the *Rosh* of *ZA*, everything is filled and completed in the holy letters, in 22 letters in all those holy trails. The *Hochma* in the 32 paths is piled and dresses in dew, *Hassadim*, and everything is filled with everything—*Hochma* as well as *Hassadim*, though the *Hochma* is concealed and the *Hassadim* are revealed. When everything is united in it—both *Hochma* and *Hassadim*—a way is made in it, to water and to bless below, to *Malchut*. That is, a *Miftacha* [key] is made in it, called "a path." Through it, it imparts illumination of *GAR* to the *Malchut*.

224-225) **Just as when a buck or a dear departs from its place, it promptly returns to that**

place, although the Creator departed upward to *Ein Sof*, He promptly returns to His place because Israel below cling to Him and do not leave Him to be forgotten and far off from them. This is why it is written, "O You my help, hasten to my assistance."

This is the reason why we must unite with the Creator and grip Him, as one who pulls from above to below, so that no one will be left from Him for even an hour.

245-246) **When Israel unite the unification** in the verse of the 25 letters, which are "Hear O Israel the Lord our God, the Lord is one," and in "Blessed be the name of the glory of His kingdom forever and ever," which are 24 letters, each of them aims in them. All the letters unite together and 49 gates in *Yovel*, *Bina*, rise in one bonding. It is so because 25 and 24 are 49, and then there is a need to rise up to *Bina* and not more. At that time, the 49 gates of *Bina* open and the Creator considers that person as though he had kept the whole of the Torah, which comes in 49 faces.

For this reason, one must aim the heart and the desire in 25 and in 24, to raise them in the heart's desire to the 49 gates. Once he has intended in that, he will aim in the unification

"Hear O Israel," and in "Blessed be the name of the glory of His kingdom forever and ever," which are the whole of the Torah. Happy is he who intends in them because he is certainly the whole of the Torah above and below. This is the complete person, male and female, since "Hear O Israel" is male, and "Blessed be the name of the glory of His kingdom forever and ever" is female, and it is the whole of the faith.

259) **"God, You are my God I shall seek You"** means that he established the light that shines in blackness, the light of *Hochma* that is governed by the left at the point of *Shuruk*, which cannot shine for lack of *Hassadim* and is therefore called "black light." It is so because the light that is in blackness does not illuminate until it is corrected below, meaning *MAN* is raised and *Hassadim* are extended for *Hochma* to clothe in, and then she illuminates. One who corrects this black light, even though it is black, is rewarded with the white light that shines, which is the light of the illuminating mirror, ZA. This is a man who is rewarded with the next world.

261) **"My soul thirsts for You; my flesh yearns for You,"** as one who is hungry for food and thirsty to drink. **"In a dry and weary land**

where there is no water." This is *Malchut* that is dominated by the left, which is black light, for lack of *Hassadim*, water. At that time she is a desert and not a habitable place. She is not a holy place, and is therefore regarded as a place without water. This is why David corrected her and extended for her water from ZA. And as we are hungry and thirsty for You after *Hassadim* in this place, "Thus I have seen You in the sanctuary, to see Your power and Your glory," since the hunger and thirst cause the raising of MAN and the extension of *Hassadim* from ZA to clothe *Malchut's* black light, and then she returns to *Kedusha* and shines.

294) **But people's folly detains them from seeing** and they do not know and do not notice why they are in this world. They are not concerned with watching over the honor of the upper King in this world, much less being concerned with the honor of the upper world, what it stands on, and how matters are interpreted.

308-309) **"And the righteous are as trusted as a young lion."** But the righteous do not trust their deeds at all. They are always afraid, like Abraham, of whom it is written, "And it came to pass, when he was coming near to enter into

Egypt." As Isaac, of whom it is written, "For he feared to say, 'My wife.'" As Jacob, of whom it is written, "And Jacob was very frightened and was distressed."

If those did not trust their deeds, it is all the more so with the rest of the righteous in the world. Thus, how does it say here, "And the righteous are as trusted as a young lion"?

Of course it is written, "As a young lion," since of all the names of the lion, only "young lion" is written, and not "lion" or *Shachal* or *Shachatz* [other names for a lion], but only "young lion," the weakest and the smallest of them all, who has no faith in its power although it is strong. So are the righteous: they do not trust their actions now, but are as a young lion: although they know that the power of their good deeds is strong, they are only as confident as a young lion and not more.

325) **The praise of the singing of the Song of Songs is the whole of the Torah**, the whole of the act of creation, the whole of the patriarchs, the whole of the exile in Egypt, and Israel's exodus from Egypt, and the song of the sea, "Then Moses sang." It is the whole of the Ten Commandments and the keeping of Mount Sinai, and includes from the time when Israel

walked in the desert until they arrived in the land and the Temple was built. It is the whole of the crowning of the upper holy name with love and with joy, the whole of Israel's exile among the nations, as well as their redemption, the whole of the revival of the dead through the day that is a Sabbath for the Lord—the day that is all Sabbath for the future, what it is, what was, and what will be afterward, on the seventh day in the seventh millennium, when it is a Sabbath for the Lord. It is all in the Song of Songs.

360) **This is so because when male and female— ZA and Malchut—are established together** under the upper King, Bina, the letters ELEH of Bina, her NHY, come down to ZA and Malchut during her Katnut. These NHY give them Mochin during her Gadlut, and then the King, ZA, rises to Bina and fills there with all the sanctities and all the blessings that extend below, imparting them below, to Malchut. This is the craving of the upper King, ZA, to be filled with sanctities and blessings to give below, to Malchut.

371-375) **Why did King Solomon see, which brought words of love between the upper world, Zeir Anpin, the lower world, Malchut,** and the beginning of the praise of love that he introduced between them, "May he kiss me"? Indeed, there is love of *Dvekut* [adhesion] of spirit to spirit only in a kiss, and a kiss on the mouth, the springing of the spirit and its outlet. When they kiss each other, these spirits cleave to one another and become one, and then it is one love.

The kiss of love spreads to the four spirits, and the four directions cleave together, and they are inside the faith, *Malchut*. And the four spirits rise by four letters, which are the letters upon which the holy name depends, and upon which the upper and lower depend. The praise of the Song of Songs depends on them, and they are the four letters of *Ahava* ["love," *Aleph-Hey-Bet-Hey*]. They are the upper *Merkava* [chariot/assembly], *HG TM*, and they are bonding and *Dvekut*, and the wholeness of everything.

The four letters *Aleph-Hey-Bet-Hey* are four spirits of love and joy of all the organs of the body, without any sadness. It is so because there are four directions in a kiss, each included in the other: the spirit of ZA is included in *Malchut*, the spirit of *Malchut* is included in ZA, and when this spirit is included in the other spirit, and the other is included in that, two spirits together are made in each—its own spirit and the spirit of the other that is included in it. Then they unite in one *Dvekut*, and they are four in wholeness—two of ZA and two of *Malchut*, springing in one another and included in one another.

When their illumination spreads into this world, a single fruit is made of these four spirits, a single spirit that consists of four spirits. It returns, ascends, and breaches firmaments until it rises and sits in the palace of love upon which every love depends. That spirit is also called "love," and when the spirit rises, it evokes the palace to unite above with the sixth palace, the palace of good will, where there the kisses are.

The four letters are for the four spirits, and they are the four letters *Aleph-Hey-Bet-Hey*, since the spirit of ZA is *Aleph*, the spirit of *Malchut* that is included in ZA is the letter *Hey*, the spirit of *Malchut* is *Hey*, and the spirit of ZA that is included in *Malchut* is *Bet*. Their fruit is called *Ahava* [love], since when they unite with one another, ZA in *Malchut* in the bonding of kisses, they immediately awaken one beside the other—the spirit of *Malchut* awakens and is included in the spirit of ZA, and the spirit of ZA is included in the spirit of *Malchut*.

For this reason, the *Hey*, the spirit of *Malchut* that is included in *Aleph*—the spirit of ZA—promptly comes out and unites with *Aleph*, clinging in *Dvekut* and in love. And two other letters awaken—*Hey*, the spirit of *Malchut*, with *Bet*, the spirit of ZA, which is included in *Malchut*—and spirits become included in spirits in the *Dvekut* of love.

383) **Rabbi Shimon wept. He said,** "Indeed, I know that the high spirit of holiness is pounding in you. Happy is this generation, for there will not be such as this generation until the time when the Messiah King arrives, when the Torah resumes its past. Happy are the righteous in this world and in the next world."

395) **"And God made the two great lights."** The two great lights are the oil of lighting, as well as the oil for lighting, the upper world, ZA, and the lower world, *Malchut*, male and female. Each time a male and a female come together, they are both referred to as masculine. And because the upper world is called great, thanks to it the lower world—which is connected and included in it—is also called "great." This is why it is written, "The two great lights."

414-415) **"And God said, 'Let there be light,' and there was light."** This light was concealed, and it is set up for the righteous for the next world, as it is written, "Light is sown for the righteous," indicating both the righteous above and the righteous below. That light never operated in the world except on the first day, and was then hidden and never used.

If it were completely hidden, the world would not exist for even a minute. Rather, it was concealed and sown as a seed that is sown and produces offspring, seeds, and fruits, and the world exists from it. There is not a day that does not come out from it in the world and sustains everything because with it, the Creator nourishes the world. Where there is engagement in Torah at night, a thread of that hidden light comes out and extends over those who are engaging in Torah, as it is written, "By day the Lord will command His mercy, and in the night His song shall be with me."

421-422) **King Solomon looked and saw** that even in that generation, which was more complete than all the other generations, it was not the wish of the high King that wisdom would be so disclosed through him, and that the Torah that was initially hidden would be revealed. And he came and opened doors for it. But although he opened, they are closed, except for those sages who were rewarded and who stutter in them, and do not know how to open their mouths in them. This generation, in which Rabbi Shimon is present, is the wish of the Creator for Rabbi Shimon for hidden matters to be revealed through him.

But I am perplexed about the sages of the generation—how they let even one moment be without standing before Rabbi Shimon and studying Torah while Rabbi Shimon is in the world. But in this generation the wisdom will not be forgotten from the world. Woe unto the world when he departs, the sages grow fewer, and the wisdom is forgotten from the world.

432) **"And behold, it was very good" is the angel of death**. Why do you say here that because of him, it does not say "It was good" on the second day? Indeed, here is the secret of secrets. Of course the angel of death is very good, since all the people in the world know that they will die and return to dust, and therefore many repent and return to their Master because of this fear. They fear sinning before Him. Many fear the King because a rope is hanging before them. Indeed, how good is the rope for people, for it

makes them good and genuine and they correct their ways properly. "And behold, it was very good," indeed, "Very."

436-438) When they come out of there to come into this world, the spirits undress the body and clothing of the Garden of Eden, and clothe the body and clothing of this world, making their abode in this world, in this clothing and body, which is from a stinking smut.

And when it is his time to go, to leave this world and go, he does not leave before the angel of death undresses this clothing and this body. Once the body has been stripped of the spirit through the angel of death, the spirit goes and dresses in the other body in the Garden of Eden, from which it undressed upon its coming into this world. There is joy for the body only in that body which is there, and he is happy that he stripped off the body of this world and wore the other, complete clothing from the Garden of Eden, which is similar to this world. He sits in it and walks and observes to know high secrets, which he could not know or observe while he was in this world in this body.

When the soul dresses in a clothing of that world, what refinements and what delights has he there? Who caused the spirit to clothe the body in the Garden of Eden? Who is it who undressed him of these clothes of this world? It is the angel of death. Thus, the angel of death is very good, and the Creator performs *Hesed* [grace] with people when He does not strip the man of the clothes of this world before He fixes up other garments for him, more honorable and better than the ones in the Garden of Eden.

440) See how merciful is the Creator over His creations: even the most wicked, who contemplates repentance but cannot repent and dies, certainly receives punishment for having departed the world without repentance, but afterwards, that desire to repent, which He placed in his heart, does not go unnoticed by the upper King, and the Creator fixes a place for the wicked in an abode in the netherworld, where he tweets in repentance. It is so because a desire comes down from before the Creator and breaks all the powers of the guards over the gates of the chambers of Hell, and reaches the place of that wicked, knocks in him, and evokes in him the desire to repent, as he had had during his life. Then that soul tweets to rise out of the abode in the netherworld.

441) There is no good will that is lost from the holy King. Because of it, happy is he who contemplates good thoughts for his Master. Even though he cannot do them, the Creator regards his will as though he did. This is for the best. However, the Creator does not consider an ill will as an act, except for contemplation of idol worship.

528-529) **The Creator created the world wisely, making it with great craftiness, blowing the breath of life in it, to know and to regard the secrets of the wisdom, to know the honor of his Master, as it is written, "Everyone who is called by My name, and whom I have created for My glory, whom I have formed, even whom I have made."** The glory below, the holy throne, *Malchut*, was established above only through the corrections of the dwellers of this world.

When people are righteous and pious, knowing how to correct corrections for the glory, *Malchut*, as it is written, "Whom I have created for My glory," for this glory of Mine, so it is established with strong pillars, *HGT*, to decorate it with corrections and decorations below, so they raise MAN from below to extend *Mochin* to her, which are called "decorations," so that My glory will rise thanks to the righteous in the land.

536-538) **Rabbi Yosi and Rabbi Hiya were walking along the way and a donkey driver was leading the donkeys behind them**. Rabbi Yosi said to Rabbi Hiya, "We should engage and exert in words of Torah because the Creator is walking ahead of us, hence it is time to make corrections for Him, so He will be with us on this way." A donkey driver stings the donkeys with a piece of wood to make them walk faster.

Rabbi Hiya started and said, "It is time to do for the Lord; they have broken Your law." Anytime when the Torah exists in the world and people engage in it, the Creator is seemingly happy with the work of His hands, there is joy in all the worlds, and heaven and earth maintain their existence. Moreover, the Creator gathers His entire household and tells them, "See the holy people that I have in the land, thanks to them, the Torah is crowned. See the work of My hands, of whom you said, 'What is man, that I should remember him?'" And they, when they see their Master's joy with His people, they promptly start and say, "And who is as Your people, as Israel, one nation in the land."

And when Israel idle away from the Torah, His might seemingly fades, as it is written, "You neglected the Rock who begot you," and then it is written, "And all the host of heaven stand." Hence, it is time to do for the Lord. Those righteous that remained should muster their strength and do good deeds, to strengthen the Creator with the righteous and with His camps and armies, since they have broken Your law and the people of the world do not engage in it properly.

560) The Creator will grant you and will hear your voice when you need Him.

561) **When the Creator created the world, He divided the world: the settled place to one side, and the desolate place to the other side.** He divided the settled place and turned the world around a single point, which is the holy land, since the holy land is the middle of the world, the middle of the holy land is Jerusalem, and the middle of Jerusalem is the house of the holy of holies. Also, all the good and nourishment of the entire settled place descends there from above, and there is not a place in the entire settled place that is not nourished from there.

567) **The governance of faith is inside the middle point of the whole of the holy land, the house of the holy of holies.** Even though now it does not exist, still, the whole world is

nourished thanks to it, and food and provision come out from there to all, throughout the place of the settled world. For this reason, even though Israel are outside the holy land, still by the power and merit of the land, there is food and provision in the world. This is why it is written, "And bless the Lord your God for the good land which He has given you." Indeed, for the good land, for thanks to it there is food and provision in the world.

590) **From the day one inherits the soul, which comprises the Creator and His Divinity, from that time he is called "a son,"** as David said in Psalms, "I will tell of the law of the Lord: He said to Me, 'You are My son, today I have begotten you.'" This applies to every person when obtaining the soul.

593) **The Creator adds a good thought to an act.** And since you are his son, everything which you have thought for your Master, He will keep through you, and you will never move from Him. Rather, you will be in His form in everything. At the time of exile, you vanish from people, while I, from this world, am an emissary of the Creator to say these words before you. I am commanded by Him never to move from

you at any time and any hour that you wish. I and all the Tannaim and Amoraim of our seminary ask of you: "Go, arise and complete the commandment of your Master."

640) **When the world was created, not a thing existed before there was the desire to create man, so he will engage in Torah, and thanks to that, the world existed.** Now, anyone who looks in the Torah and engages in it, seemingly sustains the entire world. The Creator looked in the Torah and created the world; man looks in the Torah and sustains the world. It follows that the work and the keeping of the entire world is the Torah. For this reason, happy is he who engages in the Torah, for he sustains the world.

645-647) **"To know that the Lord He is the God"** is the whole of the faith of the entire Torah, the whole of above and below. The whole of the faith, *Malchut*, since the name *Elokim* [God] is *Malchut*. The whole of the Torah is the written Torah, the name *HaVaYaH*, ZA. This is the oral Torah, the *Malchut*, the name *Elokim*. It is all one: it is the whole of the faith because *HaVaYaH* [the Lord] is the *Elokim* [God]; it is the full name.

Faith is called "a name" for in this unification it is full and complete. And He, "The Lord is one and His name One." *HaVaYaH* is one; He is "Hear O Israel, the Lord our God, the Lord is one." This is one unification. "And His name One" is "Blessed be the name of the glory of His kingdom forever and ever," which is a different unification, so His name will be one, *Malchut*. It is also written, "The Lord is the God," when they are in one unification.

How do you say that the verse, "The Lord is the God" is as it is written, "The Lord is one and His name One"? After all, is it not similar? If it were written, "The Lord is one and His name is One," I would say so. But it is written, "The Lord is one and His name One." Should it not have said here, "The Lord He is the God He," and then it would seem like "The Lord is one and His name One"?

It is all one because when uniting these two names, this in one unification and that in one unification, as it is written, "The Lord is one and His name One," the two names become one, included in one another, and everything becomes whole there, in one unification. Then, "The Lord He is the God," since everything is included in one another to be one. And as long as they have not all united, this in itself and that in itself, they are not included in one another to be all one.

666) **The Mitzvot of the Torah are parts and organs as above.** When they all join into one, they all rise to one place. The tabernacle is organs and parts, all adding up to a man, such as the Mitzvot of the Torah, since all the Mitzvot of the Torah are in man, male and female, ZON. When they conjoin, they are one, in a man, HaVaYaH filled with Alephs, which is Adam [man] in Gematria. One who omits even a single Mitzva in the Torah, it is as though he omitted the form of faith, Malchut, for all the organs are together in man. For this reason, everything rises in a unification.

680) **When a person sees the righteous or the ones who are fitting in the generation and meets them, they are certainly the face of Divinity.** They are called "the face of Divinity" because Divinity hides within them. Divinity is hidden in them, and they are revealed because those who are close to Divinity are considered her face. And who are those who are close to her? It is them with whom she is established to be seen by the high King, ZA. They are the ones who raise MAN to unite the Creator and His Divinity.

715-716) **All the gates are locked and closed, and the gates of tears do not close.** There is no tear except out of sorrow and sadness, and all those appointees over the gates break the turns of the roads and the locks, admit those tears, and that prayer enters before the holy King.

At that time, that place, *Malchut*, is pressured by the sadness and pressure of that man, as it is written, "In all their affliction He was afflicted." He called, "He was afflicted," for man's affliction moves Divinity. The craving of the upper world, ZA, to that place, *Malchut*, is as a male who always craves the female. Hence, when the King, ZA, enters the queen, *Malchut*, and finds her in sadness, then all she wants is handed to her, that man or that prayer are not returned empty, and the Creator takes pity on him. Happy is that man who sheds tears before the Creator in his prayer.

878-880) Rabbi Elazar and Rabbi Aba went inside the house. When the night was halved, they rose to engage in Torah. Rabbi Aba said, "Now is certainly a time of good will for the Creator. And we have commented many times that when the night is halved the Creator enters the Garden of Eden with the righteous and plays with them. Happy is he who engages in Torah at that time."

The Creator playing with the righteous, how does He play? At that time, when the night is halved, the Creator awakens with the love of the left for the Assembly of Israel, *Malchut*, for there is love only from the left side. That is, He clothes the *Hochma* in the left with the *Hassadim* in the middle line, and the *Hochma* is completed.

The Assembly of Israel has no gift to offer to the King, or something of importance and beauty, except those spirits of the righteous, which the Creator sees crowning in several good deeds and several merits that they did on that day. They are more desirable to the Creator than all the sacrifices and offerings because in them, the Creator smells the fragrance that Israel do.

At that time the light illuminates, meaning the light of *Hochma* illuminated after having clothed in the *Hassadim* of the middle line, and all the trees in the Garden of Eden sing, and the righteous are crowned there with the refinements of the next world, which are the illumination of *Hochma*, called "Eden." When He awoke the man from his sleep at that time to engage in Torah, He took His portion with the righteous in the Garden of Eden.

888) **Rabbi Shimon said, "Moses did not die."** But it is written, "And Moses died there." Also, in every place it reads "death" in regard to the righteous. What is death? On our part it is called so, but on the part of the upper ones, it is to the contrary: life has been *added* to him. One who is in perfection, on whom the holy faith depends, death does not depend on him and he does not die.

924) **In the early days, a man would tell his friend,** "Tell me a word of Torah and have a portion of silver." Now, a man says to his friend, "Have a portion of silver and engage in Torah." And there is no one to notice and no one to lend an ear except those few high and holy in whom the Creator is praised.

Safra de Tzniuta
[The Hidden Book]

1-2) What is the concealment of the book?

Rabbi Shimon says, "Five chapters are included in the great palace and fill the whole earth. Rabbi Yehuda said, "If these include all the wisdom, then they are better than all and do not need to learn anymore." Rabbi Shimon said, "So it is for one who enters the wisdom and comes out of it in peace, he sees here the inclusion of all the wisdom. But one who did not enter in wisdom and came out in peace is not so, since one who enters the palace of wisdom and comes out of there because of a flaw is not regarded as having entered and came out, for he did not come out of his own will. Rather, he was expelled from there due to a flaw. But one who has no flaw, and comes out of the palace of his own mind and will, is as one who enters and leaves his own house, he is as one of the family there, and Divinity shows him all her treasures and secrets, and hides nothing from him. He is considered coming and going."

It is like a person whose house was in the mountains, and who did not know city dwellers. He sowed wheat and ate the wheat as it was. One day he arrived at the city and was given good bread. That man said, "What is this for?" He was told, "It is bread to eat." He ate and found it very tasty. He said, "Of what was this made?" They told him, "Of wheat." Then he was given cakes made in oil. He tasted them and said, "Of what were these made?" They told him, "Of wheat." Then he was given a dish fit for kings, which is kneaded in oil and honey. He said, "Of what are these made?" He was told, "Of wheat." He said, "Indeed, I am the owner of all that because I eat the essence of all those," which is wheat. Because of that view he did not learn how to make all those delights and did not know the delicacies of the world, and they were lost from him. So is one who has the whole of the wisdom and does not know all the delightful refinements that come out of that whole.

39) When a person wishes to establish a prayer to his Master, his lips murmur in that manner from below upward, to raise the glory of his Master to the place of the potion of the deep well, *Bina*. Then he goes to draw from that potion

of the stream, *Bina*, from above downward to each degree through the last degree, *Malchut*, to extend donations to all from above downward. Then he must tie a knot through all, to unify all the degrees in *Ein Sof*, the knot of the aim of the faith, and all his wishes will be made, whether the wishes of the public or the wishes of an individual.

40-43) The prayer that one should ask of his Master is set up in nine ways:

1. In the order of the alphabet;

2. In mentioning the qualities of the Creator: Merciful, Gracious, and so forth;

3. In the honored names of the Creator: EKYEH, Yod-Hey, Yod-Hey-Vav, El, Elokim, HaVaYaH, Hosts, Shadai, ADNI;

4. In ten *Sefirot*: Malchut, Yesod, Hod, Netzah, Tifferet, Gevura, Hesed, Bina, Hochma, Keter;

5. In mentioning the righteous: the patriarchs, the prophets, the kings;

6. In song and praise, in which there is true reception;

7. Above them, one who knows how to properly correct corrections for his Master;

8. In knowing how to raise from below upward;

9. And there is one who knows how to extend abundance from above downward.

In all those manners of prayer, great intention is required.

And if he aims properly in all of these nine manners of prayer, it is a person who honors the name of his holy Master. It is written about it, "For I will honor those who honor Me, and those who despise Me will be despised." I will honor him in this world to keep and to do all his needs, and all the nations of the earth will see that the name of the Lord is called on him and will fear him. In the next world, he will be rewarded with being with pious, in the realm of the pious, even though he did not read in the Torah sufficiently, but because he was rewarded with looking at knowing his Master and aimed in it properly.

One who does not know how to unify the holy Name and tie the knot of faith, to extend to the place that is needed, and to honor the name of his Master, it is better for him not to be born, especially if he does not intend in the Amen. For this reason, anyone who whispers with his lips with his heart clean, with cleansing waters, it is written about him, "And God said, 'Let us make man,'" for a man who knows how to unite the similitude and image properly, where ZA is *Tzelem* [similitude] and *Nukva* is the image.

Tetzaveh [Command]

39) **"From among the children of Israel,"** since everything is called "one" being one, as it should be, only from among the children of Israel. This is so because the children of Israel stand below to open ways, to illuminate paths, to light the candles, which are the upper *Sefirot*, and to bring everything from below upwards so all will be one. This is why it is written, "But you that cleave unto the Lord."

40) **"And you, bring ... near you."** Everything is brought closer by those who know how to unite the unification and to serve his Master. This is so because when the offering is there as it should be, everything draws near together—the sides, right and left—and the illumination of the face of the Creator is in the world, in the Temple. Then the *Sitra Achra* surrenders and hides, and the side of holiness governs with light and joy.

86) **Moreover, words of Torah settle in only there, since there is no light except for that which comes out of that darkness.** This is so because when that side surrenders, the Creator rises above and His glory grows. Also, the work

of the Creator is only out of darkness, and there is no good except from within the bad. And when one enters a bad way and leaves it, the Creator rises in his glory. Hence, the perfection of everything is good and bad together, and to later depart to the good. And there is no good except for that which comes out of the bad. And in that good, the glory of the Creator increases, and this is complete work.

89) And there is a secret here, which shone for us in the desert: Why was *Din* awakened in the world on this day? Indeed, all the secrets and all the precious sanctities are dependent upon the seventh, *Malchut*, and the upper seventh is the upper world, called "the next world," *Bina*. All the candles, all the sanctities, and all the blessings shine from her to *Malchut*, and when it is time to renew the blessings and the holy things to shine, the correction of all the worlds must be observed, to renew the blessings and sanctities. Then all the corrections to sustain the worlds rise from the lower ones if their deeds are virtuous.

92) **And when Israel awaken below by the blowing of the *Shofar*,** the voice that comes out of the *Shofar* beats the air and breaks through firmaments until it rises to the strong stone, the

Sitra Achra, which covers the moon. When it observes and finds the awakening of Rachamim, the Sitra Achra that rose and stood above, covering the moon, is confused. At that time, that voice stands and removes the Din from the Malchut, and since the Rachamim was awakened below in Malchut, the high Shofar, Bina, awakens above, as well, to produce a sound, which is the Mochin de ZA, Rachamim. Then voice meets voice, Rachamim in Rachamim.

94-95) **"Serve the Lord with gladness,"** since man's joy draws another joy, the higher one. Similarly, the lower world, Malchut, as it is crowned, so it extends from above. This is why Israel hurry to awaken a sound in the Shofar, which includes fire, wind, and water, the middle line, which consists of three lines that became one and rises upwards. It strikes that good stone, which diminishes her left line, and is colored by these three colors—white, red, and green—which are the three lines included in the voice. Then, as it is fit, so it extends from above.

And since Malchut was established with this voice from below, Rachamim come out from above and are on her, hence she is mingled with Rachamim from below and from above. At that time the *Sitra Achra* is mingled, his strength wanes, and he cannot accuse. And the good stone, the *Malchut*, stands in illumination of *Panim* [face] from all sides, in illumination below and illumination above.

134-136) "You shall dwell in *Sukkot* for seven days." This is faith, *Malchut*, which receives all her *Mochin*. And this verse was said about the upper world, *Bina*. When the world was created, this verse was said.

When *Hochma*—meaning upper *AVI*, called *Aba* and *Hochma*—began to come out of the place that is unknown and unseen, from *Rosh AA*, one *Masach* emerged and struck. And that upper *Hochma* sparkled and spread to all sides in the upper tabernacle, *YESHSUT*, which is called *Bina* and *Ima*. And that upper tabernacle produced *VAK*, which are *ZA*. And then, with the sparkling of the *Masach*, it illuminated to everyone and said, "You shall dwell in *Sukkot* for seven days."

Sukkot is written without a *Vav* [in Hebrew], since this is the lower tabernacle, *Malchut*, which is like a lantern, a glass vessel in which the candle is placed so as to shine, to show all the lights. And then he said, in the sparkling of the *Masach*, "You shall dwell in *Sukkot* for seven days." The seven days are from the upper world, *Bina*, to the lower world, *Malchut*. All seven days, *HGT NHYM de Bina*, exist so as to shine for that *Sukkah* [tabernacle], which is the "Fallen tabernacle of David," the tabernacle of peace, *Malchut*. And the holy people should sit under its shade in faith, *Malchut*, and one who sits in that shade, sits in those upper days of *Bina*.

145) **The Creator "Reveals the deep and secret things."** He reveals all the deep, upper secrets. The middle line reveals the depths in the two lines of *Bina*. It reveals them because it knows what is in the darkness of the left, where the light of *Hochma* sinks for absence of *Hassadim*. And were it not for the darkness, the light would not appear later through the middle line. And it knows what is in the darkness, since it includes it in the right line. For this reason, it revealed the depths and the hidden, since were it not for the darkness of the left, the depths and the hidden would not have been revealed. And this light that appeared out of the darkness is *Hochma*.

Ki Tissa [When You Take]

54-55) All those friends, who do not love each other, depart the world before their time. All the friends in Rashbi's time had love of soul and love of spirit among them. This is why in his generation, the secrets of Torah were revealed. Rabbi Shimon would say, "All the friends who do not love each other cause themselves to stray from the right path. Moreover, they put a blemish in the Torah, since there is love, brotherhood, and truth in the Torah. Abraham loved Isaac; Isaac loved Abraham; and they were embraced. And they were both gripped to Jacob with love and brotherhood, and were giving their spirits in one another. The friends should be like them, and not blemish them, for if love is lacking in them, they will blemish their value above, that is, Abraham, Isaac, and Jacob, which are *HGT*."

In the future, when we see Divinity face to face, all the faces will be supported, for they will be shining in that secret.

106) Before Israel sinned, while they were standing at Mount Sinai, the filth of the serpent was removed from them, since then there was

the annulment of the evil inclination in the world, and it was repelled from them. At that time, they united in the tree of life and rose to the uppermost degrees and did not come down. Then they knew and saw the highest visions of ZA, their eyes shone and they were delighted to know and to hear. At that time, the Creator girded them with belts of letters of the Holy Name, which are jewels from Mount Horev, so the serpent would not be able to rule over them and would not defile them as before in Egypt.

104) **The friends came** and kissed Rabbi Shimon's hands. They said, "If we had come to the world only to hear this thing, we would have been content." They wept and said, "Woe unto us. When we depart from the world, who will shine and reveal the lights of Torah?" This thing shines to the top of the heaven, and is written in the King's throne, and the Creator is now delighted about this thing. And how much joy over joy was added before the Holy King? Who will evoke words of wisdom in the world as you do?

120) **Happy are the righteous** who know the secrets of Torah and cling to the Torah, and keep the verse, "But you shall meditate on it day and

night." By her merit, they will be rewarded with the life of the next world, as it is written, "For this is your life and the length of your days."

New Zohar, Ki Tissa [When You Take]

46) One who considers making a *Mitzva* is as though he had done it because with his thought, he caused great abundance of blessings to come from the high thought to the place called *Mitzva*, *Malchut*. For this reason, it is as though he had done it, the *Malchut*. "And you shall do them." A thought is certainly the beginning of everything.

56-59) "The heavens tell the glory of God."

Heaven is the Creator, ZA. "Tell" means that they illuminate to a place called "the glory of God." "The glory of God" is the daughter of Abraham, *Malchut*. "God" is Abraham, *Hesed*. "Tell" is as it is written, "Then he saw and told it." "And told it," as it is written, "Her stones are the place of sapphire," from the word illumination. Those heaven, ZA, correct her in all the corrections for the glory of the God, *Malchut*.

This is why Israel below bring light to the *Malchut* in secret from the fountain above, from ZA, and say, "Blessed be the name of the glory of His kingdom forever and ever," and the place called "heaven" testifies about them.

When Israel are in wholeness, they testify a complete testimony about them, the Creator and the Assembly of Israel, ZA and *Malchut*. At that time the dew of above is drawn from the place of *Atik*, *Keter*. It is so when ZA and *Malchut* are in unity, as it is written, "My head is filled with dew." Dew has the count of "The Lord is one," the Creator and the Assembly of Israel, since at that time Israel are worthy of the dew.

82-83) First, one must exert in fear, *Malchut*, who is the door to everything, and afterwards, in the written Torah, ZA who is above. It is so because any person who does not fear sin has no permission to enter that door of faith, which is *Malchut*. And once he is repelled from that door, he is repelled from everything because he has no door through which to enter everything, as it is written, "This is the gate to the Lord."

Anyone whose fear of sin precedes his wisdom, his wisdom persists, since the wisdom sits on a "Stock which Your right has planted," which is the fear, called "the glory of God."

VaYakhel [And Moses Assembled]

22) The Creator has no contentment until He enters the Garden of Eden to play with the souls of the righteous.

51) When the Creator has a time of good will, to unite the upper *Merkava* with the lower *Merkava* so they are all one, a voice comes out from the place of the high holiness, heaven, ZA, and gathers all those holy ones below—the righteous in this world—and all the holy ministers—Michael, Gabriel, Uriel, and Raphael—and all the upper camps, the angels, to all be ready together. It is written about it, "And Moses assembled," meaning the heaven, ZA. It is also written, "The whole of the congregation of the children of Israel." These are the 12 upper holy camps—the lower *Merkava* that *Malchut* rides—and they raise the *Malchut* for a *Zivug* with ZA.

71) When a person places his will for the work of his Master, that will first rises to the heart—the persistence and the basis of the entire body. Afterwards that good will rises over all the organs of the body, the will of all the organs of the body and the will of the heart join together, pulling over them the brightness of Divinity to dwell with them. And that person is the Creator's portion, as it is written, "Take from among you a donation." "From among you" is the extension, to take upon yourselves that donation, the Divinity, so that the person will be a portion of the Creator.

98-99) When the Creator created the world, He did not create it so that Israel would come and receive the Torah. The world was created with the Torah and stands on it, as it is written, "If My covenant be not day and night, I have not appointed the ordinances of heaven and earth." The Torah is the long life in this world, and it is the length of life in the next world.

Anyone who exerts in the Torah is seemingly exerting in the palace of the Creator, for the upper palace of the Creator, *Malchut*, is Torah, that is, the oral Torah, *Malchut*. When a person engages in Torah, the Creator stands there and listens to his voice.

107-108) Each day a herald calls upon all the people in the world, "This matter is up to you," as it is written, 'Take from among you a donation to the Lord.' And if you should say that the matter is hard for you, 'Whoever is of a generous heart, let him bring it.'"

Hence the meaning of the prayer: a person who fears his Master and aims his heart and will in a prayer corrects the upper correction, first by singing and praising that the upper angels say above. And in that order of praises that Israel say below, *Malchut* adorns herself in her corrections as a woman who adorns herself for her husband.

114-116) **I heard this matter among the secrets of Rabbi Shimon** and I was not given permission to disclose, except to you, the high pious ones. When *Malchut* grips people's souls and spirits in one desire for *Dvekut* [adhesion], the man places his heart and will on that, and gives his soul in *Dvekut* with that desire, to include his soul in that *Dvekut*. If at that time his dedicating of his soul is accepted in the will of the souls [*Nefashot*, pl. of *Nefesh*] and spirits [*Ruchot*, pl. of *Ruach*] and souls [*Neshamot*, pl. of *Neshama*] that she grips, it is a man who was bundled in the bundle of life in this world and in the next world.

And while the King and queen, Torah and *Mitzvot*, must include all the sides above and below, and be crowned with *Neshamot* on all the sides, she is crowned in the *Neshamot* from above, and crowned in the *Neshamot* from below, of those who give her their souls [*Neshamot*]. If a person aims his heart and will to all that, and gives her his *Nefesh* from below willingly and in *Dvekut*, the Creator calls upon him peace below, such as the peace above, *Yesod*, who blesses the queen, and includes her and crowns her on all sides.

Likewise, the Creator calls this man Peace, as it is written, "And the Lord called him *Shalom* [peace]."

118) Rabbi Aba said, "Woe Rabbi Shimon, you are alive and I am already weeping for you. It is not over you that I am weeping, but I am weeping for the friends, and I am weeping for the world that will remain orphans after your departure from the world." Rabbi Shimon is like the light of a candle that burns above and burns below. All the people of the world shine in that light that it lit below. Woe to the world when the light below departs and comes into the light of above. Who will shine the light of Torah for the world?

121) **This concerns the prayer that one should pray before the Creator, which is one great work, more honored than the work of his Master. There is the work of the Creator**

that is in the work of the body, meaning the *Mitzvot* that depend on an act, and there is the work of the Creator that is more internal work—which is the most important—meaning *Mitzvot* that depend on speech and on the will of the heart.

123) A man's prayer is the work of the *Ruach* [spirit], work from *Behina Bet*, which depends on the speech. It is in high secrets and people do not know that a man's prayer breaches airs and breaches firmaments, opens doors and rises up.

150) Happy is a man who knows how to set up his prayer properly. In this prayer, in which the Creator is crowned, he waits until all the prayers of Israel have concluded ascending and are included in the complete prayer, and then all is as perfect as it should be above and below.

163) It is called "a storm" because it storms everything above and below and there is no one who can withstand it. It comes from the north, for it is written, "Out of the north the evil will break forth." For itself, it is harsh *Dinim* of the *Masach de Malchut de Midat ha Din*. However, it comes from the north to draw *Hochma* from the left line, as do all the *Klipot*. It is so because there are several other *Behinot* outside the north,

gripping to that stormy wind. Hence, it comes from the north, meaning received the *Dinim* of the north, as well.

183-184) **When that lowermost point, *Malchut*, rises and appears,** meaning when she receives *Hochma*—called "vision"—and is adorned in the upper *Mochin*, there is every joy above and below, and all the worlds are in joy. On that night of the Sabbath, that point expands in its lights and spreads its wings on the whole world, all the other rulers pass away, and there is watching over the world.

At that time the spirit of *Neshama* is added in Israel, on each and every one, and in that added *Neshama* they forget every sadness and wrath, and there is only joy above and below. When that spirit that came down and was added in the people of the world comes down, it bathes in the perfumes of the Garden of Eden, descends, and stays over the holy people. Happy are they when that spirit awakens.

225) **"Blessed is the name of the Master of the world. Blessed be Your crown and Your place**. May Your favor remain with Your people Israel forever; may the redemption of Your right be shown to Your people in Your Temple, and

impart upon us the best of Your light, and accept our prayers with mercy. May it be Your will that You extend our lives with goodness, that I, Your servant, be numbered among the righteous, that You have mercy on me, protect me, all that is mine, and that is of Your people Israel.

"It is You who nourishes all and sustains all. You control everything. It is You who rules over kings, and the kingship is Yours. I am a servant of the Creator, and I bow before Him and before the glory of His law [Torah] at all times. Not in man do I put trust, nor on any children of God do I rely, only on God in heaven, who is the true God, whose law is true, whose prophets are true, and who executes abundant kindness and truth. In him do I trust, and to His glorious and holy name do I declare praises. May it be Your will that You open my heart with Your law, and that You give me male sons who fulfill Your wish. May You fulfill my heart's wishes and the heart of Your entire people Israel for good, for life, and for peace. Amen."

228) **One who is reading in the Torah must aim his heart and will into those things that he is reading,** for he is an emissary of his Master in words to announce to the whole nation, since he is similar to the upper one, like the Creator

at the time of the giving of the Torah. Therefore, one who ascends to read in the Torah should first put matters in his house in order, and if he did not establish order, he will not read in the Torah. How do we know? From that word of the Creator before He sounded the Torah to the holy nation. It is written, "Then He saw it and declared it; He established it and also searched it out." Afterwards, it is written, "And to man He said, 'Behold, the fear of the Lord is wisdom.'" Thus, before He sounded it to man, He set each word in itself, and so must every reader in the Torah do.

279-282) **Rabbi Aba and the rest of the friends rose and said, "Happy are we that the Creator has brought this road before us." Rabbi Aba said, "The Creator has provided me with this road in order to bond with you. Happy am I that I have been rewarded with this road."**

On the day when I went off, I saw a light splitting into three lights, which went before me and hid. I said, "I must have seen Divinity, happy am I. And now these three lights that I saw are you. You are lights and high illuminations to illuminate in this world and in the next world.

"Thus far, I did not know that all these hidden gems were in your possession. Once I saw that these words were said by the will of the commandment of your Master, I know that all the words rise on this day to the upper throne, which is *Bina*, and the minister of the faces, *Matat*, takes them and turns them into crowns for his Master. This day is crowned with 60 holy *Merkavot* [chariots/assemblies], opposite *HGT NHY*, in honor of the throne, *Bina*, by these words that were said here on this day."

In the meantime, the sun had set. At midnight, they rose to engage in Torah. Rabbi Aba said, "Henceforth, we shall say things with which to crown the righteous in the Garden of Eden, for now is the time when the Creator and all the righteous in the Garden of Eden listen to the voices of the righteous in the earth."

299) "In the middle of all the firmaments—over the land of Israel, in the middle of the world— there is a door called Gvilon." The new *Sium* in the middle of the degree became an opening for the lower one, so it could rise and receive from the upper one. Under this opening there are 70 other openings below, through which to receive the 70 names in *Malchut de Atzilut*, the illumination of the name *AB*, the 70 ministers of the 70 nations. From that opening, a road

goes up above until it reaches the upper throne because through there it is possible to ascend to *Malchut de Atzilut*.

304-309) **22 letters are inscribed and engraved in the firmament over the Garden of Eden. Each of them drips over the garden dew from the dew of above.** From that dew, which is illumination of *Hassadim*, these souls bathe and are healed after they have bathed themselves in the river Dinur to be purified. The dew comes down only from the letters inscribed and engraved in that firmament because these letters are the whole of the Torah, extending from ZA *de Atzilut*, who is called Torah, as he was made of the fire and water of the Torah, the fire and water of ZA *de Atzilut*.

For this reason, they cast dew on all those who engage in Torah *Lishma* [for the sake of the Torah] in this world. These words are inscribed in the Garden of Eden and rise up to the firmament over the Garden of Eden, taking dew from those 22 letters that are there to nourish the soul, as it is written, "Let my teaching drop as the rain, my speech distill as the dew."

In the middle of that firmament is one opening, opposite the opening of the palace above in *Yetzira*. In that opening, the souls fly out of the Garden of Eden above in a pillar that is nailed to the earth of the Garden of Eden, and reaches up to that opening.

The opening that was made in the middle of the firmament is the new *Sium* that was made in the middle of the degree of the Garden of Eden due to *Malchut's* ascent to the place of *Bina*. Because of that *Sium*, half of the degree, *Bina* and *TM*, fell to the lower degree—the earth of the Garden of Eden. At the time of *Gadlut*, when *Malchut* returns to her place and *Bina* and *TM* rise up to their degree, to the firmament, they take the lower degree along with them, those souls that are in the earth of the Garden of Eden. It follows that the new *Sium* that was made in *Bina* has become an opening for the lower one through which to rise to the upper one.

And those *Bina* and *TM* that initially fell down to the earth of the Garden of Eden, by clinging to the degree of the earth of the Garden of Eden, it is considered that they were nailed to the soil of the garden while they themselves are considered a tall pillar that reaches up to that opening in the middle of the firmament. Through that pillar, the souls rise from the earth of the Garden of Eden to the firmament of the

Garden of Eden. That is, at the time of *Gadlut*, when *Bina* and *TM*, which are considered a pillar, rise back to the firmament of the Garden of Eden, they also take with them the souls in the earth of the Garden of Eden, raising them to the firmament of the Garden of Eden.

Inside the firmament, in the opening in the middle of the firmament over the garden, three colors of light enter, included together. They are *HBD*, and they illuminate to the colors of the pillar that rose up there. At that time, that pillar sparkles and blazes in several blazing colors, and the righteous that rose with that pillar to the firmament receive the lights from the firmament through that pillar. Every hour, the righteous illuminate from that upper brightness, and this is applied always. However, each Sabbath and each beginning of a month, Divinity is revealed in that firmament more than on other times, and all the righteous come and bow to her.

Happy is he who has been rewarded with those garments. These garments are from good deeds that a man made in this world with the *Mitzvot* of the Torah, the *Mitzvot* that depend on actions. The soul stands in them in the lower Garden of Eden, and dresses in those honorable garments.

When the soul rises through the opening above, other high and honorable garments are provided to her, which are made by *Mitzvot* that depend on the will and the aim of the heart in the Torah and in the prayer. It is so because when that will rises, those who are crowned in it are crowned, a part of it remains for that person, and garments of light are made of it for the soul to dress in and rise. And although these garments of the soul in the lower Garden of Eden depend on an act, those that rise up to the firmament depend only on the will of the spirit, to stand among the angels, the holy spirits. This is what Rabbi Shimon learned from Elijah—the garments of below in the Garden of Eden of the earth depend on the action, the garments of above depend on the will and the aim of the spirit in the heart.

309) **When the soul rises through the opening above,** other high and honorable garments are provided to her, which are made by *Mitzvot* that depend on the will and the aim of the heart in the Torah and in the prayer. It is so because when that will rises, those who are crowned in it are crowned, a part of it remains for that person, and garments of light are made of it for the soul to dress in and rise. And although

these garments of the soul in the lower Garden of Eden depend on an act, those that rise up to the firmament depend only on the will of the spirit, to stand among the angels, the holy spirits. This is what Rabbi Shimon learned from Elijah—the garments of below in the Garden of Eden of the earth depend on the action, the garments of above depend on the will and the aim of the spirit in the heart.

409) **In the prayer, a man's body and soul are corrected and perfected.** A prayer is correcting corrections, which are corrected as one. There are four corrections: 1) correcting oneself to be completed, 2) correcting this world, 3) correcting the upper world in all the armies of heaven, 4) correcting the holy name in the holy *Merkavot* and in all the worlds, above and below.

417-419) **There is love after he has been rewarded with fear.** Once fear is present over a man's head from the left, then love awakens, which is right, ZA with respect to the *Hesed* in him. One who worships out of love clings to a high place above, and clings to the *Kedusha* of the next world, *Bina*, since he rises to be crowned and to cling to the right side, *Hesed de* ZA, on which there is *Bina*.

Work that comes from the side of fear is respected but does not rise to cling above in ZA. When he worships out of love, he rises and crowns above and clings to the next world. This is a man who is summoned to the next world. Happy is he, for he dominates the place of fear because no one governs the degree of fear but love, the right, the unification of ZA and *Malchut*.

One who is worthy of the next world needs to unify the name of the Creator and unite the organs, ZON, and the upper degrees, AVI, upper and lower, including them all, and bringing all of them into *Ein Sof*, tying knots, as it is written, "Hear O Israel, the Lord is our God, the Lord is one."

425-428) The aim in the word "one" is to unite everything together from *Malchut* and above, to elevate the will, to tie everything in one knot, and to elevate the will with fear and love through *Ein Sof*. The will to ascend to *Ein Sof* will not leave all those degrees and organs but will elevate his will in all of them, not one of them missing, to attach them, so they will all be one knot in *Ein Sof*.

It is a unification in correction.

One who wishes to include all the secrets of unification in the word "one" is better. Hence, we prolong the "one," [in the *Shema* reading] to elevate the will to extend from above downward, and to raise from below upwards so all will be one.

The word, "one" is above and below and the four directions of the world. Above and below, which are AVI and ZON, must be united, and the four directions of the world are the upper *Merkava* [assembly], *HGTM de* ZA above the *Chazeh* to include everything together in a single tie, one unification through *Ein Sof*.

437-438) **"Then those who feared the Lord spoke to one another, and the Lord listened and heard,** and a book of remembrance was written before Him for those who fear the Lord and esteem His name." It is written, "Then ... spoke," meaning spoke above. That is, all the holy *Merkavot* and all the holy armies spoke to one another before the Creator.

Because these holy words that they said rise up, and several rush and carry them before the holy King, and become crowned in several crowns in these upper lights, and all spoke before the holy King. Who saw joys and who saw praises that rise in all those firmaments? When these words rise and the holy king looks at them and crowns in them, they rise and sit in His lap, and

He plays with them. From there, from His lap, they rise to His head and become a crown. This is why the Torah said, "And I will be delighted each day." It does not say, "was," but "will be," in future tense. That is, each time the upper words rise before Him.

438) **However, the writing speaks of those righteous who were rewarded with repentance from love, when sins become merits.** And the greater the transgression, the greater merit it became. It follows that when these righteous were pondering the beginning, saying, "It is vain to serve God," an iniquity of which there is none worse, then these words of heresy have now become great merits due to the repentance from love that they have made. Now they are considered as though at that time those who fear the Lord spoke to one another these words of heresy, for they have become merits, and by this great inversion, great delight was made before the Creator.

463) **Happy is a man who keeps the Mitzvot of his Master, who knows their secrets.** We have no Mitzva in the Torah on which high secrets, lights, and sublime splendors do not hang. But people do not know and do not consider the

glory of their Master. Happy are the righteous, who engage in the Torah. Happy are they in this world and in the next.

481-482) **The incense ties a tie. It unites, illuminates light, and removes filth, and the letter *Dalet* becomes the letter *Hey*** for prior to the *Zivug* with ZA, *Malchut* is *Dalet*, for being without *Hassadim*, she does not illuminate and she is poor. And when ZA mates with her, the *Hochma* in her dresses in *Hassadim* and she illuminates in all the perfection and becomes the letter *Hey*.

The incense unifies a unification of ZA with *Malchut*, thus causing the *Dalet* to become *Hey*. Through it, *Hey* connects with *Vav*, ZA. *Vav* rises and is crowned in the first *Hey*, *Bina*, to receive abundance for *Malchut*. And the first *Hey*, *Bina*, shines in the letter *Yod*, *Hochma*, to give to ZA, and all raise a desire to *Ein Sof*, and all—*Hochma*, *Bina*, ZA, and *Malchut*—become *Yod-Hey Vav-Hey*, one high knot. All this is done by the incense.

Henceforth, since everything is tied in that tie, everything was crowned in *Ein Sof*, and the holy name shone and was crowned on all the sides, and the worlds were all in joy, the candles illuminated, and there were blessings and food in all the worlds. And all came in the incense.

484) **Happy are Israel in this world and in the next world because they know how to correct the correction of above and below, as the correction from above to below should be corrected, until all is tied together in one tie, in that high tie, the incense, when there is a need to correct in the correction of the inscribed letters in which the Creator is read, HaVaYaH.**

492) **In the breaking of the vessels, and later through the sin of the tree of knowledge by the serpent's seduction,** 320 sparks of holiness dispersed and fell into the Klipot. Our whole work in Torah and Mitzvot is to sort out those sparks of holiness and return them to holiness, and then will be the end of correction, as it is written, "He will swallow up death forever." However, we must sort out only 288 sparks of holiness, and we need not sort those last 32 sparks of holiness because with the sorting of the 288 sparks, they are sorted by themselves.

495-496) **At that time, when all the camps arise over the land of the Galilee, they will all go, one to the portion of his fathers, and one to**

the portion of his fathers, as it is written, "And each of you shall return to his own property," and they will recognize each other. The Creator is destined to clothe each one with embroidered garments, and they will all come and praise their Master in Jerusalem. Then multitudes will bond there, and Jerusalem shall spread to all sides, more than it had spread when they bonded there upon their return from the exile.

When they bond and praise their Master, the Creator will rejoice with them, as it is written, "And they will come and shout for joy on the height of Zion." Subsequently, it is written, "And they will flow the bounty of the Lord," each to his own portion and the portion of his fathers. And the portion of Israel will be until the high Rome, and there they will learn Torah. It is written, "You who lie in the dust, awake and shout for joy," and the portion of Israel will reach up to the great Rome, and there they learn Torah. That is, they will conquer it and return it to sanctity.

PEKUDEI [ACCOUNTS]

1) **It is written, "All the rivers flow into the sea, yet the sea is not full."** All the rivers are rivers and holy springs, the *Sefirot de* ZA, which have been filled and came out to illuminate upon the great sea, which is *Malchut*. And when the great sea is filled by those rivers, it emits water and waters all the animals of the field, as it is written, "They water every beast of the field," which are the degrees of *BYA*.

17) "Which is being shown to you." "You" is the mirror that does not shine, *Malchut*, which showed him within her all those forms. And Moses saw each of them in its corrected form, as one who sees within a crystal lamp, within a mirror that shows all the forms. And when Moses looked into them, he found them perplexing, since there, in *Malchut*, everything stood in its spiritual form, but each form equalized its form to the imaginary form in this world, in the Tabernacle.

50) It is written, "And He will be the faith of Your times, the strength of salvation of wisdom and knowledge; the fear of the Lord is His

treasure." Any person who engages in Torah in this world—and is rewarded with setting up times for it—should be with faith that his desire will be aimed at the Creator, ZA, that he will intend for the Creator. *Malchut* is called "a name," to mate with the heaven, ZA, since the faith, *Malchut*, intended to connect with ZA, as it is written, "The faith of Your times," where "Your times" are the times for Torah, ZA, and faith—*Malchut*—to bond together. "The strength of salvation," including *Hesed* in *Din*, since strength is *Din* and salvation is *Hesed*. "Of wisdom and knowledge." These are one atop the other because the *Hochma* is hidden and concealed, and they should be placed one atop the other, as *Hochma* appears only through the *Daat*.

80-81) **The right side is always posed to keep the whole world, illuminate, and bless it.** Therefore, the priest, the right side, *Hesed*, is always ready to bless the people, since all the blessings of the world come from the right side, and the priest takes first. For this reason, the priest was appointed on blessings above and below—the *Hesed* above, and the priest below.

When the priest stretches his hands to bless the people, Divinity comes over him and fills his hands. He raises the right hand over the left hand, to elevate the right and make it stronger than the left. Then, all the degrees in which the priest stretches his hands are blessed from the source of everything. The source of the well is a righteous, *Yesod*. The source of everything is the next world, *Bina*, from which all the faces, all the *Mochin* illuminate, for it is the spring and the source of everything, and all the candles and lights are lit from there.

93-94) **When the sea raises its waves in anger and the waves come up to wash the world over,** when they come and see the sand of the sea, they promptly break and turn back quiet, and cannot rule and wash the world over.

Similarly, Israel are like the sand of the sea. When the rest of the nations, the waves of the sea—angry, with harsh *Dinim*—see that Israel are connected to the Creator, they turn back and break before them, and cannot rule over the world.

109) **It is written, "While the king sat at his table, my perfume gave forth its fragrance."** "While the king sat at his table" is the Creator, *Bina*, when He gave the Torah to Israel and came to Sinai. That is, when *Bina* disclosed the

Mochin de Yechida de ZA that illuminated at the time of the giving of the Torah to Israel. There were several *Merkavot* with Him, all of which are holy *Merkavot*, left line, as well as all the upper sanctities from the upper *Kedusha* of the Torah, the right line. They were all there, and the Torah, the middle line, was given in flames of fire. Everything was of fire, written in white fire, from the side of *Hesed*, over black fire, from the side of *Gevura*. It is so because the middle line consists of *HG*, right and left, and the letters were flying and ascending through the air. In the air, the lower degrees would fly and rise up to the upper ones.

170-171) **The good deeds that one does in this world** draw light of the upper splendor to set up for him a garment for that world, to be seen before the Creator. In that garment that he wears, he enjoys and sees the illuminating mirror, as it is written, "To behold the pleasantness of the Lord and to visit in His palace."

Therefore, the soul dresses in special garments in two worlds, so she will have wholeness in all—in this world, below, and in the world above. This is why it is written, "Only the righteous will give thanks to Your name, the upright will dwell in Your presence." "Only the righteous will give thanks to Your name" is in this world; "The upright will dwell in Your presence" is in that world.

211-212) **It is written, "In the beginning God created the heaven and the earth," the heaven being ZA and the earth being *Malchut*,** since the tabernacle was made according to everything, making the similitude of the lower world, *Malchut*, and the similitude of the upper world, ZA. All of the works that the Creator worked in this world are as above. So is the tabernacle: all of His works are as the work and as the similitude of the upper world.

This is the meaning of all the work of the tabernacle. All of them are deeds and corrections of above and of below, to instill Divinity in the world, in the upper dwellers, the angels, and in the lower dwellers, people. The lower Garden of Eden, *Malchut*, is as the upper one, *Bina*. All the images and all the forms of the world are there, hence the work of the tabernacle and the work of heaven and earth, ZA and *Malchut*, are all one.

233-235) **King David always lowered himself before the Creator, for anyone who lowers himself before the Creator, the Creator raises** him above all. This is why the Creator desired David in this world and in the next world.

Similarly, one should be despised in one's own eyes and lower himself in everything, to be a *Kli* that the Creator wants.

262) It is written, "The secret of the Lord is to them that fear Him; and His covenant is to make them know it." The upper secret, which is concealed, stands only for those who fear Him, who always fear the Creator, who are worthy of these sublime secrets, and to have these secrets in them in hiding and concealment as it should be, as they are sublime secrets. However, "And His covenant, to make them know it," the secret that stands in the holy covenant. "To make them know it," since it is a place that is poised for revealing and for knowing, since the *Yesod* discloses the illumination of *Hochma* in *Malchut*. "To make them know it," through *Malchut*.

291) One who has eyes in *Tevuna* [gumption] will know and regard the wisdom of his Master, and will know these sublime matters where the keys of his Master are found, which are hidden within the holy tabernacle.

337) For this reason, the holy Israel, which is a single nation in holy unification, the Creator gives them a counsel by which to be saved from everything.

343) **All the righteous that tie the knots of unifications** and daily unify the unification of the faith, Malchut, who is called "tabernacle," raise the chair, Malchut, until they bring her to Moses, ZA. It is written about them, "And they brought the tabernacle to Moses." And since the righteous connect her with Moses, they gain blessings from the source of life by merit of the ties of unifications that they tie, tying the unification properly. It is written, "And Moses saw all the work," meaning the unification of everything, and then, "And Moses blessed them," meaning they gained the blessings from the place where the degree of Moses stands—ZA. These are the sages that do all the holy work because they know how to arrange the holy work through the unifications that they do.

344) **Anyone who prays a prayer and ties the unification is looked upon. If the prayer and the knot are proper, he is blessed first, from the place from which all the blessings come.**

349-350) **It is written, "This is the law of the burnt offering. It is that which goes up** on its firewood upon the altar all night." In the next world, *Bina*, all will be one. The burnt offering is called "the holy of holies," after the *Dvekut* [adhesion] with *Bina*. This is why *Malchut* is called "burnt offering," for it rises and crowns in ZA and in *Bina*, for everything to be one, in one connection in joy.

Because she rises up to ZA and to *Bina*, it is written, "This is the law of the burnt offering" [*Ola* means both "burnt offering" and "rising" in Hebrew], which is a male and female together. "This" is the *Nukva*, "The law" is ZA, who is called Torah [law]. The written Torah is ZA; the oral Torah is *Malchut*. "Rising" [also "burnt offering"] means rising to the next world, *Bina*, to connect within her, since *Bina* is called "the holy of holies." Also, a burnt offering is the holy of holies, as well.

359-360) **The tie of the burnt offering ties to the holy of holies, *Bina*, to illuminate. To where does the *Dvekut* of the will of the priests, the Levites, and the Israelis above, in the offering of the sacrifice, rise?**

Their *Dvekut* rises up to *Ein Sof*, since every connection and unity and perfection is to hide and conceal that which is unattainable and unknown, that the desire of all desires is in him, in *Ein Sof*. *Ein Sof* is neither about to be known nor to become a *Sof* [end], nor become a *Rosh* [head/beginning]. It is also not like the first absence, *Keter*, which elicited *Rosh* and *Sof*. *Rosh*, the uppermost point, the concealed beginning of everything, stands within the thought, *Hochma*, since *Hochma* emerged from *Keter*, as it is written, "But wisdom, from where shall it be?" He made an end, called "the end of the matter," *Malchut*, the end of all the lights. But there, in *Ein Sof*, there is no end.

361-362) There are no desires in Ein Sof, nor are there lights or candles, which are lights of Gevura. All the candles and lights in *Atzilut* depend on *Ein Sof*, to exist in them. However, it is unattainable. One who is known and unknown, in whom there is knowing but is unknown, is the highest and most concealed desire, called *Ein* [absence/null] the *Sefira Keter*. But in *Ein Sof*, not a word can be said, for there is zero attainment in it.

When the uppermost point, *Hochma*, and the next world, *Bina*, ascend in their illumination, they know only scent, *VAK* of illumination of *Hochma*, and not *GAR*, as one who smells a fragrance and is perfumed. It is not considered contentment, called "a fragrance," for it is written, "And I will not smell the savor of your sweet odors." Thus, "smell" and "fragrance" are two separate things, since a fragrance means the scent of the desire, all those desires of prayer, the desire of singing, and the desire of the priest, which are Adam. Then they all become one will, called "a fragrance," which means a desire. Then everything becomes connected and illuminates together as it should.

385-387) **When the Creator establishes His house, _Malchut_, it is written about that time, "He will swallow up death forever."** As the angel of death swallowed up the people of the world, so will the angel of death be swallowed.

And he will not be swallowed for a set time, as Israel were in exile for a set time. Rather, it is written, "Forever," for all generations.

At that time the Creator will raise the Assembly of Israel, _Malchut_, and will establish the bases and the sills, and all the ceilings of the house in their correction forever because the _Sitra Achra_ will be swallowed up, and will never rise again. Then it is written, "And He will remove the disgrace of His people from all the earth; for the Lord has spoken."

393) **The Creator chose Israel for His lot and portion, and brought them near Him**. He made of them certain degrees in this world, the patriarchs, such as above, to perfect all the worlds as one, above and below, as it is written, "The heaven is My throne, and the earth is My footstool," to perfect above and below into being one.

474-477) **Happy are you, Adam HaRishon, the chosen one among all creations present in the world**, for the Creator has made you greater than all and had let you into the Garden of Eden, and established for you seven canopies in which to play in the pleasure of the sublime delight, as it is written, "To behold the pleasantness of the Lord, and to visit in His palace." "To behold the pleasantness of the Lord" above in ZA, "And to visit in His palace" below, in *Malchut*. "To behold the pleasantness of the Lord" in those seven firmaments above, of ZA, "And to visit in His palace," in those seven firmaments below, of *Malchut*. These stand opposite those.

In all of them, the seven firmaments of ZA and the seven firmaments of *Malchut*, You stood in the Garden of Eden. The seven upper holy canopies, firmaments of ZA, stood over you, above, to be crowned in them. These are *Hassadim*. And those seven lower firmaments, of *Malchut*, you stood in them to play in them, and they are illumination, called "entertainments." In all of them, your Master complemented you, to be whole in everything, whether in *Hassadim* or in *Hochma*.

Until you were deflected by the counsel of the wicked serpent and were expelled from the Garden of Eden, causing death to you and to the entire world, for you had left those enjoyments above and below, following those impure cravings, called "vipers' head," after which the body follows, and not the spirit, as it is written, "And a cruel vipers' head," who is cruel to the spirit. Finally, Abraham the pious came and began to mend the world, and entered the holy faith, establishing above and below—in those upper firmaments, and in those lower firmaments.

The lower firmaments of *Malchut* are palaces for the upper firmaments of ZA, to unite and to connect with one another.

485-490) **The holy appointee stands over the door to all the prayers that breach airs and**

firmaments to come before the King. If it is a prayer of many, he opens the gate and lets her in, where she is detained until all the prayers of the world become a crown on the head of the righteous one who lives forever, *Yesod*.

If it is a prayer of one, it rises until it reaches the palace door, where that appointee stands. If the prayer is good for entering the holy King, he immediately opens a door and lets it in. If it is not good, he pushes it out and it descends and roams the world, standing at the bottom firmament from among those firmaments below, which lead the world. In that firmament is the appointee Sahadiel, who takes those rejected prayers, called "disqualified prayers," and conceals them until a person repents.

If he repents before his Master properly, and prays another prayer, a good one, when the prayer rises, the appointee, Sahadiel, takes that prayer, the disqualified one, and raises it until it meets the good prayer. Then they rise and mingle together, and come in before the holy King.

Sometimes, a prayer·is rejected because that man went after the *Sitra Achra* and was defiled. The appointee in the *Sitra Achra* takes that prayer, and then the *Sitra Achra* stands and mentions the man's iniquities before the Creator, slandering him above. For this reason, when the prayers and souls rise, they all rise and stand before that first palace, and that appointee stands by the door of the palace, letting the souls and prayers inside, or rejecting them.

Above the door of the palace is another door, which the Creator dug out of *Dinim de Miftacha*, as it is written, "The well that the ministers dug." It opens three times a day, meaning that three lines illuminate in it, and it does not close. It stands open for those who repent, who have shed tears in their prayer before their Master. And all the gates and doors are closed until they come in by permission, except for these gates, which are called "the gates of tears." Those are open and require no permission.

This is so because the first door is as it is written, "Sin crouches at the door," where the *Malchut de Man'ula* is found, ten thousand. In that respect, repentance does not help because it is the quality of harsh *Din*. But the Creator dug another door above it, the *Miftacha*, *Malchut* that is mitigated in *Bina*, and from there the repentance helps.

When this prayer in tears rises through these gates, that *Ophan*—who is an angel from *Malchut*, called *Ophan*—comes. He stands over 600 big animals, and his name is Yerachmiel. He takes the prayer in tears, the prayer enters and is connected above, and the tears remain here. They are written in a door that the Creator dug.

The prayer in tears raises MAN for correction of the *Miftacha*, to raise *Malchut* to *Bina*; hence, the prayer is accepted and the tears remain carved on the door, where they cause the mitigation of *Malchut* in *Bina*. *Dema* [tearing] comes from the word mixing, for it mixes and mingles *Malchut* in *Bina*.

576-577) **Happy are the righteous who know how to set up their prayer properly because when that prayer begins to rise, those angels rise along with that prayer and enter the firmaments and palaces up to the gate to the upper door, and a prayer enters to be crowned before the King.**

All those who pray prayers and sanctify their Master wholeheartedly, that prayer should elicit from the thought and by the will of speech and spirit. Then the name of the Creator is sanctified, and when the prayer reaches the angels, who are friends, they all take the prayer and go with it up to the seventh palace, to the door that is there.

Those angels praise the Creator when Israel pray prayers and sanctify to the Creator. At daytime, they are the appointees during the day, who were appointed to praise along with the people of Israel, to be friends with them. At night, they are friends to those other ones, who say poems at night.

647-652) **The sixth palace is called "the palace of desire," a desire called "[that which] proceeds out of the mouth of the Lord." This is a joy of *Dvekut* of everything, and here is the desire of all the desires, as it is written, "Your lips are like a thread of scarlet." It is a desire of all the souls that come out from what proceeds out of the mouth of the Lord.**

In the palace of desire, all the wishes and all the requests in the world are granted because it is the wish of all the wishes, when there are kisses, as it is written, "And Jacob kissed Rachel." Then, when they kiss one another, it is called "a time of good will," since then there is the wholeness and all the faces illuminate. When the prayers rise, it is a time of good will to be present. It is written about it, "And I, my prayer is to You, O Lord, a time of good will," which is bonding in kisses.

There are six doors in that palace, four doors to the four directions, *HG TM*, one above, and one below, *NH*. In those doors, Raziel—a great spirit—was appointed over all the appointees in all the doors. He was appointed and deposited with all the upper secrets that are spoken mouth to mouth, which kiss one another in the love of love.

These secrets are not about to reveal, but when the gates open, all the palaces, all the spirits, and all the camps know that the gates of good will have been opened. But only desires of the prayers enter those gates, desires of praises, desires of the high, holy souls.

It is a palace of Moses. In this palace, Moses was gathered in love and kissed kisses in a death of kiss. In this palace, "Moses spoke and God answered him with a voice."

When those who kiss kisses cling to one another in a kiss, it is written about it, "Let him kiss me with the kisses of his mouth." There are kisses of joy and love only when clinging to one another mouth-to-mouth, spirit-to-spirit, satiating each other with every indulgence and with joy from the upper illumination.

705-706) **From this palace, all the secrets and all the upper and lower degrees begin to unite,** so that all will be in wholeness, above and below, so that all will be one, one bonding, to properly unify the holy name, and to be completed so the upper abundance illuminates in the lower one, and the illuminations of the candles illuminate as one, not parting from one another. At that time, those who are drawn and affected are drawn—who was unknown and unrevealed, so he would draw near and unite with one another, so that all will be in the complete unification as it should be.

Happy is he who knows the secrets of his Master, to know him properly. They eat their part in this world and in the next world. It is written about it, "Behold, My servants shall eat." Happy are the righteous who engage in Torah day and night because they know the ways of the Creator, and know how to properly unite the sacred unification, for anyone who knows how to unify the holy name in wholeness, as it should be, happy is he in this world and in the next world.

706) **Happy are the righteous who engage in Torah day and night** because they know the ways of the Creator, and know how to properly unite the sacred unification, for anyone who knows how to unify the holy name in wholeness, as it

should be, happy is he in this world and in the next world.

742) **When the righteous Joseph, _Yesod_, is about to correct everything, he takes everything.** And when he connects in his palace, everyone awakens to take craving and desire, the upper ones and lower ones, and it is all in one will and one wholeness, to delight the upper ones and lower ones in one desire, as it should be, and all the lower ones persist through him. This is why it is written, "And the righteous is the _Yesod_ [foundation] of the world," since the world stands on this foundation.

747) **There are things that the body enjoys, that enter the body, but not the soul, and there are things that the soul enjoys and not the body. This is why the degrees differ from one another. Happy are the righteous who take the straight path and avoid that side, clinging to the side of _Kedusha_.**

752-760) **The seventh palace** is the innermost palace. It is hidden, there is no real form in it, and there is no _Guf_ at all here, only a _Rosh_. Here is the concealed of the secret of secrets, the place to enter the channels of above, of _Atzilut_. Here is a spirit who includes all the spirits in all the palaces. Here is a desire that includes all the desire, to unite all the palaces as one. In this palace is the spirit of life, from *Bina*, so that all will be one correction.

That palace is called "the house of the holy of holies," the place to receive the upper soul, *Bina*, who is called so to evoke in him the next world, *Bina*.

This world, *Malchut*, is called "world." "World" means ascent, where the lower world, *Malchut*, rises to the upper world, *Bina*, hides in it, disappears in it, and appears in hiding. *Malchut* ascends with all the palaces that have approached her and hides within the upper concealment, *Bina*. The upper world, *Bina*, means that *Bina* rises and hides within the upper desire, within the most covered of all that are covered, who is completely unknown, unrevealed, and there is none who knows him, who is *AA*.

The curtain, the *Parsa*—between the sixth palace, holiness, and the seventh palace, the holy of holies—was spread and covers to conceal the hidden one, the seventh palace. The ark-cover was spread in high concealments over the ark of the testimony in the holy of holies, *Yesod* of *Malchut de Atzilut*, clothed in the seventh palace, to conceal the concealed inside the ark of the covenant, for they are hidden and concealed.

Inside the ark-cover, which is the ark, there is a hidden place, concealed and covert, in which to gather the upper anointing oil, the spirit of life, through a river that stretches out of Eden, *Yesod de ZA de Atzilut*. The river is called "the fountain of the well," *Malchut*, whose waters never stop. When *Yesod* lets in and extends every holy ointment from above, from the place of the holy of holies, *Bina de Atzilut*, the illumination and extension come down into those hoses of *Yesod* of *Malchut de Atzilut*, and *Malchut de Atzilut* is filled from there, like a female is impregnated and filled by the male.

The seventh palace, too, is established to receive the lights of *Yesod de ZA de Atzilut* through *Malchut de Atzilut*, which is clothed in it, like a female who receives from the male. The reception that she receives are all those spirits and holy souls who come down to the world to clothe in people. They are detained there as long as it is necessary, until they come down and clothe in people. After their demise from this world, they return to the seventh palace.

They are detained in the seventh palace until the arrival of the Messiah king, when all those souls are satisfied and come to *Atzilut* to their places, and the world will rejoice as before, prior to the diminution of the moon and the sin of the tree of knowledge, as it is written, "The Lord will rejoice in His works."

It is so because after their demise from this world, the souls cannot rise above the seventh palace, for that is where the *Parsa* separates between *Atzilut* and *BYA*. Hence, they are detained in the seventh palace until the end of correction, when the boundary of the *Parsa* is cancelled and they can climb up to *Atzilut*, to their root, to *Bina de Atzilut*, since the light of *Bina* is called *Neshama* [soul]. This is why at that time it is written, "The Lord will rejoice in His works."

In this palace are pleasures, delights and entertainment of the spirits with which the Creator is entertained in the Garden of Eden. Here are all the lusts and all the pleasures, for all the palaces to unite in Him as one, and they will all become one. Here it is the connection of everything in one unification.

When all the organs, all the *Behinot* in the palaces, unite in the upper organs of the seventh palace, each according to what he deserves, they have neither passion nor delight other than the unification in that palace. It all hangs here. When the bonding here unites in a single unification, then all the illuminations in the organs, all the illumination of the *Panim*, and all the joys illuminate and rejoice.

Happy is he who knows how to set up orders and to properly correct the corrections of the wholeness. He is the Creator's loved one in this world and in the next world, and then all the *Dinim* and all the bad decrees are revoked from the world.

764) The fountain of the well, *Yesod*, never ceases from the well, which is *Malchut de Atzilut* clothed in the seventh palace. Hence, that place is the perfection of everything, the persistence of the whole body to be complete in everything, as it should be. Here, in the seventh palace, is the unification and the connection as one, to be one above and below, in one connection, so the organs, *Behinot*, and the degrees in the palaces do not depart from each other, and so all will be in a *Zivug PBP* [*Panim be Panim* (face-to-face)].

771) **When they are all completed together,** when all the palaces are included in the seventh palace, and the upper organs, ZON *de Atzilut*,

illuminate to the lower ones, the palaces, a high soul awakens—*Bina de Atzilut*—enters everyone and illuminates to all. Then everyone is blessed: the upper ones, *ZON de Atzilut*; the lower ones, all the palaces, and what is within them. The one who is not known and which did not enter the calculation of the desire, who is never perceived, *Atik*, dresses inside of them, and then everything rises through *Ein Sof* and all connects in one connection.

786-787) **It is written, "And they had the hands of a man under their wings."** Spirits, animals, and *Ophanim* are all winged. The hands under their wings are to receive prayers and receive those who repent. "The hands of a man" means places and receptacles to accept people in their prayers and litanies, and to open doors to receive them, to unite and to tie ties, and to do as they wish.

These places and receptacles are called "The hands of a man" because they are for man. These are holy names that rule over each degree, in which people come in with their prayers and litanies through all the high gates. By that, the lower ones rule above.

788) **Happy are those who know how to set up the unification of their Master properly**

and to go by the path of truth, so they will not err in faith.

812-813) This is why he must connect to the *Kedusha* of his Master and not part from Him. And when he asks, the beginning of the pleading should be to know his Master, to show his passion for Him, which is the first request, "Grant us from You wisdom, understanding, and intelligence." Henceforth, he will part a little and ask the pleas that he needs to ask.

All his questions will be after he arranges the order. Likewise, all his questions will be in litanies and requests before his Master, and He will not remove Himself from him, meaning be angered. Happy is he who knows how to arrange that order, to go by the straight path as he should.

832) **Anyone who does not know how to establish the praise of his Master, it is better for him not to be born** because the prayer must be complete above, out of thought, the will of the heart, the voice, and the word of the mouth, to make wholeness, connection, and unification above. As it is above, and as the wholeness comes out from above downward, so it should be from below upward, properly tying the connection.

833-835) **The secret is for the friends to walk on the straight path.** Thought, will, voice, and speech are four that tie the ties, opposite HG TM. Thought and will are HB, voice and speech are TM. Once they all tie ties together, they all become one *Merkava*, to instill Divinity upon them—the speech—and then all become four pillars to crown in them, and Divinity relies on them in all those high connections.

The thought, which is *Hochma*, elicits and begets the will, *Bina*. The will that comes out of the thought begets and elicits the audible voice, ZA, and the audible voice ascends to tie ties from below upward, the lower palaces in the upper ones. The voice—which ties connections between the two lines in *Bina*, and extends blessings from above downward, from *Bina*, in secret—relies on those four pillars—thought, will, voice, and speech, HB TM. The reliance is at the *Sium* [end] of the tie, in the speech, *Malchut*, the place where everything is tied together and they all become one, since *Malchut* receives everyone into her.

Happy is he who ties the ties of his Master, authorizes supports properly, and intends in all those matters. He is happy in this world and in the next world. Thus far the palaces on the side of *Kedusha* have been perfected.

VaYikra

[Leviticus]

VaYikra [The Lord Called]

10) **The Zohar explains the matter of, "He called unto Moses."** Certainly, this calling has no resemblance to a corporeal call, but as it is written, "The Torah speaks as the language of people." Hence, we should understand the inner meaning of this calling.

18) **Since man's merit is not told in his presence.** This means that the Creator does not reveal the merit of a degree to the one who attains it until that degree has gone and he has been rewarded with a new degree. Then He reveals before him the praise and wholeness of the first. Thus, the Creator does not reveal the praise of the degree to its face, while it still exists.

70) **The thought of the Creator, which is the *Sefira Hochma,* is superior and the *Rosh* [head] of everything.** This is so because *Partzuf* ZA begins from *Hochma* and its *Keter* is from *Ima.* From that thought, ways and paths extend to devise the Holy Name and to correct in its proper corrections. The potion of the Garden of Eden extends from that thought to water everything, and the upper and lower exist from that thought.

Also, the written Torah, ZA, and the oral Torah, *Malchut*, were emanated from that thought.

88) **There is nothing in the Torah that is weak or broken. When you observe and know it, you will find it as strong as a hammer that breaks the rock. And if it is weak, it is from you, as it is written, "For it is no vain thing for you," and if it is empty, it is from you.**

99) **"How good and how pleasant it is for brothers to dwell together, as well."** Happy are Israel, for the Creator did not hand them over to a minister or to a messenger. Rather, Israel grip to Him and He to them. For their love, the Creator calls them, "servants," as it is written, "For unto Me the children of Israel are servants; they are My servants." Afterwards He calls them "sons," as it is written, "You are the children of the Lord your God." After that He calls them "brothers," as it is written, "My brothers and my friends." And because He called them "brothers," He wished to place His Divinity in them and He will not stray from them. Then it is written, "How good and how pleasant it is for brothers to dwell together, as well."

109) **"Serve the Lord with gladness."** Any work that a person wishes to do for the Creator should

be done with gladness, willingly, so that his work will be whole.

200-201) **"Bless the Lord, all you servants of the Lord." This is a praise for all those with faith.** Who are those with faith? They are the ones who engage in Torah and know how to unite the Holy Name properly. And the praise of those with faith is that they stand at midnight to engage in Torah and adhere to the Assembly of Israel, *Malchut*, to praise the Creator with words of Torah.

When one rises at midnight to engage in Torah, a Northern wind—meaning illumination of the left—awakens at midnight, which is the deer and *Malchut*, and stands and praises the Creator, ZA. And when she stands, several thousands and several tens of thousands stand with her in their existence, and they all begin to praise the holy King.

246) **When the Creator watches over the world and sees that the acts of people below are upright,** *Atik*, which is *Keter*, appears in ZA, *Tifferet*, and all those *Panim* of ZA look at the hidden *Panim* of *Atik*. Then, all are blessed because they look at each other in an upright way, in the middle line, which leans neither to the right nor to the left. It is written about that,

"The upright shall behold His face," meaning that the faces of *Atik* and ZA look at each other in an upright way, in the middle line. And then they are all blessed and water each other until all the worlds are blessed and all the worlds are as one. At that time, it is considered that "The Lord is one and His name One."

249-250) **And when the people of the world improve their actions below**, the *Dinim* are perfumed and impregnated, and the *Rachamim* awaken and rule over that evil that has awakened from the harsh *Din*. And when the *Rachamim* awaken, there are joy and comfort because they rule over that evil, as it is written, "And the Lord repented of the evil." He repented because the harsh *Din* has surrendered and the *Rachamim* ruled.

When the *Dinim* are perfumed and *Rachamim* rule, each *Sefira* returns to existence and all are blessed together. When each returns to its place, all are blessed together, and *Ima* is perfumed with bonding the engravings that returned to her, then repentance is considered whole and the world is atoned for, since *Ima* sits in complete joy, as it is written, "As a joyful mother of children."

288) **As long as the Assembly of Israel is with the Creator, the Creator is in wholeness and willingly**

pastures Himself and to others. To Himself means that He nurtures Himself by sucking the milk of upper *Ima*. He receives the abundance of *Bina* and from that nursing that He sucks, He waters all the others and nurtures them.

When the Assembly of Israel is with the Creator, the Creator is in wholeness and joy, and there are blessings in Him, which come out from Him to all the others, to all the worlds. And any time when the Assembly of Israel is not with the Creator, the blessings are devoid of Him and of all the others.

311-312) **The prayer and the voice of the *Shofar* that the righteous produces in the *Shofar* comes out of his spirit and soul [*Nefesh* and *Ruach* respectively] and rise upwards.** On that day, there are slanderers above, and when that voice of the *Shofar* rises, they are repelled by it and cannot exist. Happy are the righteous, for they know how to aim their will before their Master and know how to correct the world on that day with the voice of the *Shofar*. This is why it is written, "Happy is the people that knows the joyful shout," "Knows," and not "Blows."

On that day, the people should see that a man is complete in everything—knowing the ways of the holy King and knowing the King's honor, to pray the prayer for them on that day and summon the voice of the *Shofar* in all the worlds through the intention in the heart, with wisdom, will, and wholeness. Thus, through him, the *Din* would depart from the world. Woe unto those whose emissary is unworthy, since they will come to remind the iniquities of the world because of him. This is the meaning of, "If the anointed priest should sin" who is the emissary of the whole of Israel, hence the fault of the people, since the *Din* is over the people.

315) **How much should one regard the glory of one's Master to be a whole creation before the Creator? When the Creator created man, He created him whole, as it is written, "That God made the man upright."**

324) **Happy are the righteous, for the Creator teaches them profound secrets of above and below,** and it is all for the Torah, since anyone who engages in the Torah is crowned in the crowns of His Holy Name. This is so because the Torah is the Holy Name and one who engages in it is registered and crowned in the Holy Name, and then he knows the hidden ways and the deep secrets above and below, and he never fears.

342) **One who makes a request of the King** must unite the holy Name in his will from below upwards, from *Malchut* to *Keter*, and from above downwards, from *Keter* to *Malchut*—uniting everything in one unification in *Ein Sof* [infinity], and in this unification he will include his plea. Who is so wise as to make his pleas like King David's, who was keeping the King's door? He was a *Merkava* [chariot/assembly] to *Malchut*, which is called "the King's door." So it is, and this is why the Torah teaches us the ways of the holy King, so we will know how to follow Him, as it is written, "After the Lord your God shall you walk."

373-374) **The Assembly of Israel does not stand before the King, ZA, unless in the Torah.** As long as Israel that are in the land engage in Torah, the Assembly of Israel is with them. When they are idle from words of Torah, the Assembly of Israel cannot be with them for even an hour. For this reason, when the Assembly of Israel awakens to the King in the Torah of the lower ones, her strength grows and the holy King is delighted to greet her.

And as long as the Assembly of Israel comes before the King and the Torah is not with her,

her strength withers. Woe unto those who weaken the force of above. And for this reason, happy are those who engage in Torah.

379-380) **"When the morning stars sang together, and all the sons of God shouted for joy."** When the Creator comes to entertain with the righteous in the Garden of Eden, all things, meaning degrees in the lower world, *Malchut*, and all the upper ones and lower ones awaken toward Him. And all the trees, meaning degrees, in the Garden of Eden begin to praise before Him, as it is written, "Then shall all the trees of the wood sing for joy before the Lord, for He has come." And even the birds in the land all utter praise before Him.

At that time, a flame comes out and strikes the wings of the rooster, who calls and praises the holy King. He calls upon people to exert in Torah, in praising their Master, and in His work. Happy are those who rise from their bed to engage in Torah.

When the morning comes, the doors on the south, meaning *Hesed*, open and the gates of healing come out to the world. And Eastern wind, *ZA*, awakens and *Rachamim* are present. And all those stars and signs, meaning degrees, which are appointed under the governance of that morning, which is *Yesod* that shines *Hassadim*, they all begin to praise and to sing for the High King.

387) **After Moses died, it is written, "And this people will rise up, and go astray."** Woe unto the world when Rabbi Shimon departs it, when the fountains of wisdom are blocked in the world and a man seeks a word of wisdom, but none shall be found to speak. And the whole world will be erring in the Torah and there will be no one to evoke in the wisdom.

It is written about that time, "And if the whole congregation of Israel shall err," meaning if they err in the Torah and do not know her ways and what they are because "and the matter is hidden from the eyes of the assembly," meaning that there is none who knows how to reveal the depth of the Torah and her ways, woe unto those generations that will be in the world at that time.

388) **At the time of the Messiah, the Creator will reveal profound secrets in the Torah, "For the earth shall be full of the knowledge of the Lord, as the waters cover the sea."** It is written, "And they shall teach no more every man his neighbor, and every man his brother, saying, 'Know the

Lord'; for they shall all know Me, from the least of them unto the greatest of them."

397-399) **When the rooster calls and people sleep in their beds and do not awaken,** the rooster calls, strikes his wings and says, "Woe unto so and so; he is cursed by his Master, he is abandoned by his Master," since his spirit has not awakened and he did not observe the King's honor.

At the rise of day, a herald declares about him and says, "But no one says, 'Where is God my Maker, who gives songs in the night,'" to help him with those praises so that all will be in one assistance. The *Malchut* sings to ZA at night, to help man so he, too, will awaken with these praises. And when one praises and engages in Torah, she raises MAN, he helps the *Malchut*, and they are both in one assistance.

What is "My Maker"? When a person rises at midnight, he engages in the song of the Torah, since the song of the Torah is read only at night, when he engages in the Torah. When the day rises, the Creator and the Assembly of Israel correct him with a single thread of grace that was saved from all, to illuminate him among the upper ones and lower ones.

"Where is God my Maker." It should have said, "Makes for me"; why "My Maker"? When he rises at midnight to engage in Torah, when the day rises, Abraham awakens with his thread of grace and the Creator and the Assembly of Israel correct him. They make him a new creation every day, as it is written, "God, my Maker."

433-436) **When he has acquired Ruach,** that Ruach comes out and breaks mountains and rocks, which are the external forces, and rises and spreads, and enters among the high and holy angels. This is because the Ruach extends from the world of Yetzira, where the angels are. There, he knows what he knows and learns things from them and returns to his place. At that time, this is man's connection to holiness until he is rewarded with Neshama and acquires it.

When he acquires a Neshama, she rises to the world of Beria, from which the Neshama extends, and the guards at the gates do not detain her. She spreads and rises further up among those righteous who are bundled in the bundle of life, Malchut, where she sees the pleasure of the King and enjoys the upper brightness.

When the holy doe [deer] awakens, meaning Malchut, in the Northern wind at midnight, she comes down and that righteous who has acquired a *Neshama* rises and gains strength in the Torah like a mighty lion, until the morning rises. Then he walks with that holy doe to be seen before the King and to receive from him a single thread of grace, the thread of Abraham, the light of *Hesed*.

And when that righteous comes with the doe, *Malchut*, he is crowned with her before the king.

448-449) **"My heart is for the governors of Israel that offered themselves willingly among the people, bless the Lord."** All the willingness and all the heart that a man needs to extend blessings from above downwards to unite the Holy Name, he needs to extend in a prayer to the Creator, willingly and with the intention of the heart, from a deep stream, *Bina*. It is written about it, "Out of the depths have I called You, O Lord," where it is the depth of all in the high valleys, which are the high beginning, where AVI, *Hochma* and *Bina*, mate. Here, too, "My heart is for the governors of Israel" refers to AVI, who are the governors that give *Mochin* to the holy Israel, ZA, who extends from between them.

"That offered themselves willingly among the people" are the patriarchs, HGT *de* ZA, who are called "princes," as it is written, "The princes of the peoples are gathered together, the people of the God of Abraham," meaning the patriarchs that extend from Abraham, *Hesed de* ZA. Then, "Bless the Lord," extend blessings from Him downwards and there will be blessings in the whole world.

This is so because when there are blessings from above in this world below, everything is in gladness, all is in perfection, since no light is complete unless when it is extended down to this world. Happy are Israel for the Creator imparts upon them blessings and listens to their prayer. It is written about them, "When He has regarded the prayer of the destitute, and has not despised their prayer."

TZAV [COMMAND]

60) **An uneducated one is called "a beast."** And once he places himself under the discernment of "a man" in the Torah, the words "O Lord, You preserve man and beast" will come true in him. If he is as a horse, whose master is riding him, and the horse tolerates him and does not kick his master, so he should be—as a horse under the wise disciple.

67) **And like all the *Kelim* [vessels] of the Temple, which are called "holy,"** all those who serve the wise disciples are called "holy." And the disciples of the rav, which correspond to the organs of the body of the rav, are called "the holy of holies."

71) **A wise disciple should see himself equal to all the students of Torah.** This is how he should consider himself from the perspective of the Torah, from the perspective of the noetic NRN. But from the perspective of the organs of the body, the perspective of the beastly NRN, he should regard himself equal to all the uneducated people, as it is written, "One should always see himself as though the whole world depends on him." For this reason,

he should aim his mind, spirit, and soul to make those sacrifices with all the people in the world, and the Creator adds a good thought to the act. By that, "Man and beast You deliver, O Lord."

89) **"The Lord is righteous in all His ways and kind in all His deeds."** People should regard the glory of their Master and they will not stray from their ways outwards.

129-130) **In the altar, Uriel rises and appears as a mighty lion lying over its prey.** And priests and Israel saw and were delighted, for they knew that their offering was welcomed by the holy King. And another fire, high and holy, descended from above. It is Angel Uriel, opposite the bottom fire that they placed on the altar. At that time, one would be startled before one's master and return in complete repentance.

It is similar to a king whose people sent him a gift which he welcomed. He said to his servant, "Go and take that gift that they brought me." This is what the Creator said to angel Uriel, "Go and receive the gift that My sons have sacrificed before Me." What joy was there in everything, and what sweetness was in all when the priest and the Levite and the one who made the offering would aim to make the offering as it should be, in complete unification.

144) **For this reason, sages said, "Repent one day prior to your death,"** since each day, one must repent and give one's spirit to Him, so he will depart in one, as it is written, "Into Your hand I commit my spirit."

151) **This holy flesh, *Malchut*, burns in several flames from the side of *Gevura* with the love of her husband, ZA.** She is burning in love, the love of the reading of *Shema* [Hear], the love of unification. She will not quench day or night; and friends, please give him—the Creator—no rest until he is in the flame of love of His unification at the reading of *Shema*, to keep in it the words, "A continual fire would burn on the altar and would not quench."

151) **And once the righteous has taken upon himself not to nurse the beastly *Guf* and NRN, and they are regarded as "a poor man is regarded as dead," then he is rewarded with the permanent instilling of Divinity, where Divinity burns the evil in the Noga in them until they are fit for the end of correction.**

165) **"For with You is the source of life; in Your light we shall see light."** "For with You is the source of life" is the upper oil that is drawn and never stops, which is present within the uppermost *Hochma*. It is written, "For with You," meaning that it is with You in love that is above all, and never parts from you. "The source of life" is *Bina*, since *HB* are attached together in a never ending *Zivug*. *Bina* is called "the source of life" because she is the source and the fountain of life, which is imparting of the *Hochma*, life, to elicit life from the *Hochma* for the upper tree, *ZA*, and to light the candles of *Malchut*. This is why the tree, *ZA*, is called "the tree of life," a tree that is planted and rooted in the source of life, *Bina*.

182) Anyone who engages in Torah, whose lips speak Torah, the Creator covers him and Divinity spreads her wings over him, as it is written, "I have put My words in your mouth and have covered you with the shadow of My hand." Moreover, he sustains the world and the Creator delights with him as though on that day, He was planting the heaven and earth.

184) **"Bind up the testimony, seal the law [Torah] among my disciples."** Bind up the testimony is the testimony of David, *Malchut*,

as it is written, "And My testimony which I will teach them." "Bind up" means bonding, as one who binds a knot in one place. "Bind up the testimony" means the bound *Malchut*. "Seal the law [Torah]," which is ZA, meaning that all the abundance and *Gadlut* extended from above, its sealing, the completion, is in "My disciples," who are *NH*, and are called "the disciples of the Creator."

This is so because there the *Gadlut* and the oil gather between two pillars, *NH*, to be there. They are the place of all the *Gadlut* and the oil that pours from above, from *Tifferet*, who is called Torah, to pour it into the *Peh* of *Yesod*, and to pour it in this testimony, *Malchut*. Then, everything binds into one strong bond, and will be as it is written, "Bind up the testimony," tying the *Malchut* by sealing the law "Among my disciples," where the abundance of Torah is sealed, ended in *NH*, and from them to *Yesod*. Then, *Malchut* is tied to *Yesod*, to receive the abundance, and everything becomes one knot.

186) Happy are those who engage in Torah, for they are at a higher degree than everyone. One who engages in Torah needs neither sacrifices nor burnt offerings, since the Torah is better

than anything; it is the bond of the faith of everything, the bond of *Malchut*. This is why it is written, "Her ways are ways of pleasantness, and all her paths are peace."

190) **Two candles, one above and one below.** If one lights that candle below and puts out that candle above, that smoke, which rises from the candle below, lights that candle above. Thus, the smoke of the offering that rises from the offering causes the extension of illumination of *Hochma* above and lights up the upper candles, ZA and *Malchut*, and they light up together. Thus, all the *Sefirot* grow close together by this scent. This is why it is written, "A sweet savor unto the Lord."

New Zohar, Tzav [Command]

1-6) On the left side stands a degree from the side of *Tuma'a* [impurity] called "evil thought," since the degree over it is evil. Here are all the evil desires and thoughts in the world. The evil thought stands over all those desires by which a man is defiled.

There are several impure degrees in this evil thought, and all are poised to defile the man with those desires and thoughts of the evil thought. Then the man is defiled in them and clings to that side. For that, we should offer a burnt-offering to be purified. When he offers it, he should lean his will toward the holy thought, and when smoke rises from those fats and entrails, it first rises to that evil thought, who takes them all and feeds on them so she does not approach the holy.

Afterwards another fine smoke rises and all the upper ones—the *Partzufim* of *Kedusha* in BYA, among which are the litigants—gather and enter deep inside until they gather one inside the other until they all rise, and all mingle with one another complementing one another, and body connects to body.

Then that man crowns his will with the will of the pure thought, the priest from the right side and the Levite from the left side tie organs to organs until that pure thought rises between right and left, and they connect to one another, connecting with each other and becoming one. Then it is called "sweet savor," meaning contentment and a desire to bond and enter one into the other.

When all are connected to one another, the next world, *Bina*, emits great light to illuminate everyone together. Great joy is present, all the faces shine, and everything is in sweetness. Then the man parts from the evil thought and clings to the pure thought until everything clings to the hidden, highest thought of all, and all will be one.

ON THE EIGHTH DAY

1) Happy are Israel for the Creator gave them the holy Torah, which is the joy of everything, the joy of the Creator and the place where He roams, as it is written, "and I was daily all delight," and the whole Torah is one holy name of the Creator. And the world was created in the Torah, as it is written, "Then I was beside Him as trusted [Amun]." Dot not read it as Amun, but as Uman [a master craftsman], as she was His tool for creating the world.

8) **All those who engage in Torah** cling to the Creator and are crowned in the decorations of Torah. They are loved above and below, and the Creator offers them His right hand, mercy. It is even more so with those who engage in Torah at night, as well, for they have established that they partake in Divinity and join together. And when the morning comes, the Creator decorates them with a single string of grace, so they will be among the higher and among the lower.

42) **"Remember, O Lord, Thy compassions and Thy mercies, for they are from the world."** "Remember... Thy compassions" is Jacob, and

"Thy mercies" is Abraham. "...they are from the world" means that the Creator took them from the world and raised them, and made them into a holy chariot to protect the world. And because they are from the world, He remembers them, to protect the world and to have mercy on it. Similarly, the Creator takes righteous from the world and raises them, to protect the world.

117) **The Creator is destined to purify Israel.** With what will He purify them? With what is written, "And I will sprinkle clean water upon you, and you shall be pure." These are the waters of mercy, which clothe and include the illumination of the left, from which the purity comes. And since they are purified, they are sanctified, for they cling to the sanctity of ZA, which has the *Mochin* of AVI, called, "holiness." And Israel, who cling to the Creator, are called, "holiness," as it is written... "And you shall be holy men unto Me."

KI TAZRIA [WHEN A WOMAN DELIVERS]

1-3) "On my bed night after night I sought him whom my soul loves."

"On my bed night after night," said the Assembly of Israel, Divinity. "On my bed I was angered before Him, asking Him to mate with me to delight me—from the left line—and to bless me—from the right line—with complete joy—from the middle line." When the king, ZA, mates with the Assembly of Israel, several righteous inherit inheritance of a holy legacy, upper *Mochin*, and several blessings are found in the world.

101) "And I saw that wisdom excels over folly." The benefit for the wisdom comes from the very folly, for if there had not been folly in the world, wisdom and its words would not have been known. And we learned that it is mandatory for a man who learned wisdom to learn a little bit of the folly and to know it, for it is for that that wisdom has come, just as there is benefit to light from darkness, for without darkness, light would not have been known and no benefit would come from it.

105) **"As light excels over darkness." The benefit of the light comes only out of the darkness.** The correction of the white is black, for without the black, the white would be pointless. And because there is black, the white is elevated and respected. It is like sweet and bitter. A person cannot know the taste of sweetness before he has tasted bitterness. Thus, what makes it sweet is the bitter.

In things where there are opposites, the one reveals the other, such as in white and black, light and darkness, sick and healthy. If there were no sickness in the world, the term healthy would be unattainable, as it is written, "God has made the one opposite the other." And it is also written, "It is good that you grasp the one, and also not let go of the other."

139) **Hence, the coupling of people is at set times, to aim their desire to adhere to the Creator.** And they already commented that at midnight, the Creator enters the Garden of Eden to entertain with the righteous, and the Assembly of Israel, *Malchut*, praises the Creator. This is a good time to cling to them, to the Creator and His Divinity.

145) **Happy are Israel who adhere to the Creator, and whom the Creator loves, as it is written, "I have loved you, says the Lord."** And for His love, He brought them into the holy land, to instill His Divinity among them and to dwell with them, so Israel will be holier than all the people in the world.

Metzorah [The Leper]

1-3) People should guard their way and fear the Creator so they do not stray from the straight path or breach the words of Torah or move away from it.

Any one who does not engage in Torah and does not exert in it is reproached by the Creator. He is far from Him, Divinity is not over him, and those guardian angels that walk with him to guard him, depart him. Moreover, they declare before him and say, "Do not be around so and so for he does not care for the glory of his Master." Woe unto him, for the upper ones and lower ones have left him, and he has no part in the path of life.

And when he exerts in the work of his Master and engages in Torah, several guards are ready to guard him, and Divinity is over him, and they all declare before him and say, "Give honors to the form of the King, Give honors to the king's son," and he is kept in this world and in the next. Happy is he.

5) People do not know, do not hear, and do not observe their Master's will. The herald calls

before them daily, and there is no one to listen and no one to awaken one's spirit to the work of his Master.

6-8) **When the night grows dark and the gates close,** the *Nukva* of the great abyss awakens, and several armies of damagers are in the world. At that time, the Creator puts all the people in the world to sleep. He puts to sleep even all those who have awakening of life, meaning the righteous. And the spirits roam the world and announce things to people in their dreams. Some of them are lies and some of them are true. And people become connected in their sleep.

And when the north wind awakens and the night divides, a flame bursts out and strikes under the wings of the rooster, and he calls. Then the Creator enters the Garden of Eden to play with the righteous, and an announcer comes out and calls, and all the people in the world awaken in their beds. And those with awakening of life rise up from their beds to the work of their Master, and engage in Torah and in praising the Creator until the morning comes.

When the morning comes, all the armies and camps above praise the Creator. Then, several gates open to all sides, and Abraham's gate, *Hesed* [mercy], opens in the Assembly of Israel, to summon all the people in the world to enjoy the *Hassadim* [mercies]. It is written, "And Abraham planted a tamarisk tree in Beersheba," since *Malchut* is called Beersheba, and Abraham planted the tree of *Hesed* in it.

20) **"She is a tree of life to those who take hold of her, and happy are all who support her."** The tree of life is the Torah, a high and mighty tree. She is called Torah because it instructs and reveals what was hidden and unknown. She is called "life" because all the upper life is included in her and stem from her.

"To those who take hold of her," meaning those who are gripped to her, for one who is gripped unto the Torah is gripped unto everything—gripped above and below.

AHAREI MOT [AFTER THE DEATH]

30-31) Rabbi Shimon said, "I am surprised at the people of the world, who have no eyes to see or a heart to notice, and who do not know nor pay attention to looking into their Master's will. How are they asleep and not rising from their sleep before that day comes when darkness and murkiness cover them, and the creditor collects their debt.

"The herald calls on them each day and their soul testifies to them each day and night, and the Torah raises voices to all sides, saying, 'Until when will fools love foolishness?' 'Whoever is a fool, let him come here. 'Heartless,' she said to him, 'Come, eat of my bread and drink of the wine that I have mixed," but there is no one to lend an ear or awaken his heart."

32) In the last generations that will come, the Torah will be forgotten from them and the heartless will gather to their place, and there will be no one to close or open in the Torah. Woe unto that generation. Henceforth, there will not be such as that generation until the generation when the Messiah comes and knowledge awakens

in the world, as it is written, "For they shall all know Me, from the least of them to the greatest of them."

38-40) There are times for finding favor in the Creator, for finding blessings, and for making pleas. And there are times when there is no favor, blessings do not come, and harsh *Dinim* awaken in the world. Sometimes the *Din* persists. There are times in the year when the favor is present, and times in the year when the *Din* is present. There are times in the year when the *Din* is present and persists and threatens the world but does not operate. There are times in the month when there is favor, and times when there are *Dinim*, which persist over everything.

There are times in the week when there is favor, and there are times in the week when there are *Dinim* in the world. There are times in days when the favor is present in the world and the world is perfumed, and there are days when *Dinim* persist and exist. There are different times even in an hour. This is why it is written, "And a time for will."

65-66) "How good and how pleasant it is for brothers to dwell together in unity, as well." These are the friends, as they sit together inseparably. At first, they seem like people at war, wishing to kill each other. Then they return to a state of brotherly love.

The Creator, what does He say about them? "How good and how pleasant it is for brothers to dwell together in unity, as well." The words, "as well" indicate the presence of Divinity with them. Moreover, the Creator listens to their words and He is pleased and content with them.

And you, the friends who are here, as you were in fondness and love before, you will not part henceforth, until the Creator rejoices with you and summons peace upon you. And by your merit there will be peace in the world. This is the meaning of the words, "For the sake of my brothers and my friends let me say, 'Let peace be in you.'"

92) "My dove, in the clefts of the rock," in the concealment of the degree.

My dove is the Assembly of Israel, *Malchut*. As a dove never leaves her mate, the Assembly of Israel never leaves the Creator. "In the clefts of the rock" are disciples of the wise, who are not at rest in this world. As they hide themselves from their enemies in the clefts of the rocks, in the concealment of the degree, the humble disciples of the wise, who hide their degree from people, among whom are pious, who fear the Creator, from whom Divinity never parts. Then the Creator demanded of the Assembly of Israel for them and said, "Let me see your looks; let me hear your voice, for your voice is sweet," since no sound is heard above but the sound of those engaging in Torah.

94) "That which is has been already, and that which will be has already been."

"That which is has been already." Before the Creator created this world, He was creating worlds and destroying them, which is the breaking of the vessels, until the Creator desired to create this world and consulted with the Torah, who is the middle line. Then He corrected in His corrections, crowned in His crowns, and created this world. All that was in this world was at that time in front of Him, at the time of creation, and was corrected before Him.

95) Before the leaders of the world in each generation came to the world, they all were before the Creator in their forms. Even all those souls of people, until they come to the world, they are all engraved before Him in the firmament in their very form of this world, and all that they

learn in this world, they know everything before they come to the world.

96) At the time of the creation of the souls, while they were still above, before they came to this world under time, they were in eternity, above time, when present and future act at once, as is the nature of eternity.

It follows that all the deeds that the souls will do one at a time when they come into this world are already there at once, as their actions in this world, since all the Torah that they will learn in this world during the days of their lives is already there entirely, and all their evil works are already depicted in their souls. And as they will cast the part of *Kedusha* in this world, likewise there. If they are destined to sin in this world and repent one at a time, it is depicted above at once, as is the nature of eternity, that this, too, is already depicted there.

99) All true righteous, before they come into this world, they are all corrected above and are called by names. Since the day the Creator created the world, Rabbi Shimon was ready before the Creator and was with Him, and the Creator called him by his name. Happy is he above and below. It is written about him, "Let your

father and your mother be glad," "Your father" being the Creator and "Your mother" being the Assembly of Israel.

115) Happy are Israel more than all the idol-worshipping nations for the Creator wishes to purify them and have mercy on them, for they are His lot and inheritance, as it is written, "For the portion of the Lord is His people." They unite above, in ZA, hence the love of the Creator clings to them, as it is written, "I have loved you, says the Lord."

144) Anyone who has been rewarded with the Torah and satiates his soul with it, the Creator declares several benefits for him, to benefit him in this world and in the next world, as it is written, "And a good rumor." From which place is it good? "From a faraway land," for initially, the Creator was far from him, for he was hateful of him at first, from that place he is greeted, as it is written, "From afar the Lord appeared unto me."

155-156) When half the night is through, all those who engage in Torah unite with Divinity. When the morning comes and the queen, Divinity, bonds with the king, ZA, they are with the king and the king spreads his wings over all of them, as it is written, "By day the Lord will command grace [Hesed], and at night, His song is with me."

When the morning rises, the patriarchs, HGT de ZA, come with the queen and rush to speak with her and bond with her. And in them the Creator, ZA, speaks with her and calls her to spread His wings over her.

174-175) "God, God the Lord has spoken and called the earth." "God, God the Lord" are HGT, the wholeness of everything. "Spoken" means bestowal. "Earth" is Malchut, to be in the Assembly of Israel in wholeness, in joy, from Yesod de Malchut, called Zion.

When the Creator wished to create the lower world, He made it as perfect as above. He made Jerusalem the middle of the whole earth, and a place on it, called Zion, Yesod, a place from which it is blessed. From that place of Zion, the world began to be built, and from it, it was built. "Out of Zion, the perfection of beauty, God appeared." That is, "Out of Zion," who is "The perfection of beauty," of the world, "God appeared." Jerusalem, Malchut, was blessed only from Zion, Yesod, and Zion was blessed from above, ZA. Everything connects one in one, ZA and Malchut, one in one, unite through Zion.

206-208) "As the deer yearns for the water brooks, my soul yearns for You, O God."

Happy are Israel more than all the nations because the Creator has given them the holy Torah and has inherited them holy souls from a holy place to do His commandments and to delight in the Torah. Anyone who delights in the Torah is afraid of nothing, as it is written, "Were Your law [Torah] not my delight, I would be lost in my affliction."

"My delight" is the Torah, for the Torah is called "delights," as it is written, "And I will be delighted day by day." We learned that the Creator comes to delight in the Garden of Eden, to delight so He would rejoice in them. Happy are the righteous, of whom it is written, "Then shall you delight in the Lord," to be delighted with that potion of the stream, which is Bina. It seems that the Creator delights in them from that potion of the stream in which the righteous delight. This is why He comes to be delighted with the righteous, and anyone who engages in Torah is rewarded with being delighted with the righteous from that potion of the stream that is Bina.

"As the deer yearns by the water brooks." This is the Assembly of Israel, *Malchut*. "Yearns by the water brooks" means to be given the potion of the spring of the stream, *Bina*, by the righteous, *Yesod*, will yearn. "So my soul yearns for You, O God," to be watered by You in this world and in the next world.

216) A person needs to worship the Creator in wholeness, "And you shall love the Lord your God." He should love the Creator truly with his soul. This is complete love, love of his soul and spirit. As they, the soul and the spirit, clung in a body, and the body loves them, so should man love the Creator and cleave to Him, as the love of his soul and spirit, as it is written, "My soul, I have desired you at night," truly my soul, clothed in a body.

217-218) "With my spirit within me have I sought You," that I may cling to You with great love in the night. A man should rise each night out of love of the Creator to engage in His work until the morning rises and draws upon him a thread of grace [*Hesed*]. Happy is a man who loves the Creator with this love. Those true righteous who love the Creator so, the world exists because of them and they govern all the harsh decrees above and below.

That righteous one who clings above to the holy king with his spirit and soul—with love as it should be—rules the earth below, and everything he sentences for the world comes true.

244-245) Before the Creator created the world, He created repentance.

The Creator said to repentance, *Bina*, "I wish to create man in the world provided that if they return to you from their iniquities you will be willing to pardon their iniquities and atone them." Each and every hour, repentance is ready for people. When people repent from their iniquities, this repentance, *Bina*, returns to the Creator giving *Mochin* to ZA and atones for everything. Then the *Dinim* surrender and all are perfumed, and the man is purified from his iniquities.

When is one purified from his iniquity? When he properly enters repentance. When he repents before the upper king and prays a prayer from the bottom of the heart, as it is written, "From the depths I have called You, O Lord."

245) Happy are the righteous in this world and in the next world, for they are all holy. Their *Guf* [body] is holy, their *Nefesh* [soul] is holy, their

Ruach [spirit] is holy, and their *Neshama* [soul] is holy of holies.

368) Woe unto people for they are all obtuse and blind, and do not know nor hear or notice how they are in the world. But there is counsel and healing before them, yet they do not look because people can be saved only by the counsel of the Torah.

391) Happy are the righteous in this world and in the next world, for the Creator desires their glory and discloses to them high secrets of His holy Name, which He did not disclose to the high and holy angels.

412) It is written, "One thing I have asked of the Lord, that shall I seek: That I may dwell in the house of the Lord all the days of my life, to behold the pleasantness of the Lord."

Happy are the righteous, for whom several high treasures are hidden in that world, *Bina*, for the Creator plays with them in those worlds, for which He asked to behold the pleasantness of the Lord, the illumination of *Atik* extended in *Bina*. "But in a flood of great waters they will not reach him," indicating lights of *Atik*, who is unattainable. However, there are righteous who are rewarded with that, as well. This means that there are righteous who are rewarded with the light of *Atik*, as it is written, "Neither has the eye seen a God besides You, will do for he who waits for Him." "Will do" implies *Atik* because life extends from luck, from *Dikna de Atik*. Thus, they can receive and draw abundance from *Atik*, too.

New Zohar, Aharei Mot [After the Death]

51-54) "My beloved went down to his garden, to the beds of perfume, to pasture in the gardens and to gather lilies."

All the songs are holy, and the Song of Songs is the holy of holies. The Assembly of Israel, *Malchut*, praises the Creator and says to Him: "My beloved," as it is written, "My beloved is white and ruddy."

When it is midnight, a flame awakens and comes under the wings of the rooster, who calls. At that time the Creator goes down to His garden, which is the upper Garden of Eden, and at that time the rooster above awakens and says, "Arise, all who have sleep in the holes of their eyes. It is time for the deer, *Malchut*, to unite with her husband, ZA." Happy is a man who rises at midnight to engage in Torah, for the Creator and all the righteous listen to his voice, as it is written, "You who sits in the garden, friends are listening to your voice, let me hear it."

At that time, a thread of grace is poured over one who engages in Torah, and at that time the Creator goes down to His garden, *Malchut*. "He went down to the beds of perfume." Perfumes are illumination of *Hochma*. *Rosh* [head] is GAR, and those righteous who have those *Mochin* of perfumes of the *Rosh* are called "the beds of perfume."

"To pasture in the gardens," in two gardens, the Garden of Eden of above, *Bina*, and in the Garden of Eden of below, in *Malchut*. They are called "this world," *Malchut*, and "the next world," *Bina*. "To gather lilies" means the righteous who engage in Torah, whose lips whisper the Torah. It is written, "lilies"; do not pronounce as *Shoshanim* [lilies], but as *Sheshonim* [repeating], for they repeatedly delve in the Torah. That is, even in the grave their lips whisper the Torah. It is said about them, "To gather lilies," that he gathers them from this world prematurely so they would not sin.

64) There are three "I will be." "I will be with you in the first exile." It was said, "When they

exiled into Egypt, Divinity was with them." And "I will be with you in the second exile." It was said, "When they exiled into Babel, Divinity was with them." And "I will be with you in the third exile." It was said, "When they exiled into Greece, Divinity was with them." He did not reveal to them the "I will be" of the fourth exile." Rather, "In its time, I will hasten it." If they are rewarded, I will hasten it. If they are not rewarded, in its time.

KEDOSHIM [HOLY]

1-2) Several times did the Torah testify to people, several times did she raise her voice to all sides to awaken them, yet they are all asleep in their slumber in their iniquities, neither looking nor noticing with which face they rise to the upper judgment day, when the upper king claims from them the affront of Torah, who yells against them. They do not turn their faces to her because they are flawed in everything, not knowing the faith of the upper king. Woe unto them and woe unto their souls.

The Torah testifies to him and says, "Whoever is a fool, let him come here, 'Heartless, she said to him.'" Heartless is one who has no faith because one who does not engage in Torah, there is no faith within him and he is flawed in everything.

4) Happy are the righteous who engage in Torah and know the ways of the Creator. They sanctify themselves in the sanctity of the King and are holy in everything. Because of it, they draw a spirit of *Kedusha* from above, their sons are all true righteous, and are called "sons of the king," "holy sons."

7-8) When the Creator created the world and wished to discover depths out of the concealments, and light out of darkness, at that time they were mingled in one another. For this reason, out of darkness came forth light, and out of concealment came forth and revealed the deep. One came out of the other. Out of good came forth bad, and out of *Rachamim* [mercy] came forth *Din* [judgment]. Everything is included in one another, the good inclination and the bad inclination, right and left, Israel and the rest of the nations, white and black. Everything depends on one another.

The whole world is seen only in one bonding, attached in its entanglement: *Midat ha Din* [quality of judgment] and *Midat ha Rachamim* [quality of mercy], *Malchut* and *Bina*, attached and entangled in one another. Therefore, when the world was sentenced in the inclusive *Din*, it was sentenced with *Rachamim*, with *Malchut* included in *Bina*. Were it not so, the world would not have been able to exist for even one moment.

11) Man is never purified unless with words of Torah. This is why words of Torah do not take *Tuma'a*, since she, the Torah, is poised to purify the impure. There is healing in the Torah, as it

is written, "It will be health to your navel and marrow to your bones." There is purity in the Torah, as it is written, "The fear of the Lord is pure; it stands forever." "Stands forever" means that it always stands in this purity and it is never removed from it.

13-14) The Torah is called "holy," as it is written, "For I the Lord am holy." This is the Torah, the high and holy name. For this reason, one who engages in it is purified and then sanctified, as it is written, "You shall be holy." "Shall be," which is a promise that through the Torah you will be holy.

"And you will be unto me a kingdom of priests and a holy nation." The sanctity of the Torah is holy, more than all other holinesses. The holiness of the upper hidden *Hochma* transcends all. There is no Torah without *Hochma* [wisdom], and there is no *Hochma* without Torah. It is all in one degree and all is one.

18) One who wishes to be sanctified with his Master's will should serve only from midnight onward or at midnight because at that time the Creator, ZA, is in the Garden of Eden, *Malchut*, and high *Kedusha* awakens. Then is the time for the rest of the people to be sanctified. Disciples of

the wise, who know the ways of Torah, midnight is their time to rise and engage in Torah, to bond with the Assembly of Israel, *Malchut*, and to praise the holy name, *Malchut*, and the holy king, ZA.

22) Let one come and exert in the one. The Creator, who is one, will exert in one, who is Israel, since the king exerts only in one who is worthy of him. This is why it is written, "And He is at one, and who can return Him?" That is, the Creator is present and found only in one, as one who was established in high *Kedusha* to be one, in Israel. Then he is in one, and not in another nation.

25) "You will be holy for I the Lord ... am holy."

Happy are Israel for not establishing this matter in another place, for not wanting anything for their *Kedusha* but to cling unto Him, as it is written, "For I the Lord ... am holy," to cling unto Him and not to another. This is why "You will be holy for I the Lord your God am holy."

31) It is written, "And you who cleave to the Lord." Happy are Israel, who cling to the Creator. Because they cling to the Creator, everything clings together to one another.

52) There is no separation between Torah and *Mitzva* because the Torah is the whole and the

Mitzvot in her are her details, and they are one. The Creator is true, His law is true law, He is His law and commandment as they are one.

53-55) "The glory of God is to conceal a matter." From those who do not exert in this glory, the *Mitzvot*, conceal the matter from them. It is said about them, "The fools carry disgrace." These are the ignorant who do not exert in the glory of Torah, and how do they say, "Our Father in heaven, hear our voice, have compassion and mercy on us and accept our prayer"? The Creator will tell them, "And if I am a father, where is My glory," meaning where is your exertion in My Torah and *Mitzvot* to do My commandments, for one who does not know the commandments of his Master, how will he serve Him?

The exception is he who hears from sages and does, although he does not know of his own. This corresponds to "We shall do and we shall hear," that he hears from sages and does.

54) Rabbi Shimon came and kissed Moses' hands. He said, "You must be a son from the world of *Atzilut*, as in His firstborn son, *Tifferet*, the son of upper *AVI*, that *Atzilut* is His undoubtedly. No other son preceded you in thought, speech, or action." Moses said, "You and the friends, and

the heads of the seminary that are here with me are without any cessation at all and without mixture of the *Sitra Achra*, in the form of the world of *Atzilut*." They all kissed each other and were known in brotherhood, and wept.

57-58) One who puts himself to death over the Torah, who is precious, the Torah exists in him and does not part from him. But one who does not exert in it, even though he follows the commands of sages, hearing from sages and doing, he is their servant, a slave and not a son. But if he is a faithful servant, his master makes him ruler of all that he owns.

But one who does not engage in Torah and does not serve the sages, to hear the *Mitzvot* from them, to keep "We shall do and we shall hear," but sins and transgresses in "You shall not do" is similar and equal to the idol-worshipping nations of the world, the children of SAM and the serpent, of whom it was said, "The fools carry disgrace," for they did not wish to receive the Torah. Anyone in whom there is no Torah, there is no glory, as it was said, "The wise shall inherit glory."

74) David's beauty shines to all the worlds. His head is a skull of gold, embroidered with seven

decorations from seven kinds of gold, and the fondness of the Creator is before him. For his love for Him, he said to the Creator to turn His eyes back and look at him, when he said, "Turn to me and pardon me," because they are beautiful in everything, as it is written, "Turn your eyes away from me." It is so because when those eyes of *Malchut* look at the Creator, arrows of love awaken in this heart from mortars in supernal love. For the great flame of the supernal love for Him, he said, "Turn your eyes away from me," meaning turn Your eyes from me to another side, for they are burning me with a flame of love. It is written about it in David, "And he was ruddy, with beautiful eyes and a handsome appearance." And because of this high and beautiful David, with whom the Creator's love and passion is to cling to him, David said, "Turn to me and pardon me."

92) One who walks on the straight path in the Torah, and one who engages in it properly always has a good portion for the next world, since the words of Torah that he utters from his mouth go and roam the world and rise up. And several high and holy angels connect to that speech, which rises on a straight path, crowns in a holy crown, and bathes in the river of the

next world, *Bina*, which stretches out of Eden, *Hochma*. It is received in it and swallowed within it. And that high tree, ZA, delights around the river causing ZA to receive the illumination of the river from *Bina*. At that time, an upper light extends and comes out, and crowns in that person the whole day.

94) One whose passion is to engage in Torah but finds no one to teach him, and for the love of Torah, he speaks in it and stutters in it in stuttering, not knowing, each word rises and the Creator is happy with that word and accepts it, planting it around that stream, *Bina*. Those words become big trees, great lights that are called "willows of the brook," as it is written, "In her love she always errs."

95-96) Happy are they who know the ways of Torah and engage in it honestly, for they plant the trees of life above, extending *Mochin* to ZA, the tree of life, and they are all healing to his soul. This is why it is written, "There was a true law [Torah] in his mouth." But is there a Torah that is not true? Indeed, as it was said that if one who does not know instructs teaching, it is not truth. And one who learns something from him learns something that is not true. This is why it is written, "There was a true law [Torah] in his mouth."

Yet, one must learn the Torah from any person, even from one who does not know, since by that, he will awaken in the Torah and will come to learn from one who knows. Afterwards, it will be found that he has been walking in the Torah on a true path. One should always engage in the Torah and its commandments even if he does not work *Lishma* [for Her sake], because from *Lo Lishma* [not for Her sake] he will come to *Lishma*.

100) The Creator rebukes the man with love in concealment. If he accepts His rebuke, good. If not, He rebukes him and leaves him among those who love him. If he accepts, good. If not, He rebukes him openly, in front of everyone. If he accepts, good. If not, He leaves him and does not rebuke him any longer, for He leaves him to go and do as he pleases.

122) *The Zohar* explains three discernments:

1. The governance of the middle line, which sustains the two lines—right and left—and makes peace between them by setting up the illumination of the

right from above downward, and the illumination of the left from below upward. The great punishment of one who blemishes the order of the middle line is that he draws illumination of the left from above downward. This was the sin of the eating from the tree of knowledge.

2. The measure of the flaw of one who connects *Dinim de Nukva* and *Dinim de Dechura* [female judgments and male judgments respectively] with one another, unlike the way of the correction of the middle line, when *Dinim de Dechura* were added to *Dinim de Nukva*, and the ruin is great.

3. The bonding of two kinds of *Dinim* with one another in the way of the complete correction of the middle line. At that time the *Dinim* of both are cancelled and the perfection of the two lines—right and left—properly appears.

108) When the Creator created the world, He established every single thing, each in its side, either on the right or on the left, and appointed

high forces on them. Hence, you have not even a tiny blade of grass on earth that does not have a superior force over it in the upper worlds. And all that they do with each one, and all that each and everyone does is all by intensification of the upper force appointed over it from above.

130) Happy are the righteous in this world and in the next world. It is written about them, "The path of the righteous is as the light of dawn," for in the future the serpent that was initially in the *Nukva*, suckling from *Malchut*, will be gone and *Dechura* will come to be in his place, as in the beginning, in a never ending *Zivug*, for there will no longer be someone to separate the *Zivug*, and everything will be complete.

EMOR [SPEAK]

3) "How abundant is Your goodness, which You have concealed for those who fear You."

"How good is Your goodness," how sublime and honorable is that upper light called "good." It is written, "And God saw that light, that it was good." This is the hidden light with which the Creator has done good in the world. There is no hindrance of it each day, and the world exists by it and stands on it. "Which You have concealed for those who fear You." The Creator made the upper light when He created the world and concealed it for the righteous in the future. There are two lights: 1) the hidden light for the righteous in the future, which never illuminates, 2) the light called "good," which extends from the hidden light that illuminates in the world each day, and on which the world stands.

5) When a person is poised to leave into that world and he is on his sickbed, three emissaries come to him, and he sees there what a person cannot see when he is in this world. That day is the day of the upper judgment, when the king asks for his deposit back—the soul. Happy is a

man who returns the deposit to the king as was given to him, without corruption.

26) Happy are Israel, whom the Creator has chosen out of all the idol-worshipping nations, and out of the love of them has given them the true Torah [law] to know the way of the holy king. Anyone who engages in the Torah is as though he exerts in the Creator, for the whole of the Torah is the name of the Creator. For this reason, one who engages in Torah engages in His name, and one who departs from the Torah departs from the Creator.

31) Anyone who engages in Torah at night and rises at midnight, when the Assembly of Israel, *Malchut*, awakens to correct the king's house, to extend illumination of *Hochma* for Him, will build a house with wisdom. That man partakes with it and is considered to be from the king's house, and each day he is given of these corrections of the house.

36) Happy are Israel in this world and in the next world, for it is written about them, "And I will divide you from the nations to be unto Me."

How divided are Israel in *Kedusha* from all, to serve the Creator, as it is written, "And you shall be sanctified and be holy for I the Lord am holy."

37) "Salvation belongs to the Lord; Your blessing is upon Your people, Selah."

Happy are Israel for wherever they exiled, Divinity exiled with them. When Israel came out of exile, to whom will be the redemption, to Israel or to the Creator? After all, Divinity will also come out of exile. It will indeed be salvation to the Lord. When? When "Your blessing is upon Your people, Selah," when the Creator watches over Israel with blessings, to deliver them from exile and to do good to them. Then salvation is certainly the Lord's, since Divinity will come out of exile. For this reason, they will return with Israel from exile, as it is written, "And the Lord your God will return your captivity, and have compassion on you." "Return" means that He, too, will return with Israel from exile.

45) Seal the Torah. In which place is the sealing of the written Torah, ZA? It is in my studies. These are prophets, called "Taught of the Lord," *Netzah* and *Hod*, as it is written, "He set up the right pillar and named it Yachin," which is *Netzah*, "And he set up the left pillar and named it Boaz," which is *Hod*. From there, paths extend to the faithful prophets who receive from *Netzah* and from *Hod*. Those *NH* stand and remain

existing for the body, ZA, for the six lights in it, as it is written, "His legs are of marble." His legs, *Netzah* and *Hod*, stand for ZA, in whom there are six *Sefirot*, and everything stands in wholeness. The *Kedusha* of all is present only when they are in wholeness because when ZA bonds with *Malchut*, everything is perfect, everything is one, and no place is blemished. This is why the Assembly of Israel is called "whole."

46) The Creator is present only in a broken place, a broken *Kli*. That place is the most complete because he lowers himself so that everyone's pride will be on him, the pride of the upper one. He is the one who is whole because one who lowers himself, the Creator makes him upright.

50-51) The Creator is destined to complement Israel, so they will be complete with everything, so they will not be flawed at all because at the time of revival there will be the correction of the world. Such are the *Kelim* and the clothes of man, which are the corrections of the body, and hence he will complement them.

When they awaken from the dust, at the revival of the dead, they will rise as they had entered the grave. If they entered lame or blind, they will rise lame and blind. They will rise with the same clothing, which is the body, so it will not be said that it is another who has awakened for the revival. And afterwards the Creator will heal them and they will be whole before Him. Then the world will be complete with everything. And then, "On that day, the Lord will be one and His name, One."

70) Israel ascend from below upward, as it is written, "And your seed will be as the dust of the earth." Thus, they rise from the dust of the earth to the stars of the heaven, and then rise above everything and cling to the highest of all places, as it is written, "And you who cleave unto the Lord your God."

83) Happy are Israel in this world and in the next world; they know how to cling to the holy king, evoke the force of above, and extend their master's *Kedusha* over them. This is why it is written, "Happy are you, Israel, who is like you?" "And you who cleave to the Lord your God are alive everyone of you this day."

91-92) It is written, "And I will be sanctified among the children of Israel," first, when Israel raise *MAN* to evoke the three sanctities above. And then, "I the Lord sanctify you," when Israel receive the high *Kedusha*.

In which place does man sanctify himself in *Kedusha*, to include himself in it? When a person reaches "The Lord of hosts" mentioned after the third "Holy," *Netzah* and *Hod*, "I the Lord sanctify you." And we, after three times holy, say only "The Lord of hosts," not including ourselves there. Afterwards, when a person reaches "The whole earth is full of His glory," the *Kedusha* is drawn to *Malchut*, and then he includes himself in the *Kedusha* to be sanctified below, inside that glory of below, *Malchut*, as it is written, "Shall be sanctified by My glory."

Afterwards he will make the way in private, first including himself in *Malchut*—the honor of below, in the words, "The whole earth is full of His glory," including the whole earth and all the nations—and then he will extend the *Kedusha* in particular, only to Israel, so everything is sanctified and the *Kedusha* expands from Israel to the entire world.

129) Open for me an opening like the tip of a needle, and I will open the high gates for you.

Open for me, my sister, because the door for my entrance is in you. My sons can enter only in you. If you do not open your door, then I am locked; I will not be found. Hence, "Open for me." Certainly, open for me. This is why when David wished to come into the King, he said, "Open to me the gates of righteousness ... This is the gate of the Lord." The gates of righteousness is *Malchut*; it is the way to enter the King. "This is the gate of the Lord," to find Him and to adhere to Him. Hence, "Open to me, my sister, my love," to mate with you and forever be at peace with you.

129) For itself, ZA is in *Hassadim* covered from *Hochma*. And *Malchut* in and of herself is in *Hochma* without *Hassadim*. She is called "night" because *Hochma* does not shine without *Hassadim*. Hence, there is complete abundance for the redemption of Israel only through *Zivug* of ZA and *Malchut*. This is because then the *Hassadim* of ZA are mingled with the *Hochma* of *Malchut*, and Israel receive the complete abundance from GAR.

BaHar [On Mount Sinai]

32) **Man without a woman is half a *Guf*, one where Divinity is not present.** Similarly, when the Creator is not near Divinity and in the whole of Israel—who are virtuous people, which are His organs—then the cause of causes, *Keter*, is not there. It is as though the Creator is not one, since He is not united with Divinity.

Because the Creator is not called "One" unless He is in *Zivug* with Divinity, and when abroad, Divinity is far from her Husband, they said that all who live abroad are as one without a God. This is so because there are no sacrifices abroad, which is the *Zivug* of the Creator with Divinity, and when the Creator joins Divinity, the words, "In that day, the Lord will be one and His name, One," will come true. Then the cause of causes, *Keter*, will be over them.

52) **One should always be cautious with one's Master, and let his heart adhere to sublime faith, so he may be whole with his Master. When he is whole with his Master, no person in the world can harm him.**

56) The faithful ones lead *Malchut* according to their wish everyday. She observes what they command. The faithful ones are the ones who evoke good, meaning *Yesod*, opposite her, by giving alms and by not sparing what is theirs. They know that the Creator will give them more, since *Yesod* evokes blessings opposite it. And one should not say, "If I give this now, what will I do tomorrow?" Rather, the Creator will give him endless blessings.

83-84) When a son always clings to his father without any separation, there is no one who can protest against him. A servant does his master's work and corrects the corrections of the worlds. One who has both, a son and a slave included as one, in conjunction, this person corrects all the faith, the *Malchut* into one whole with ZA without any separation and unites everything together. This is a man of whom the Creator declares in all the armies and camps of all the worlds and firmaments, "Notice so-and-so, who is the King's trusted one, who has all his Master's secrets in his possession." Happy is he in this world and happy is he in the next world.

From that day forth, that man is known and is registered in all the worlds, for all the armies and

camps should be with him, and the Creator no
longer needs a thing from him, other than himself,
since all the worlds stand on him. Then a voice
awakens and declares of that man, "He is comely
for the Only One, to be with the Only One," the
Creator, "and to engage One in One."

New Zohar BaHar [On Mount Sinai]

7) One should place one's heart and desire and
cling to the Creator.

9) Rabbi Shimon says, "Anyone who performs
righteousness and clings to the tree of life will be
saved in this world, and even from the death in
the world of the rest of the people, the corporeal
death, and all the more so from spiritual death.

15-17) Happy is the man who is among the first
ten at the synagogue because what is completed
is completed in them.

There is no congregation of less than ten, who
are the instilling of the ten *Sefirot* of Divinity,
which sanctify in Divinity first. There must be at
least ten at the synagogue at once, and not come
few at a time so the wholeness of the organs is not
delayed. It is so because the Creator made man at
once and established for him all the organs at the

same time, as it is written, "He has made you and established you." Once all of man's organs were completed, each organ was established properly by itself. But before he was entirely completed, not a single organ was established.

Likewise, since Divinity came first to the synagogue, there must be ten there at once, opposite the ten *Sefirot* of Divinity, who is a complete level, and then what is completed is completed. And as long as there are not ten there, none of them is complete. Afterwards everything was corrected. "The king is glorified in the multitude of the people." This is why the people come next, after the first ten, when they have already completed the organs of Divinity, her ten *Sefirot*, who are all a correction of the body of Divinity because "The king is glorified in the multitude of the people."

When Divinity comes first and people are still not ten together, the Creator calls, "Why have I come and there is no person?" "And there is no person" means that the organs have not been established, for even if there are nine people there, even one of them is not established and the body of Divinity is not completed, for when the body is not complete with ten, there is certainly no person, not one of them is whole.

For this reason, "And there is no person" is precisely so.

When the body is completed below, when there are ten, the upper Divinity comes and enters the body, and the lower one is made, precisely as above. It is so because the ten *Sefirot* of Divinity clothe the ten of the congregation, and then everyone must not open their mouths to speak of worldly matters because Israel are now in the upper wholeness, sanctified in the upper *Kedusha*, and happy are they.

BeHukotai [In My Statutes]

20) Woe unto people who do not know and do not consider the glory of their Master.

21) The poor is gripped in *Din* and all his feeding is in *Din*, in a place called "justice," which is *Malchut* ...When she is not in a *Zivug* with ZA, she is poor and she is called "justice," and one who gives *Tzedaka* [alms, but also righteousness in Hebrew] to the poor makes the Holy Name above properly whole, connecting her with ZA, which gives her everything. Because *Tzedaka* is the tree of life, ZA, and *Tzedaka* gives and bestows upon justice, *Malchut*, when she gives to justice, ZA and *Malchut* connect with one another and the Holy Name is complete.

30-31) There is an allegory about a man who loved his friend. He told him, "Certainly, because of the sublime love that I have for you, I wish to dwell with you." His friend replied, "How will I know that you will dwell with me?" He went and took all the good things in his home and brought them to him and said, "My pawn is with you, so I will never part from you."

So is the Creator. He wished to dwell with Israel. He took His treasure, Divinity, and lowered it down to Israel. He told them, "Israel, here is My pawn with you, so I will never part from you." And although the Creator was removed from us, He left the pawn in our hands because Divinity is with us in exile and we keep His treasure. And when He asks for His pawn, He will come to dwell with us. This is why it is written, "And I will set My tabernacle among you." "I will give you a pawn so I will dwell with you." And even though Israel is in exile now, the Creator's mortgage is with them and they have never left it.

42) **How beloved are Israel by the Creator**. The Creator wishes to reprove them and to lead them in the straight path, as a father has mercy on his son. And out of his love for him, his cane is always in his hand, to lead him in the straight path and so that he will not stray to the right or to the left, as it is written, "For whom the Lord loves He reproves, even as a father corrects the son in whom he delights." And the one whom the Creator does not love and loathes, He removes His reproach from him, removes the scepter from him.

BaMidbar

[Numbers]

BaMidbar [In the Desert]

19-20) It is written, "Out of Zion, the perfection of beauty, God appeared." "Appeared" means illuminates. When He illuminates, He illuminates to all the worlds. And when this light—blessing and life—awakens, everything is in unity, in *Zivug*, and all is in love, all is in perfection, and then it is peace for all, peace of above and of below, as it is written, "Peace be within your walls, and prosperity within your palaces."

21) "**Be joyful with Jerusalem and rejoice for her, all you who love her.**" How favored is the Torah by the Creator because wherever words of Torah are heard, the Creator and all His armies listen to His words. And the Creator comes to dwell with him.

22) **The *Mitzvot* of the Torah are sublime, superior**. A man comes and performs a *Mitzva*. That *Mitzva* stands before the Creator and crowns before Him and says, "So and so made me," and "I am from so and so," since he awakened it above. This is so because as he evoked the *Mitzva* below, it is awakened above and makes peace above and below. This causes

Zivug between ZA and *Malchut*, who are called "above" and "below."

75-76) **Happy is the man who knows how to lure and to serve his Master with the desire and the intention of the heart.** Woe unto one who comes to lure his Master with a far away heart and unwillingly.

For this reason, one needs to attach one's soul and desire to one's Master, and not approach Him with a false desire.

Nasso [Take]

1) It is written, "Time to do for the Lord; they have broken Your law."

The days are few, and the owner of sins, the slanderer, is pressing. The herald calls each day for repentance, and the harvesters of the field—those who have been rewarded with the crop of the upper field, the attainment of the secrets of the Torah—are few. And even those who did attain are at the end of the vineyard and do not properly notice or know to which place they are going.

17) Happy is a man who has been rewarded with the Torah, to walk and to cling to His ways. When a person walks in the paths of Torah, he draws upon him a high and holy spirit, as it is written, "Until the spirit be poured upon us from on high." And when a person strays from the path of Torah, he draws upon him another spirit, from the other side, from the side of *Tuma'a*, and the side of *Tuma'a* awakens from the side of the hole of the great deep, the abode of the evil spirits that harm people, and which are called "harm-doers of the world."

18-19) Anyone who clings to the Creator and keeps the commandments of the Torah seemingly sustains the worlds—the world above and the world below, as it is written, "And do them."

And anyone who breaches the commandments of the Torah seemingly blemishes above, blemishes below, blemishes himself, and blemishes all the worlds. There is an allegory about sailors who were sailing in a boat. One fool among them rose and wished to puncture the boat. His friend told him, "Why are you puncturing the boat?" He replied, "Why should you care? I am drilling under me!" He told him, "But we are both drowning in the boat together!"

90) "And the educated ones will shine as the brightness of the firmament" with this composition of yours, Rabbi Shimon, *The Book of Zohar*, from the brightness of upper *Ima*, who is called repentance.

90) Israel are destined to taste from the tree of life, which is *The Book of Zohar*. Through it, they will come out of exile in mercy and it will exist in them.

98-99) As the Creator divided them at Mount Sinai, He will divide them in the last redemption.

This is so because it is said about Israel, "And the children of Israel went up armed out of the land of Egypt." "Armed," from the side of the tree of life, ZA, which are fifty [spelled like "arms" in Hebrew] years of the *Yovel* [fifty years' anniversary], *Bina*, which ZA receives from *Bina*. It is said about them, "They shall come up to the mount." And among them was "the angel of God, who went before the camp of Israel." Also, it is they who were told, "And how I bore you on the wings of eagles," which are clouds of glory, "And brought you unto Myself," "And the children of Israel were going out boldly." Thus, He will bring the disciples of the wise out with all this glory.

As it was said about the ignorant from the side of the good, "And they stood at the foot of the mountain," so they will be in the last redemption—under the disciples of the wise, as a servant who walks by the feet of his master's horse. At the foot of the mountain they were told, "If you accept the law, good. If not, there will be your burial place." Similarly, they will be told in the last redemption, "If you take upon yourselves a disciple of the wise at the end of the exile, like a man who is riding a horse and his servant serves him, good. If not, there—in the exile—will be your burial."

105) How loved are Israel before the Creator, wherever they are, the Creator is with them because He does not remove His love from them, as it is written, "And let them make Me a Temple, that I may dwell among them."

106-107) Happy is the man who is among the first ten at the synagogue because by them is the congregation completed, when it is not less than ten. They are the ones who are sanctified by Divinity first. But there must be ten at the synagogue at the same time, and not come bit by bit, so that the wholeness of the organs is not detained, for all ten are as organs of a single body in which Divinity dwells, for the Creator has made man at once and established for him all the organs at the same time.

Once all of the man's organs were completed at that time, each organ was properly established in itself. Likewise, since Divinity came to the synagogue first, there must be ten there together, and then it is completed because there is no congregation of less than ten, who correspond to *Malchut's* ten *Sefirot*. As long as there are no ten together there, none of them is completed. Afterwards, the whole congregation is corrected, as it is written, "The king is glorified in the multitude of the people." Hence, the people, who come after the first ten are all the correction of the body, the correction of the congregation, since the multiplication of the people increases the glory of the king.

109) "When a man utters a vow." "Utters" means he retires from the rest of the people in the world to be sanctified as above and to be whole. When a person comes to be purified he is purified. A man who comes to be sanctified is sanctified and the *Kedusha* of above is spread over him, the *Kedusha* with which the Creator is sanctified.

110) Oh how should one observe and know the work of his Master, for each day the clarion calls out and says, "How long, you fools, will you love foolishness?" "Return, O backsliding children," "I will heal your backsliding," and there is no one to lend an ear. The Torah declares before them and there is no one to notice.

167) The Creator called Israel Adam, such as above, ZA, and He called them "beast." It is all in one verse, as it is written, "And you are My sheep, the sheep of My pasture, you are men," for Israel are called man and beast. This is why "Man and beast You save, O Lord." If they are rewarded,

they are called "man," such as above. If they are not rewarded, they are called "beast."

189) Rabbi Aba said, "I have seen the face of Divinity, and one who sees the face of Divinity must walk and run after her." It is written, "And let us know, let us eagerly pursue to know the Lord." It is also written, "And many peoples shall go and say, 'Come and let us go up to the mountain of the Lord ... for out of Zion shall go forth the law [Torah]." And I wish to follow you and learn from those good things that you are tasting each day from the holy splendor of Rabbi Shimon.

299) The discernments whether there is *Din* or not are only with respect to the lower ones. But with respect to the *Atzmut* [self (Himself)], everything is Godliness, above time, place, or change. All those degrees and corrections that we discern in Godliness are but kinds of concealments and covers with regard to the lower ones because the ten *Sefirot* are ten kinds of covers over Himself. Similarly, all the imaginary images of time, place, and deeds are all but kinds of covers over His Godliness that seem that way in the eyes of the lower ones. It is as one who is not impressed or changed at all by the covers in which he is

covered, for only his friends are impressed by his disappearance or appearance.

Likewise, Godliness does not change or is in any way affected by those degrees and corrections and names in time, place, and change of action that the lower ones discern in His covers. Rather, we should know that these covers also serve for disclosures. Moreover, by the measure of the cover in each name and correction, so is the measure of disclosure in it. One who is rewarded with receiving the measure of covers properly is later rewarded with these covers becoming measures of disclosures for him.

One who studies should remember these words during the study, and he will not fail in his thought.

329) Happy are the righteous, for all those holy words that are said in the spirit of the high and holy spirit—the spirit in which all the upper holy ones are included—have been revealed to you. These are words to which upper and lower listen.

Happy are you who sit at the throne of Midian, harvesters of the field, who know these matters and regard them. You will know your masters face to face, eye to eye, and with these words you will be rewarded with the next world, as it is written, "And you shall know this day and reply to your heart." *HaVaYaH, Atik Yomin, Elokim, ZA* are all one. Blessed be His name forever and for all eternity.

New Zohar, Nasso [Take]

3) Woe unto he who comes to seduce his Master with a faraway heart and an incomplete desire, as it is written, "And they deceived Him with their mouth and lied to Him with their tongue, and their heart was not steadfast with Him."

4) The unification of the prayer and the blessing depend on the speech and the uttering of the mouth, and everything depends on the root of the deed. One who does not know the root of the deed, his work is not work. If he blemishes the deed of the speech, there is no place for the blessing to be, and his prayer is not a prayer.

BeHaalotcha [When You Mount the Candles]

1) Happy are Israel for the Creator desired them and gave them the true law, the tree of life, by which man inherits life in this world and life in the next world. Anyone who delves in the Torah and clings to it has life, and anyone who leaves the words of Torah and becomes separated from the Torah, it is as though he has parted with life because she is life and all her words are life.

5) Happy are Israel, for the Creator gave them the holy Torah and taught them His ways so as to adhere to Him, to keep the commandments of the Torah and to be rewarded with the next world. He brought them near when they came out of Egypt, for then he brought them out of the other authority and raised them to unite in His Name. Then, the children of Israel were called "Free from everything," for they did not sit under another authority, and He raised them to unite in His Name, which is above everything, and which governs upper and lower.

13) **How pleasant are the words of Torah, for in each and every word are sublime secrets, and the whole Torah is called "superior."**

14) **Happy are Israel, for they were given the superior law, the law of truth. And one who says that that story in the Torah [in Hebrew, Torah means law, too] points only to that story, damned be he, for if this is so, then the Torah is not the superior Torah, the law of truth. Certainly, the holy, superior Torah is a true law.**

24) When the deepest of all—upper *Aba*—shines, He shines in the river, in upper *Ima*, and the river stretches directly through the middle line, ZA, to water everything, all the degrees in *Malchut*. It is written about that time, "When you mount," since everything stems from the deepest of all. "When you mount" means that it comes from the Upper One, the deepest of all, called "thought," which is *Aba*, and all is one thing. At that time, the Assembly of Israel is blessed, and the blessings are in all the worlds.

58) **Woe unto one who says that the Torah comes to tell literal tales** and the uneducated words of such as Esau and Laban. If this is so, even today we can turn the words of an uneducated person

into a law, and even nicer than theirs. And if the Torah indicates to mundane matters, even the rulers of the world have among them better things, so let us follow them and turn them into a law in the same way. However, all the words of the Torah have the uppermost meaning.

59-60) The Torah created the angels and all the worlds, and they exist for it. Moreover, when it came down to this world, the world could not tolerate it if it had not clothed in these mundane clothes, which are the tales and words of the uneducated.

Hence, this story in the Torah is a clothing of the Torah. And one who considers this clothing as the actual Torah and nothing else, damned will be his spirit, and he will have no share in the next world. This is the reason why David said, "Open my eyes, that I may behold wondrous things out of Your law," that is, gaze upon what lies beneath the clothing of the Torah.

61-62) There is an openly visible clothing, and when fools see a person dressed handsomely, whose dress seems elegant, they look no further and judge him by his elegant clothes. They regard the clothes as the man's body and regard the man's body as his soul.

Such is the Torah. It has a body, which is the *Mitzvot* of the Torah, which are called "the bodies of the Torah." This body clothes in dresses, which are mundane stories, and the fools in the world consider only that clothing, which is the story of the Torah. They do not know more and do not consider what exists underneath that clothing.

Those who know more do not consider the clothing, but the body under that clothing.

64) **Woe unto the wicked ones who say that the Torah is nothing more than fables and consider only the clothing.** Happy are the righteous who consider the Torah as they should. As wine sits only in a jar, the Torah dwells only in that clothing. Hence, one needs to regard what is found under the clothing, which is why all these tales are dresses.

88) "And the wise shall shine as the brightness of the firmament" are the authors of the Kabbalah. They are the ones who exert in this brightness, called *The Book of Zohar*.

88) **"Every son that is born you shall cast into the river."** The Torah is called "a son." The newborn is the attained. "Into the river"

means the light of Torah. "Cast" is like "You will study it" [it's an anagram in Hebrew], where you study each insight that is born in you by the light of Torah and by its soul. This is the light of this *Book of Zohar*, and it is all because of you.

SHLACH LECHA [SEND]

41) Oh how should people regard the work of the Creator, how they should regard the words of Torah. Anyone who engages in Torah seemingly sacrifices all the sacrifices before the Creator. Moreover, the Creator atones for all his iniquities and several thrones are established for him in the next world.

55) The Creator praises in the Torah and says, "Go in My way and engage in My work, and I will bring you to good worlds, to upper worlds."

62) Those who are faithful rejoice in words, and the words are blessed within them. They observe that they are one root and one core, and there is no separation in them. Those who are not faithful and do not study the Torah *Lishma* [for Her sake], make the faith, *Malchut*, separated from ZA, since they blemish the *Zivug* of ZA and *Malchut*, who are the written Torah and the oral Torah because they do not believe that they are one core and one root.

67) "If the Lord desires us ... then He will ... give it to us." This is what the faithful ones say.

When one exerts for the Creator with the desire of the heart, he will be rewarded with her because all He wants of him is the heart. He will be kept by the holy impression, which is the holy covenant.

We must not rebel against the Torah because the Torah does not require wealth or vessels of silver and gold. If a broken body engages in the Torah, it will find healing for everything, as it is written, "It shall be healing to your navel and marrow to your bones." It is written, "And health to all their flesh." All the slanderers over a person turn into his helpers and declare, "Make way for so and so, the King's servant!" That is, let no one stop him from coming to the King to serve Him.

68) Happy are those who engage in Torah *Lishma* [for Her sake] because they truly connect to the Creator. They are called "brothers and friends," as it is written, "For the sake of my brothers and friends I will now say, 'Peace be within you.'"

83) Israel are happier than all the nations in the world for the Creator wanted them, called His name by them, and was glorified in them, for the world was created only for Israel, so they may engage in Torah. It is so because one connects to one, ZA and *Malchut*, and Israel below, in this

world, are His existence, where by their good deeds they raise MAN for their *Zivug*, and they are the existence of all the other nations, who exist for Israel, who do their Master's will.

84-85) When the Creator created the man in the world, He established him such as above, and placed his power and might in the midst of his body, where there is the heart, the strength of the whole body and from which the whole body is nourished. The heart grips and strengthens in a high place above, in the brain that is in the head above, and connects to the other.

In this manner, the Creator established the world. He made it one body, and established the organs of the body around the heart, and the heart is inside of the whole body, and all the organs are nourished by the heart, who is the strength of all and on whom everything depends. And the heart connects and unites with the upper brain that is above.

183) "A lovely hind and a graceful doe, let her breasts satisfy you at all times; with her love be you ravished always."

Torah, Torah, the light of all the worlds, several seas and streams, origins, and springs spread out from you to all sides. From you is everything; on you stand the upper and the lower; the upper light comes forth from you. Torah, Torah, what shall I tell you, a lovely hind you are, and a graceful doe. Above and below are your lovers, who will be rewarded with nursing from you properly? Torah, Torah, the enjoyments of your Master, who can reveal and tell your secrets and concealments?

202-203) If you were not Rabbi Shimon, it would not be conveyed to be revealed.

The *Zivug* in that world bears fruit more than a *Zivug* that is done in this world. With their *Zivug*, the *Zivug* of that world, with their passion as one, when the souls cling to one another, they bear fruit and lights come out of them and become candles, and these are the souls for the proselytes who convert. All those souls that are born out of these *Zivugim* [couplings] enter the same hall.

When one proselyte converts, a soul flies out of that palace and enters under the wings of Divinity, and Divinity kisses her because she is an offshoot of the souls of the righteous, and sends her into that proselyte, and she stays within him. From that time, he is called "a proselyte of *Tzedek* [justice]." That is, the meaning of what is written, "The fruit of a righteous is a tree of life," who is ZA, elicits souls. This is also the fruit of the righteous—he makes souls.

210) Happy is he who lowers himself in this world, how high he is in that world. One who is small is great, and one who is great is small. The Creator increases only one who lowers himself, and the Creator lowers only one who increases himself. Happy is he who lowers himself in this world, how great he is in ascension in that world.

303) There is no GAR except through illumination of *Hochma* on the left, and only by inclusion of the right together with the left—when *Hochma* clothes in *Hassadim* and illuminate the GAR, and all the reward and all the good in the future is only in the illumination of the GAR. However, through the sins of the lower ones, the left overcomes the right and wishes to govern alone. Then a dispute is made between the right and the left, and the right line removes his *Hassadim* from the left line. At that time the left is quenched because *Hochma* cannot illuminate without *Hassadim*, and the harsh *Dinim* in it appear. Likewise, the right remains in VAK without GAR for there is GAR only from the illumination of *Hochma* in the left. This is

why the Temple was ruined and Israel were exiled among the nations.

It was said about the verse, "I the Lord, in its time I will hasten it," if they are rewarded, "I will hasten it"; if they are not rewarded, "In its time." How can Israel be redeemed if they have not even been rewarded and are still rebellious? The thing is that the exile was because through their sins, they caused the left to overcome the right and rule by itself, for then the right removes the *Hassadim* from it. Hence, when Israel repent and cling to the Creator, who is the middle line, the middle line returns and unites the right with the left, sustains the lights of both of them, the *Hochma* clothes in *Hassadim*, and the GAR appear, meaning that Israel are redeemed with their illumination and receive all of their good reward. It was said, "If they are rewarded, I will hasten it," and on that there is no set time. Rather, when they repent, they are redeemed.

However, if they do not repent, there is a set time that brings redemption even though they have not made repentance, which is once it is possible to gather all the harsh *Dinim* that Israel suffered during the exile into a complete measure in a way that they suffice that Israel will fear and never sin again, making the left prevail over the right, as they did at the time of the ruin. At that time they are worthy of redemption even without repentance for even without repentance they are guaranteed, "And let them not return to folly" for the many harsh *Dinim* that they had suffered.

It was said, "If they are not rewarded, "In its time," which happened by itself along with the disclosure of the *Dinim* in the exile for a sufficient amount, and there is no need at all for Israel's awakening for repentance. It is so because all the exile and the harsh *Dinim* in the exile come from the domination of the left without the right, the north side. Through the left, the GAR appear, from which there are all the reward and all the good that is destined to come to Israel.

At the time of redemption, the Creator awoke Abraham, the right line, south, and even though they were not rewarded and did not make repentance of clinging to the middle line, it was already time to redeem them even without repentance.

1-2) **"They are more desirable than gold, yes, than much fine gold, and sweeter than honey and the drippings of the honeycomb."** How sublime are the words of Torah, how precious they are. They are lovely above; they are lovely for all. It is so because they are the Holy Name, and anyone who exerts in Torah, exerts in the Holy Name and is delivered from any harm. He is delivered in this world and delivered in the next world. Anyone who engages in Torah grips to the tree of life. And because he is gripped to the tree of life, he is gripped to everything, as it is written, "She is a tree of life to those who take hold of her."

Anyone who engages in Torah has freedom from everything, freedom from death. This is because freedom, *Bina*, is upon him and grips him.

30) **"Whatever your hand finds to do with your strength, that do"** means that a person should contain the left in the right, and everything he does should be included only in the right. "Whatever your hand finds" is the left, which is called "hand." "To do with your strength" is

right, as it is written, "Your right hand, O Lord, glorious in power." And when a man is watchful to make all his actions toward the right side and to include the left in the right, the Creator is inside him in this world and will gather him to Him in the next, other world.

31) **One should not say, "When I come into that world, I will beg for mercy of the King, and will repent before Him."** Rather, it is written about that, "There is no deed or contemplation or knowledge or wisdom" once a person departs this world. If one wishes for the Holy King to shine for him in that world and give him a share in the next world, he should engage in including his deeds in the right in this world, and that all his actions will be for the Creator.

42) And if he does not redeem his *Nefesh*, *Ruach*, and *Neshama* in the Torah before he goes to that world, he will reincarnate into this world as before, as it is written, "He returns to the days of his youth," receiving *Nefesh*, and *Ruach*, and *Neshama*.

HUKAT [THE STATUTE]

1) **"This is the statute of the law." "And this is the law that Moses set before the sons of Israel."** These are holy words of Torah. They are superior; they are sweet, as it is written, "They are more desirable than gold, yes, than much fine gold, and sweeter than honey." One who engages in Torah, it is as though he stands by Mount Sinai each day and receives the Torah, as it is written, "This day you have become a people."

27-29) **"Who sends forth springs in the streams ... they give drink to all the animals of my fields."** King David said these verses in the spirit of holiness and they should be regarded. When the upper *Hochma* beat in its engravings, when the upper *HB* mated, although the upper *Hochma* is the most hidden of all that are hidden, since the *Yod* does not come out of the *Avir* in the upper *HB*, which are upper *AVI*, it is an opening from which a river stretches out. It is filled with high gates, which is *Bina*, *YESHSUT*, in whom the *Yod* comes out of the *Avir* and *Hochma* and *Hassadim* flow out of them.

He compared this matter of upper *AVI* and *YESHSUT* to a fountain and a water-source that fills a great lake from which springs, streams, and rivers extend to the right and to the left. Similarly, *AVI* and *YESHSUT* are for a thin one that is unknown, in the *Zivug* of *Yesodot* [pl. of *Yesod*] of upper *AVI*, who are unknown, in whom the *Yod* does not come out of the *Avir*. That river stretches out, stretching out of Eden, *Bina*, who went out of *Rosh AA* at the time of *Katnut* and returned to *Rosh AA* at the time of *Gadlut*.

Through this exit and coming, it fills that deep stream, *YESHSUT*, like the great water lake that is filled by the fountain and the source, who are upper *AVI*. From there, springs and streams extend to *ZA* and *Malchut*, and are filled by it with *Hochma* and *Hassadim*, as it is written, "Who sends forth springs in the streams." These are the high and holy rivers of *ZA*, the pure persimmon, pure air that *HGT* of *ZA* receive, the pure persimmon from upper *AVI*. It is written, "They go among the mountains," *HGT de ZA*, who are called "mountains," and from whom *Malchut* receives. Also, *ZA* and *Malchut* both drink from that spring of the upper holy stream that stretches out, who is *YESHSUT*.

Once ZA and *Malchut* have drank, "They give drink to all the animals of my fields," as it is written, "And from there it parted and became four heads." These four heads are "All the animals of my fields," which are four animals, ox, eagle, lion, and man, which are *Malchut's Merkava* [structure/chariot].

They are the whole of the camps and hosts in *BYA*.

57) **Righteous, who are rewarded with being attached to the bundle of life**, *Yesod de ZA*, are rewarded with seeing the glory of the high and holy King, as it is written, "To behold the pleasantness of the Lord, and to visit in His palace." Their abode is higher than all the holy angels and all their degrees, since neither the upper nor the lower are rewarded with seeing that high place, as it is written, "Neither has the eye seen a God besides You," which is the upper Eden.

61) **Best of all is one who comes to this world and does not part from the Creator, who is not revealed, and whose every word is in humbleness.** This is a worthy pious, who observes the *Mitzvot* of Torah and keeps them, and engages in Torah day and night. He unites and enjoys a higher

degree than all the people, and all burn from looking in the *Huppah* [canopy] of this one.

68) **Happy are the righteous in this world and in the next world.** And although they are in another place, in another, upper world, their merit remains in this world for all generations. When Israel repent before the Creator and are sentenced to a decree, the Creator summons the righteous who stand before Him up above and informs them, and they revoke that decree, and the Creator takes pity over Israel. Happy are the righteous, of whom it is said, "And the Lord shall guide you always."

78) **From this we learn that anyone who wishes to evoke things of above—in an act or in a word— if that act or that word is not done properly, nothing is evoked.** All the people in the world go to the assembly-house to evoke a matter above, but few are the ones who know how to evoke. The Creator is near to all those who know how to call Him and to evoke a matter properly. But if they do not know how to call upon Him, He is not close, as it is written, "The Lord is near to all those who call upon Him, to all who call upon Him in truth." "In truth" means that they know how to properly evoke a true matter. So it is in everything.

81-83) Anyone who knows how to properly set up an act, and properly set up words, it is certain that they awaken the Creator to extend high and upright matters. If not, he does not reconcile with them. Hence, the whole world knows how to arrange the act and set up the words. What is the importance of the righteous, who know the root of work and action, who know how to aim the heart and will more than those other ones who do not know so much?

Those who do not know the root of the act so much, but only an arrangement and not more, pull toward them a pull behind the Creator's shoulders, meaning that their prayer does not fly in the air, which is called "Providence." That is, it is Providence of the face, and they are only worthy of the "behind the shoulders."

Those who know and aim the heart and desire find blessings from the place of thought, *Hochma*, and come out in all the trunks and roots of the degrees properly, as it should be, until the upper ones and lower ones are blessed, and the holy upper name is blessed by them. Happy are they because the Creator is near to them and is before them. When they call Him, He is ready for them. And when they are in trouble, He is with them. He respects them in this world and in the next world, as it is written, "Because he has loved Me, therefore I will deliver him; I will set him on high, because he has known My name."

New Zohar, Hukat [The Statute]

11-12) How strong is repentance, superior to everything. When a person repents before his Master, the well of living waters, *Malchut*, is filled and her fountains flow to all sides, and a rod extends to all in 12 gates, to water small animals with great ones, which are the 12 tribes called "lion and wolf," the great animals, and "lamb and kid," which are small animals.

When Israel repented they said psalms. Those seven degrees that they returned brought them back with their psalms and elevated the upper well, *Malchut*, up to *Bina*, since from *Malchut* to *Bina* are seven degrees. The serpent parted from the world, as it is written, "Then shall Israel sing ... 'Spring up, O well,' they replied to it," since the well, *Malchut*, rose up above to *Bina* and the lower mother, *Malchut*, connected to the upper one, *Bina*.

60) "And the children of Israel sighed." When they saw the hard work, until the upper covenant was mentioned to them and upper *Ima*, *Bina*, awakened in mercy for her children, as it is written,

"And their cry rose up to the God," upper *Ima*—in whose hands is all the freedom—and opened to Israel the upper doors, which are 50 gates, bringing them out of there, and the lower *Ima*, *Malchut*, was filled with mercy over them. Then Moses came out to the world, appointed, a father, to shepherd Israel in the Torah.

102-103) The love of *Tzedek* [justice], since *Tzedek*, *Malchut*, is Your love, a small love. It is so because *Malchut* is called "small love," and when she unites with ZA above, in *Hassadim*, she becomes big, since *Hesed* is called "great love." Also, ZA is great by bonding with her, as it is written, "Great is the Lord and greatly glorified in the city of our God," when He is connected to *Malchut*, who is called "The city of our God." For this, the queen pulls him with these words of love.

"Tell me, the one whom my soul loves." This means that You, in whom is all the love of my soul, if You do not bond with me, how will You feed the world? How will you feed yourself from the upper depth, from *Bina*, for you and for others? After all, the blessings above are present only in a place of male and female.

107-108) "How good and how pleasant it is for brothers also to dwell together." Dwelling together means bonding of the brother, *Zeir Anpin*, with *Tzedek* [justice], *Malchut*. "Also" comes to include Israel, who are the *Merkava* [chariot/assembly] for this unification. This is why she told him, "How will you feed yourself, how will you rest these herds of Jacob? "Oil of gladness from your friends" are the upper fathers who joined within you first.

Israel are brothers and friends of ZA, anointing him with the oil of gladness over their heads in their prayers. The oil of gladness are those 12 rivers of pure persimmon that illuminate in her, from the 12 *Behinot* in ZA. Then there is joy in the worlds, desire in the worlds, and the anger departs from the world.

111) There is no joy before Him from all of His *Merkavot* [chariots/assemblies] as the joy of the souls of the righteous that are near Him.

119-121) "Listen, daughter, and see." "Listen," since hearing depends on you, for when Israel return in repentance before Me, "Listen," bring their prayers before Me, for the door to everything is in you. I have placed it in your hands to lead the lower world, hence "Listen, daughter, and see," for you are the mirror of everything, since the *Hochma*, called "mirror," appears only in *Malchut*. For this reason, you are called "A well for the living who see." Hence, you should ask about the deeds of the people of the world each day, to give to each person according to his works.

When the Creator created the world, He placed His palace in the hands of the queen to watch over the world. When the people of the world are worthy, joy is added above.

"Lend your ear to receive the prayer of everyone." So she did as well with all the prayers, to bring the crown to the righteous, *Yesod*, since all the prayers are to bring the crown to the righteous. These are the forms of *MAN* over which the righteous will pour *MAD*.

131) In the days of the Messiah, the knowledge will be renewed in the world and the Torah will illuminate before everyone, for it is written, "They shall all know Me from the least of them unto the greatest of them."

139) The Creator is destined to reveal supernal wisdom, which is the existence of all the worlds, to His children, when knowledge awakens in the world, when each and everyone of Israel attains attainment in the upper *Hochma*, who is the meaning of the name of the Creator. This is a benefit that never stops, forever and ever.

7) We should pay attention to the faith of the Creator, whose every word is true and great faith.

The words of a man are small, and all his words are transient, as he himself is as transient as a fleeting shadow. But repentance, prayer, and good deeds with many tears are holy because the great one, the superior one over the entire world, shines His light and restricts His *Kedusha* unto the man to do His will.

187) Three are called prayer:

1. A prayer for Moses the man of God. This is a prayer that there is none like it in another person.

2. A prayer for David. This is a prayer of which there is none like it in another king.

3. A prayer for the poor.

Of those three, the most important is the prayer for the poor. This prayer precedes Moses' prayer, precedes David's prayer, and precedes all the other prayers in the world.

188) The poor is brokenhearted. It is written, "The Lord is near to the brokenhearted." The poor always quarrels with the Creator, and the Creator listens and hears his words. When the poor has prayed his prayer, He opens all the windows of the firmament and all the other prayers that rise up, the brokenhearted poor pushes them away. It is written, "A prayer for the poor, for he will wrap." It should have said, "For he will wrap himself"; what is, "For he will wrap"? He causes delay, delaying all the prayers in the world, which do not enter until his prayer enters. Wrapping means delaying.

190) All the hosts of heaven ask one another, "What does the Creator do? In what does He exert?"

They are told, He unifies in passion with His *Kelim*, with the brokenhearted. None of them know what is done with the prayer of the poor and with all his complaints, for there is no passion to the poor unless when he sheds tears in complaints before the holy king, and there is no passion to the Creator unless when He accepts them and they are poured out before Him. This is a prayer that causes delay and stalling to all the prayers in the world.

192) One who prays his prayer should make himself poor so that his prayer will enter among

the prayers of all the poor, for all the gate-guards do not let any prayer in the world enter as they let the prayer of the poor, for they enter without permission. And if one always makes himself and makes his desire like the poor, his prayer rises and meets the prayers of the poor, bonds with them and rises with them, enters in their midst, and is willingly accepted by the holy king.

214-217) When *Malchut* is in great love for her loved one, ZA, for her pressing love she cannot tolerate the separation. She diminished herself in a great diminution until only a single, tiny point of her was seen. Then she is concealed from all her hosts and camps and says, "I am black and comely," and I have no place to put you under my wings.

For this reason, "Do not see me," do not see me at all for I am a tiny point. What do her mighty brave ones do? They roar as mighty lions, as it is written, "The young lions roar for prey." Out of the sounds and the roaring that they roar as strong and mighty powerful lions, her lover above hears and knows that His love is in love with Him, as He is, that she diminished herself for His love, until none of her form and beauty was seen.

Then out of these sounds and roars of those mighty powerful ones of hers, her beloved loved one comes, ZA out of his palace, with several gifts, several presents, with fragrances and with perfumes. He comes to her and finds her black and small without any form or beauty. He approaches her, embraces her, and kisses her until she gradually awakens because of the fragrances and the perfumes, and for the joy of her lover, ZA, who is with her. She is built and made in her correction, in her beauty, and she becomes the *Hey de HaVaYaH* as before.

290) He who loves the king calls at the gate. The king said, "Who is it?" They said, "Someone who loves you." He said, "My love, My heart's favored one, no other voice shall call him but Me." The king shouted and said, "So and so, come in, My heart's favored one, My beloved, set up the palaces to speak with him."

346) Israel have a writing and a tongue. In each letter they can look at a form and depiction properly to understand the upper secrets in them. "But He shall not regard the nations," since they have no authentic writing or tongue that are depicted by the upper forms. They have nothing to look and to know in the form of

their writing, for they are vain, a fraud, for their writing and language are but agreements, a form and language to which people agreed. He shall not regard their thought, their looking at the forms of their letters, since they have no writing. Happy are Israel.

426) Rabbi Shimon said, "Several times have I said that thing, yet the friends are not looking. The Creator places His Divinity only in a holy place, a place which is worthy of being in it."

439-441) "Go forth, O daughters of Zion, and gaze on King Solomon with the crown with which his mother has crowned him."

King Solomon is ZA. His mother is *Bina*. At that time she rejoices with all the king's sons, who are all those who come from the side of Israel, for they do not bond with the *Zivug* of ZA and *Malchut*. They are not standing with them, except Israel, who are the dwellers of the house and serve them, raising MAN through their Torah and prayer, which evoke toward the *Zivug*. Therefore, the blessings that come out from the *Zivug* of ZA and *Malchut* are Israel's.

Israel take all the blessings that come forth from the illumination of the *Zivug* of ZA and *Malchut*, and send some of them to the rest of the nations, and the rest of the nations feed on that part. From among the side of the portion of the appointees over the rest of the nations, a very thin trail comes out, from which the portion of the external ones and the nations of the world extends, and from which it divides into several sides. This is what we call, "the extract" that comes out of the side of the holy land, *Malchut*.

For this reason, the entire world drinks of the extract of the land of Israel, for the land of Israel is *Malchut*. Whether above or below, all those other idol-worshipping nations feed only on that extract, and even the bottom *Sefirot* drink from that extract.

441) Only Israel were chosen out of the entire world to cling to the middle line. This is why they take all the illumination of the *Zivug*, and the rest of the world only the extract, the path of a hairbreadth trail, called "The trail of the vineyards," since the ministers of the nations of the world are called "vineyards." That hairbreadth trail is from the left line, they are blessed by it, and it is called "The trail of the vineyards."

New Zohar, Balak

56-57) There has never been a day since the day when the world was created that the Creator had to be with Israel as that time when Balaam wished to obliterate Israel's enemies from the world. The Creator said about it, "Balaam wished to obliterate you from the world, but I will not do so. Rather, I will destroy all the nations to which I have driven you down, and I will not destroy you."

That is, if all the nations of the world should come, they will not be able to obliterate you from the world. Laban came first and wanted to uproot only Jacob from the world. The Creator came and protected him. Pharaoh came and wished to obliterate them from the world. The Creator came and protected them. Haman came and wished to obliterate them from the world. The Creator came and turned everything back. Likewise, in every generation the Creator always protects Israel.

70-71) When the Creator found Abraham in the land, they were practicing idolatry and did not know the faith of the Creator, but all were straying after idol-worship. Abraham rose and grew among them and became one complete branch before the Master of the world, and He found him there.

The Creator took that branch, planted it, watered it, toiled with it, uprooted it from there, and planted it in another land, as it is written, "Go forth out of your land and out of your homeland, and from your father's house," and He made of him a holy nation.

PINHAS

2) Anyone who engages in Torah in this world is rewarded with several gates being opened to him, several lights to that world. Hence, when he passes away from this world, the Torah walks before him and goes to all the gate-keepers, declares and says, "Open the gates and let the righteous gentile in, set up a chair for so and so, the King's servant," for there is no joy to the Creator except in one who engages in the Torah. It is even more so with a man who awakens at night to engage in Torah, for all the righteous in the Garden of Eden listen to his voice and the Creator is among them.

91) A man who dwells in a city where there are bad people, and cannot keep the *Mitzvot* of the Torah, and does not succeed in the Torah changes his place, uproots himself from there, and strikes root in a place where good people with Torah and with *Mitzvot* dwell. The Torah is called "a tree," as it is written, "It is a tree of life for they who hold it." Also, man is a tree, as it is written, "For man is the tree of the field." The *Mitzvot* in the Torah are as fruits, and it is written about it, "Only the trees of which you

know that they are not trees for food, them you should destroy and cut down," destroy from this world and cut down from the next world. This is why he must uproot himself from that place where there are wicked, for he will not be able to succeed in Torah and *Mitzvot* there. He will plant himself elsewhere, among righteous, and will succeed in Torah and *Mitzvot*.

109-111) The righteous are indeed caught by the iniquities of the generation, but the righteous are caught by illnesses or sores to atone for the iniquities of the world, for then all the iniquities of the generation are pardoned, and by that the side of *Kedusha* rises and the *Sitra Achra* surrenders.

How do we know all that? From all the organs of the body. When all the organs are in trouble, and a great illness lies upon them, they need to strike one organ so that all will be healed. And which organ is struck? The arm. The arm is struck, blood is drained from it, and then there is healing to all the organs of the body.

So are people—they are organs with one another. When the Creator wishes to give healing to the world, He strikes a righteous one among them with diseases and afflictions, and for him, He gives healing to all. How do we know it? It is written, "And he was wounded because of our transgressions, oppressed because of our iniquities ... and by his bruising we are healed." "His bruising" means bloodletting, as one lets out blood from an arm, for by that bruise we are healed; it is healing for us, to all the organs of the body. He never strikes the righteous, except to heal a generation and to atone for their iniquities.

118) Oh how Israel are loved by the Creator. Their joy and their praises are only about Him, for so we learned—that any joy of Israel in which they do not include the Creator is not joy.

143-145) One day, a sage from the nations came to Rabbi Eliezer and said to him, "Old man, old man, three questions I would like to ask you:

"One: You say that another Temple will be built for you, but there can only be building twice, a first Temple and a second Temple that are written. You will not find a third Temple in the Torah. That which was for you to build had already been built, and there is never more in it, for the writing called them 'The two houses of Israel.' Also, it is written about the second Temple, 'The glory of that last house will be greater than the first.'

"Also, You say that you are closer to the High King than all other nations. One who is close to the King is always happy, without sorrow, fear, or troubles. But you are always afflicted, in trouble, and in more grief than all the people in the world. We, however, no affliction, trouble, or grief come upon us at all. Thus, we are close to the High King and you are far from Him, and this is why you are having sorrow, troubles, mourning, and grief, which we do not.

"And also, you do not eat carcass or none kosher so that you will be healthy and your body will be healthy. We eat whatever we want and we are robust in strength and in health, and all our organs exist. You, who do not eat, are all weak from bad illnesses and are more shattered than all the other nations. You are a people whom the Creator hates in every way. Old man, old man, tell me nothing for I will not hear you or take from you." Rabbi Eliezer raised his eyes, looked at him, and turned him into a pile of bones.

152) Israel were made by the Creator, the heart of the whole world. Hence, so are Israel among the nations, like a heart among the organs. And as the organs of the body cannot exist even a minute without the heart, all the other nations

cannot exist in the world without Israel. And so is Jerusalem among the rest of the countries, like a heart among the organs. Hence, it is in the middle of the whole world, like a heart, which is in the middle of the organs.

187) The evil inclination was given to every person so he may conquer it and ride on it. All the wholeness comes through the evil inclination, if he conquers it, as it is written, "With all your heart," meaning with both your inclinations—the good inclination and the evil inclination. It follows that if he is rewarded and rides on the evil inclination, he is rewarded.

It is written, "Who is mighty? He who conquers his inclination." If he conquers it, he is rewarded with all the wholeness. One who is rewarded with conquering it to a certain extent, the evil inclination becomes for him an ass to ride on, and the evil inclination never again afflicts him.

Then the evil inclination becomes for them an ass [Heb: Hamor], since Homer [matter/substance] has the letters of Hamor, as it is written about Abraham, "And [Abraham] saddled his ass," a poor riding an ass. It is so because they were rewarded with conquering the evil inclination until it became for them an ass to ride on to bring them to the wholeness.

442) The friends wept and said, "Woe Rabbi Shimon, when you part from the world, who will disclose such hidden and profound secrets, which have not been heard since the days of King Solomon until now? Happy is the generation that hears these words; happy is the generation that you are in it; woe unto a generation orphaned of you."

500) Once it was said, "Let us make man in our image after our own likeness," why does it say afterwards, "And God created the man in His own image"? He asked the angels about the creation of man. Some of them said, "Let him be created," and some of them said, "Let him not be created." The Creator created him, as it is written, "And God created the man in His own image." Thus, he did not place one portion in him from the angels, and he was not done in their form, but in the form of the king, in His image and after His own likeness, which is only the image of the likeness of His pattern.

504) Happy is he who exerts in the last exile to know Divinity, to honor her in all the *Mitzvot*, and to suffer for her several afflictions, as it is

written, "The bride's reward is affliction and sorrow," that is, "According to the sorrow, so is the reward," as it is written, "And he lied in that place." *Vayishkav* [and he lied] has the letters of *VeYesh* [and there are] *Chaf-Bet* [22], for if there are 22 letters of the Torah, meaning that he is complete in the Torah, Divinity lays with him.

546) The friends said, "If the Torah were not given on Mount Sinai, but the Creator would say, 'Here is Rabbi Shimon to give you My Torah and My secrets,' it would suffice the world. Woe, when you part from the world, who will light the candle of Torah? Everything will darken after that day, for until the arrival of the Messiah king, there will not be a generation as that generation that Rabbi Shimon is in."

709) Moses said, "These words are unclear and need to be explained for the friends, for one who closes before them the secrets of the Torah pains them. For the wicked, the lights of the secrets become darkness to them.

This is like concealed money. For one who digs until he finds it, and it is not his, it turns in his mind into darkness and gloom. But for the one that it is his, it shines. This is the reason why one should reveal the hidden secrets of Torah to the friends."

858) The *Ein Sof* is called "wise in all kinds of wisdoms, understanding in all kinds of understandings, devout in all kinds of *Hassadim* [mercies], mighty in all kinds of mighty deeds, a counsel in all kinds of counsels, righteous in all kinds of righteousness, and king in all kinds of kingships through *Ein Sof* [infinity] and unfathomably."

DEVARIM

[DEUTERONOMY]

VaEtchanan [I Pleaded]

1-2) How powerful is the force of Torah, and superior she is to everything. Anyone who engages in Torah does not fear upper ones or lower ones, and does not fear ill happenings in the world because he grips to the tree of life, the Torah, and eats from it each day.

The Torah teaches a person to walk in the path of truth. She teaches him counsel how to repent before his Master, and even if he is sentenced to death, everything is cancelled and departs from him, and does not stay over him. Therefore, we should engage in Torah day and night, and never part from her, as it is written, "And you shall meditate therein day and night." If he removes the Torah from himself or parts from her, it is as though he has parted from life.

8-9) When a person rises from his bed at midnight to engage in Torah, a herald calls on him and says, "Behold, bless the Lord all the servants of the Lord who stand in the house of the Lord in the nights." In the morning, when he stands in prayer before his Master, that herald calls on him and says, "And I have given you ways among them that are standing."

After he concludes his prayer with favor before his Master, he should devote his soul with the heart's desire to *Malchut*. There are several counsels for a person in everything. When he is in prayer, all those words that one utters from his mouth in that prayer rise up and breach airs and firmaments until they reach the place that they reach and crown in the head of the king, who makes a crown out of them.

32) In all of one's actions, he should see the Creator before him. Anyone who is walking along the road, who fears robbers, should aim for three things—a gift, a prayer, and a war—as did Jacob when he feared Esau. However, the most important of them is the prayer. But even though prayer is the most important, two or three friends engaging in words of Torah is the most important of all, for they do not fear robbers because Divinity is connected to them, for they are engaged in Torah.

35) The Creator is destined to open the eyes, for there has never been wisdoms that would gaze upon the upper wisdom and attain what they did not attain in this world, so they would

know their Master. Happy are the righteous who are rewarded with that wisdom, for there is no wisdom like that wisdom, no knowing like that knowing, and no adhesion like that adhesion.

47) One who loves the king does a great *Hesed* [grace/kindness]. He does *Hesed* with all. A greater *Hesed* is called "a true *Hesed*," when he does not desire reward for his works, but works only because of the love of the king, whom he loves dearly. For this reason, *Hesed* depends on the love of the king, which is why he is called "Abraham, who loves Me," for because he loved Him dearly, he multiplied *Hesed* in the world.

62) When a person comes to unify the name of the Creator, all the hosts of heaven stand in lines to be corrected and to all be included in that unification, to stand in one, in one unification. They are all properly corrected in their corrections through that unification.

69-70) It is a commandment [*Mitzva*] to love. The love of the Creator means that one should love Him with great love, as did Abraham, who loved the Creator with a great love and devoted his body and soul to Him. From this we learn that one who loves the Creator keeps ten utterances, ten *Sefirot*, above and below. For this reason, all those ten trials by which Abraham was tried and succeeded in all of them correspond to ten utterances because each trial is one utterance, one *Sefira*, an utterance by which he was tried and succeeded.

For this reason, there are ten trials opposite the ten *Sefirot*, and Abraham succeeded in all of them because he was tied and clung to the right of the Creator, which is called "great love," *Hesed de ZA*. It is called "great love," because one who stands in this love is tied to the upper world, which is ZA.

An everlasting love is the lower world, *Malchut*, to which the love of the Creator is tied. Everything—great love, everlasting love—are one without separation between them. The love transcends all the works in the world. With love, the Creator's name is glorified and blessed more than anything.

138) Since the day when Israel were exiled from their land there has not been joy before the Creator, and it is all because of the love that the Creator loved them, as it is written, "'I have loved you,' said the lord." This is why it is written, "And you shall love the Lord your

God." "And you shall love" means that one should connect to Him with sublime love, that any work that one should do for the Creator should be done with love, as there is no work like the love of the Creator.

139) There is nothing more favorable in the eyes of the Creator than one who loves Him properly, as it is written, "With all your heart." What does "With all" mean? It should have said "With all your heart," as well as "With all your soul," and "With all your might"; what is "With all your heart"? It comes to include both hearts—one good and one bad. "With all your soul" means with two souls—one good and one bad. "With all your might" means whether one comes into wealth by inheritance or whether he has earned it.

140-141) One who loves the Creator is crowned with Hesed [grace/mercy] from all sides, does Hesed to all, and cares not for his body or means. How do we know it? From Abraham, who because of his love for his Maker, cared not for his heart, for his soul, or for his means.

"For his heart" means that Abraham did not look after his own will for his love for his Master. "For his soul" means that he had no mercy for his son and his wife for his love for his Master. "For his means" means that he stood at a crossroads and offered food to the whole world. This is the reason why he was crowned with a crown of the *Sefira Hesed*, as it is written, "Mercy to Abraham."

One who is tied with the love of his Master is rewarded with it, and moreover, all the worlds are blessed for him. This is the meaning of what is written, "And Your pious ones shall bless You." Do not pronounce it "Shall bless You," but "Shall bless *Koh*," since the pious ones, those who have been rewarded with the *Sefira* of *Hesed*, will bless Divinity, who is called *Koh*. Thus, even Divinity is blessed because of them.

144) Happy are those in whom the love of their Master clung. There is no measure to the portion of those in that world.

145-147) The righteous have several sections above sections in that world. The highest among those sections is for those to whom love is their Master is connected, since their section ties to the palace that rises above all because by that, the Creator is crowned with love.

This palace, the highest of all, is called "love," and everything stands on love, as it is written, "Many waters cannot quench the love." Everything stands with love because the holy name, HaVaYaH, is so. The upper tip, Keter of Yod of HaVaYaH, Hochma, never parts from her because the Keter is on her with love, and never part from her. The letter Hey of HaVaYaH is Bina, from which the Yod, Hochma, never parts and they are always together in love, never parting from one another. Likewise is the Hey of HaVaYaH, as it is written, "And a river comes out of Eden," where the river, Bina, comes out of Eden, Hochma. Bina always comes out of Hochma, and they forever cling with love.

When Vav-Hey, Zeir Anpin and Malchut, cling to one another, they cling together in love, the groom with the bride, whose way is always in love. It follows that Yod with the first Hey, the first Hey with Vav, and Vav with the last Hey always connect to one another with love, and everything is called "love." Hence, one who loves the King becomes tied to that love, and this is why it is written, "And you shall love the Lord your God."

150-151) The evil inclination, what is it like? When it comes to bond with a person, it is like iron before it is placed in the fire. Once it is heated, it returns being entirely like fire.

When the evil inclination comes to bond with a person, it is like a person who sees the opening and sees that there is no one at home to stop him. He enters the house and becomes a guest there, and he sees that there is no one to stop him from leaving there to go on his way. Since he entered the house and there was no one to stop him, he became appointed over the house and became the landlord of the house, until he finds that the whole of the house is in his possession.

197) The amount of pleasure is according to the amount of the will to receive. However, it must be straightened so it is limited to receiving in order to bestow, and this is done by the lights of *Bina* because the will to receive will be corrected and straightened into being reception in order to bestow, and then the will to receive will not be corrupted as before. By that he is healed from all the blemishes that were in him.

New Zohar, VaEtchanan [I Pleaded]

11-13) The word *Ehad* [one] in "*Shema* Ysrael [Hear O Israel]."

The *Dalet* of *Ehad* is higher and bigger than the other letters. Likewise, the *Reish* of

Aher [other] is bigger than the other letters, to make a distinction so as to not replace the high and holy one, One God, and include the other side with Him, another god. The sign is that *Ayin Dalet* in "Hear O Israel" are big: the *Ayin* of *Shema* [hear], and the *Dalet* of *Ehad* are the letters *Ed* [witness] implying the need to testify a testimony to the secret of secrets, to elicit one measure for measuring the faith. One who knows that secret knows the secret of his Master and inherits two worlds—this world and the next world. Also, the measure is called "the measuring line."

This was given to the high and holy sages who know the meaning of their Master and exert in His glory. It was not given to the wicked of the world who do not know and do not care for the glory of their master. Those true righteous, on whom the meaning of the upper faith depends, were permitted to know and to look because they stray neither to the right nor to the left, but cling to the middle line.

93) One who knows the meaning of the wisdom can attain and make merits on all sides until he knows the upper secrets, the secrets of his Master, the secrets of the wisdom to know and

to attain. One who knows and regards, happy is he in this world and in the next world because that rule will correct a man's legs to enter the presence of the king and to walk on a straight path. Happy is he in this world and happy is he in the next world.

EKEV [BECAUSE]

1) **Each pleasure that a person enjoys from the Creator,** if he blesses for it, he raises that pleasure with the aim of the blessing for MAN to *Malchut*. By that, ZA and *Malchut* rise to *Bina*, where they receive *Mochin* and *Kelim* from which the abundance comes down to all the worlds, and for which the Creator delights the man.

7) **The Creator desires those who bless Him and His desire is for the blessing below** because that blessing rises and shines for the candle that does not shine, the *Malchut*, strengthening her with a great force to rise up to ZA for a *Zivug*. It is written about it, "I will honor those who honor Me," referring to those who honor the Creator.

8) **The secret of secrets for those who know the wisdom of their Master**—to know the secret of the blessings on the *Mitzvot* [commandments] of the Torah and on all the pleasures and delights of this world—is to impart blessings from above to below.

12) **Since the *Masachim* [screens] that separate between the halves of the degrees, between *KHB*,** and *Bina* and TM of each degree, are

considered doors. Without them it would not be possible for the lower one to rise to the upper one, since the whole ascent of the lower one to the upper one is only because of the *Bina* and *TM* of the upper one that fell to the lower one and clung to him.

For this reason, when they return to their degree in the upper one, they take the lower one along with them. And since that fall is done through the *Masach*, which is the connection of *Malchut* in *Bina*, and the ascent of *Bina* and ZON is done by fissuring the *Masach*, through the descent of *Malchut* from *Bina*, the *Masach* is considered a door because when it fissures, the lower one rises to the upper one through there. Thus, if the one who blesses aims in the blessing—in the word "Blessed"—to extend the name of the 42 letters, the *Masachim* open and fissure, meaning the doors in each degree, to raise the lower one to the upper one. At that time the blessing rises from *Bina* and *TM* at the end of the degrees through doors of all the degrees until it arrives in *Malchut de Atzilut*, since they all open and the blessing rises through them until it arrives in *Malchut de Atzilut*.

22) **There are three *Behinot* [discernments]: kneeling, bowing, and straightening up.**

1. **Kneeling** is the bending of the knees with his head held up. It means lack of GAR because the bending of the knees is annulment of NHY de Kelim, and one who lacks NHY de Kelim, lacks GAR of lights due to the inverse relation between lights and vessels. The straightening up of the head indicates desire to receive Hochma, which is that kneeling that we kneel in the word "Blessed," Malchut, indicating that Malchut needs Hochma because this is why the head is held straight, showing that she is devoid of Hochma. Hence, the knees are bent, showing that there is no GAR there.

2. **Bowing** of the head only indicates that he does not need Hochma, but Hesed, because he desires mercy. This is why he bows his head, which are Kelim de GAR. It is the right line of ZA, which receives from AVI and does not desire Hochma but Hassadim, and this is why we bow in the word "You," right line.

3. **Straightening up** is when all three parts of the body, HBD, HGT, NHY,

are upright. It indicates that he has *Hochma* and *Hassadim* together, hence his head is held up and his knees are straight. This is the middle line, *Tifferet*. This is why we straighten up in the word *HaVaYaH*, middle line, which includes everything.

KI TETZE [WHEN YOU GO OUT]

52) It is not the study that is the most important, but the act. Anyone whose fear of sin precedes his wisdom, his wisdom lasts.

105) It is with reason that the Creator said, "Anyone who engages in Torah, in doing *Hassadim*, and prays with the public, I commend him as though he has redeemed Me and My sons from among the idol worshippers."

But a number of people engage in Torah and in doing *Hassadim* and praying with the public, yet the Creator and His Divinity, Israel, are not redeemed? Indeed, it means that he should engage in Torah to unite Divinity with the Creator and not for any other aim. Doing *Hesed* [mercy/kindness] means that there is no *Hassid* [devoted/reverent/pious] except one who does *Hesed* with his Maker, when all the *Mitzvot* that he keeps are to redeem Divinity from exile through them, and not for any other aim. By that, he does *Hesed* with the Creator and he is called *Hassid*.

106) One who does *Hesed* with Divinity—to raise her from the exile—does *Hesed* with the Creator.

When Israel sinned and the Creator wished to afflict them, *Ima*—Divinity—was lying over them and prevented the Creator from afflicting them until they went astray. What did the Creator do? He exiled the king's children, Israel, along with the queen, Divinity. He swore that He would not return to His place until the queen returns to her place. Thus, one who does *Hesed* with Divinity and repents, and in all the Torah and her *Mitzvot* aims only to redeem Divinity from exile, does *Hesed* with his Maker and is seemingly redeeming Him and His Divinity and His children from the exile.

107-108) Elijah said, "Moses, you are that man. You are the son of the king and the queen, whose work toward the Creator is not even as one who does *Hesed* with his Maker, but as a son who is committed to brace himself and muster his strength to redeem his father and mother, who puts himself to death over them. One who is not the king's son and does *Hesed* with the king and the queen, it is certainly considered doing *Hesed* with his Maker. But you, who are the king's son, it is your duty, and not *Hesed*."

Moses rose and bowed to the ground before the Creator. He said, "So be it that I should be

considered a son, that my works for the Creator
and His Divinity will be to them as a son who
exerts among them for his father and mother,
whom he loves more than he loves himself,
his soul [Nefesh], his spirit [Ruach], and his soul
[Neshama], and regards all that he has as null and
nothing, to do with them the will of his father
and mother and to redeem them with them.
And although I know that everything is in His
possession and I have nothing to give Him, still,
the Merciful one desires man's heart—for it to
be ready for anything." At that time the Creator
came, kissed him, and said, "Moses, you are
indeed a son of Mine and of Divinity. Sages and
angels, kiss the son." All rose and kissed him, and
accepted him as great and as king over them.

128-129) Although the *Hey* of *Atzilut*, of the
name *HaVaYaH*, *Malchut*, supports everything,
you must not fly up and come down except
with *Malchut*.

As the organs of the body have no movement
but in the soul, the organs she has—her *Sefirot*—
spread over you to support you with them. So
is the *Hey*, like the sea. If she has *Kelim* to fill,
they are filled by her and she spreads in them
like streams extending from the sea to the earth.

If she has no *Kelim*, she is only *Hey*, without expansion of the streams.

So are Divinity's *Kelim*. Above they are holy angels, and below they are Israel. There are virtuous ones among them, with *Hesed*, mighty *Hassidim*, with Torah, Prophets, and Hagiographa, men of kingship of whom it was said "And who had strength to stand in the king's palace"—in the standing of the prayer in the king's palace, who is *ADNI*, her king—is *HaVaYaH*. They are wise and understanding, the heads of Israel, and not the heads of the mixed multitude, *Malchut*, spreading over them in her ten *Sefirot*. At that time the cause of causes comes down over her in *Yod-He-Vav-He* to come down on them, to raise Divinity over them.

142) The mother lies on the chicks. Israel tweet her with several tweets of prayers, yet she does not wish to come down to them to illuminate from above downward. She does not wish to change from *Katnut*, when she is lying and illuminates only from below upward. What do Israel do? They take the mother with them, meaning Divinity, and tie her with a knot of *Tefillin*. When they reach the *Shema* reading, her sons call out the six words of unification, "Hear

O Israel, the Lord our God, the Lord is one," *HGT NHY de* ZA from *Gadlut*. They come down to their mother, Divinity, and tie her with them in the unification, "Blessed be the name of the glory of His kingdom forever and ever."

It is written, "Which you shall call," calling the *VAK de Gadlut de* ZA to illuminate in Divinity. At that time she will illuminate the *Hassadim* from above downward, for it is her season and the time of her *Zivug*. It is written, "Seasons," "Which you shall call in My seasons," in my season.

New Zohar, Ki Tetze [When You Go Out]

2-3) One should place words of Torah over the evil inclination so it will break, for the evil inclination needs only words of Torah. This is why it is written, "And these words that I command you this day shall be upon your heart," meaning on both your inclinations, two hearts.

The good inclination, why does it need words of Torah? The good inclination crowns in words of Torah, and the evil inclination surrenders through words of Torah.

KI TAVO [WHEN YOU COME]

New Zohar, Ki Tavo [When You Come]

1) Rabbi Shimon escaped to the desert of Lod and hid in a cave, he and his son, Rabbi Elazar. A miracle happened to them and a carob tree came out, and a fountain of water. They ate of that carob and drank of those waters, and Elijah would come to them twice each day and teach them, and no one knew of them.

10) Come out and see, a king who loved his son, even though he cursed him and smote him, he loved him deeply. When he shows great anger, his mercy is over him. So is the Creator: although He cursed, His words are with love. On the surface, they seem as curses, but they are great good, because those curses were with love.

18-20) Since the day when the world was created the Creator did not disclose His might so it is seen in the world, nor a time of good will, except on the way to Egypt. "For whereas you have seen Egypt," in that same way and same manner will it be done to you.

Once all the other sides from the nations of the world gather over Israel, Israel will think that at that time they will be lost, and that they will be sold to their enemies, as it is written, "And there you shall sell yourselves." It does not write, "And you were sold," but "And you shall sell yourselves," meaning that you will think in your hearts that you have been sold. But it is not so, as it is written, "And no man shall buy," as there is no one who can rule over you.

All that will be at the end of days, and it all depends on repentance. One who has a heart will look and know to return to his Master.

21-22) Rabbi Shimon told him, "In which place did the redemption of Israel appear in those curses?" Elijah told him, "Look and behold the place that is worse than all the curses, there is the revelation of the time of redemption." He looked, beheld, and found.

37-39) "The fruit of the tree which is in the midst of the garden." This is the place in which spirits of people are concealed, the place called "the treasury of the souls," and it is with the Creator. He told them, "You will not exert to know how the spirits spread from My precious *Zivug*." The souls are born from a *Zivug* of ZA and *Malchut*. For this reason, there are males and females in the souls. It is known that the male light is poured from above downward in *GAR*, and female light is poured only from below upward, in *VAK*. For this reason, *Adam HaRishon* was commanded not to look at the elicitation of the souls from *Malchut*, who is the tree in the midst of the garden, for perhaps he would cling to male souls and he, too, would extend illumination of *Hochma* from that *Zivug* from above downward in the male light, for extension of *Hochma* from above downward is left without right and causes separation of ZA, the middle line, from *Malchut*, so that *Malchut* remains in left without right.

We learned about it, "If a woman inseminates and delivers a male child" is written, and not, "Comprising male and female," as in the souls, in which each soul consists of male and female. It is as is done in the world, where in this world the males and females do not conjoin as they came out above, in the souls that emerge from ZON, who come out in pairs—male and female together.

For this reason, pairs do not come out in this world, too, since *Adam HaRishon* and his *Zivug* sinned before the Creator. For this reason, when the souls come out from above and descend to this world, the males part from the females until the Creator desires to reunite them.

VaYelech [And Moses Went]

1) **Happy are Israel, whom the Creator desires. And because He desired them,** He called them, "Holy firstborn sons," brothers, as though He came down to live with them, as it is written, "And let them make Me a sanctuary, that I may dwell among them." He wished to correct them such as above, placed seven clouds of glory over them, and His Divinity walks before them.

16) **Woe to people who do not notice and do not engage in their Master's glory, nor regard the upper Kedusha [holiness], to be sanctified in this world and to be holy in the next world.**

27-28) **There it said "song," and here, "singing." "Song" is male, ZA, and "singing" is Nukva, Malchut.** Compared to Moses, all the prophets are as a monkey in the eyes of people. They said, "song," meaning "The Song of Songs," "A psalm, a song for the Sabbath day," and Moses said "singing." But should Moses not have said, "song," and they, "singing"? Yet, Moses did not say it to himself, but for Israel.

It is therefore clear that Moses was at a higher degree than all of them. Moses rose from below upward and they descended from above downward. Moses rose from below upward, as we learn that sanctity is increased, not decreased. Moses rose from below upward, saying the singing, which is the praise of the queen, who praises the king, and he began with *Malchut*, while Moses himself united with the king.

It follows that his singing rose from below upward, and they descended from above downward, saying a song, male, the praise, that the King praises the queen, and they united in the queen. It follows that their song is from above downward, from ZA to *Malchut*. Hence, by that, Moses' merit is recognized as more than all the others.

34-35) For this reason, a man should establish his Master's praise in the same way. First, from below upward, raising his Master's glory, *Malchut*, to a place from which the potion of the depth of the well pours forth, the place of *Bina*, and then to extend from above downward, from the potion of the stream, *Bina*, to every degree of ZAT, through the last degree, *Malchut*, to extend blessings to all from above downward. Afterwards a tie of faith must be tied to all, to connect everything to *Ein Sof*. This is a man who respects the name of his Master, to unify the holy name. This is why it is written, "For them that honor Me I will honor," meaning for those who honor Me in this world, I will honor in the next world.

"And they that despise Me shall be esteemed lightly." This is one who does not know how to unify the holy name and tie the knot of faith, to extend blessings to the required place, and to honor the name of his Master. Anyone who does not know how to honor his Master's name would be better off not being born.

37-39) When Israel below keep their answering of Amen and aim their hearts as they should, several doors of blessing open above, there is much goodness in all the world, and there is joy in everything. What is Israel's reward for causing it? Their reward is in this world and in the next world.

In this world, when they are afflicted and they pray their prayer before their Master, the voice declares through all the worlds, "Open the gates and let in the righteous, loyal nation." Do not pronounce it "loyal," but Amens [a similar pronunciation in Hebrew], who observe their answering Amen. "Open the gates," as Israel opened the gates of blessings for them, now open the gates and let the prayer of those who are afflicted be answered.

This is their reward in this world. What is their reward in the next world? When a man who observed answering Amen departs this world, what does he observe? That is, he observe that blessing which the sayer blesses and he waits for him to answer after it, "Amen," as he should? At that time, his soul rises and declares before him, "Open the gates before him," as he opened the gates each day when he was loyal, meaning Amens.

What is Amen? Amen is the spring of the stream that extends, *Bina*. It is called Amen, as it is written, "And I was beside Him as an apprentice." Do not pronounce it *Amon* [apprentice], but Amen. Keeping all the degrees—that river that stretches out, *Bina*—is called "Amen," as it is written, "From the world and to the world," from the world above, *Bina*, to the world below, *Malchut*. Here, too, Amen and Amen, Amen of above, *Bina*, Amen of below, *Malchut*. Amen means keeping of them all.

9) Israel are happier than all the idol-worshipping nations because all the other nations were given to appointed ministers to rule over them, but holy Israel are happy in this world and in the next world, for the Creator neither gave them to an angel nor to another ruler. Rather, He held them in His own portion, as it is written, "For the portion of the Lord is His people."

24) Happy are Israel, for the Creator leads them. It is written about them, "For the Lord has chosen Jacob for Himself, Israel for His *Segula* [virtue/remedy/merit]." It is also written, "For the Lord will not abandon His people." "The Lord will not abandon His people" for His great name because they clung to one another, for Israel clung to His great name. This is why the Creator will not leave them, for wherever they are, the Creator is with them.

25-27) Rabbi Shimon arose, sat, laughed, and was merry. He said, "Where are the friends?" Rabbi Elazar arose and let them in. They sat before him. Rabbi Shimon raised his hands and prayed a prayer and was merry. He said, "Those friends who were at Idra Raba [Aramaic: "Great Circle" or "Great Assembly," see appendix], let them come in here. Everyone left, and Rabbi Elazar, his son, Rabbi Aba, Rabbi Yehuda, Rabbi Yosi, and Rabbi Hiya remained. In the meantime, Rabbi Isaac came in. Rabbi Shimon said to him, "How good is your portion, what gladness should be added to you on this day." Rabbi Aba sat behind his shoulders and Rabbi Elazar before him.

Rabbi Shimon said, "It is a good time now and I would like to come to the next world without shame. Thus, I wish to disclose before Divinity sacred things that I have not disclosed thus far, lest it is said that I departed from the world deficient. Thus far, they have been hidden in my heart to enter with them into the next world.

"This is how I am arranging you: Rabbi Aba will write, Rabbi Elazar will learn orally, and the rest of the friends will speak in their hearts."

29-31) Rabbi Shimon said, "How odd is this hour, from Idra Raba [Aramaic: "Great Circle" or "Great Assembly," see appendix] in the portion *Nasso* [take], since in the Idra, the Creator and His *Merkavot* [chariots/assemblies] came, and now, the Creator is here, for he came with the righteous in the Garden of Eden, which did not happen in the Idra. The Creator desires the glory of the righteous more than His own glory, and now the Creator desires our glory, for all the righteous in the Garden of Eden have come with Him."

Rabbi Shimon said, "But Rabbi Hamnuna Saba is here with 70 righteous around him engraved in crowns, each illuminating from the radiance of the brightness of Holy *Atik*, the most hidden of all that are hidden, and he comes with joy to hear those words that I am saying." While he was seated, he said, "But Rabbi Pinhas son of Yair is here, set up his place." The friends who were there shook up, arose, and sat at the corner of the house, and Rabbi Elazar and Rabbi Aba remained before Rabbi Shimon. Rabbi Shimon said, "We were in the Idra Raba when all the friends would speak and I was with them. Now only I am speaking and everyone will listen to my words, upper and lower. Happy am I on this day."

He said, "I am for my beloved and on me is His passion. All the days that I was tied to this world, I was tied in a single tie to the Creator. For this reason, now, 'On me is His passion,'" for He and His entire camp have come with joy to hear hidden words and the praise of Holy *Atik*, the most hidden of all that are hidden, the secluded and separated from all, which is not separated because everything cleaves to him and he cleaves to everything; he is everything."

91) Rabbi Shimon said, "I have not disclosed everything, and all those words were hidden in my heart thus far, and I wanted to conceal them for the next world because in the next world we are asked a question with wisdom, for wisdom is what they want from us." This is why he concealed the words for the next world. But now I see that the Creator's wish is to disclose them so I may enter His palaces without shame.

95-97) All the words in the Idra Raba [Aramaic: "Great Circle" or "Great Assembly," see appendix] are good, and all are holy words, words that do not stray to the right or to the left. They are all hidden words that are revealed to those who entered the wisdom and came out of it in wholeness. All the secrets are like that—revealed only to those who came in and came out. Until now, these words that I have disclosed here were covered because I feared revealing them, but now they have been revealed. The holy *Atik* is revealed before me, for it is not for my own glory nor for the glory of my father's house that I had done it. I did it so I would not enter His palace in shame, for I saw that the Creator and all those true righteous that are here all permitted me to disclose them, for I saw that they were all glad with this joy of mine. All are summoned in that world to my joy, happy am I.

Now I testify about me that all the days that I was standing in the world, I craved to see that day when I would have permission to disclose the secrets, but it did not come to me until now, for in this crown of disclosure of secrets is this day crowned. And now I wish to disclose matters before the Creator, for all the secrets I am revealing are crowned in my head, and that day will not go far from coming to its place in that world as another day. It is so because I have the whole of this day in my possession, and not more, and now I am beginning to disclose the matters so that I may not enter the next world with shame. Here am I beginning to speak.

98-102) "Justice and law are the foundation of Your throne; mercy and truth go before You."

Whoever is wise will look at it to see the ways of the high and holy one, that they are true *Dinim* [judgments], *Dinim* that are crowned by the upper *Sefirot*. I see that all the lights illuminate from the upper illumination that is more hidden than all that are hidden, *Atik*, all the degrees in which to illuminate, and each with a unique illumination. In the light within each degree, a unique revelation is revealed, and all the lights grip that light to this light, and this light to that light, illuminating in one another and never parting from one another.

The light within each illumination, which are called "the king's corrections," the king's *Sefirot*, each light illuminates and grips to that light that is deep within, the light of *Ein Sof*, which does not spread out, and in which there is no perception whatsoever. For this reason, everything rises by one degree and everything is crowned by one thing, and one does not part from the other, He and His name are one. He is the light that appears, called "the king's garment." The light that is deep within all the lights is a hidden light, and in it is that one which does not spread out and does not appear, *Ein Sof*.

All the illuminations and all the lights illuminate from the holy *Atik*, the most hidden of all that are hidden, the upper illumination. When looking, it is not present in all the lights that expand from *Atik*, but only the upper hidden illumination, and it is not revealed.

There are two illuminations in those garments of glory, garments of truth, corrections of truth, and illuminations of truth, the correction of the king's throne, *Bina*. They are called "justice and law." ZA is law, *Malchut* is justice. They are the beginning and the wholeness of all the faith. Justice is initially, and the disclosure of the wholeness in justice is called "law." All the *Dinim* above and below are crowned in them, and everything is hidden in law, in ZA, and in justice, in *Malchut*, nourished by the law, ZA. Sometimes *Malchut* is called as it is written, "Melchizedek king of Shalem [whole]."

When *Dinim* awaken from the law, they are all *Rachamim*; they are all in wholeness, since the law perfumes the justice, *Dinim*, the *Dinim* are mitigated, and all come down to the world in wholeness, in *Rachamim*. That is the time when male and female unite and all the worlds are in mercy and joy.

110) All my life I have been looking at the verse that reads, "My soul shall be glorified in the Lord; the humble shall hear and be merry," and now the verse has come true. "My soul shall be

glorified in the Lord," for my soul is gripped to Him. In Him she blazes, to Him she cleaves and exerts, and in that exertion she will rise to her place. "The humble shall hear and be glad." All those righteous and all those at the great seminary, and the righteous who now came with Divinity are hearing my words and are glad. For this reason, "O magnify the Lord with me, and let us exalt His name together."

201) When he entered the cave they heard a voice inside the cave. That man was quaking the land, irritating from *Malchut*, several slanderers in the firmament are quieted on this day for you. This is Rabbi Shimon, whose Master praises every day. Happy is he above and below. Several high treasures are kept for him. It was said about him, "And you, go to the end and rest and rise again for your fate at the end of the right."

209) "For I will call on the name of the Lord."

The end of the verse ties the knot of faith to what is written, "He," as it is written, "For He is righteous and just." That is, He is everything; He is one, without separation. If you say that all those names in the texts are many, he repeated and said that it is written, "He," that all rise and connect and unite in the One. He is everything;

He was, He is, and He will be; He is one. Blessed be His name forever and for all eternity. This is why the words connect, and the holy words of the name of the Creator unite.

210) Happy is he who calls on the king and knows how to call on Him properly. If he calls and does not know whom he is calling, the Creator moves away from him, as it is written, "The Lord is near to all who call Him." To whom is He close? He repeats, "To all who call Him in truth." But is there anyone who would call Him falsely? It is one who calls and does not know whom he is calling.

How do we know? Because it is written, "To all who call Him in truth." What is "In truth"? In the seal of the king's ring, the middle line, the seal of the *Mochin* with the *Malchut*, who is called "the king's ring, for she is the wholeness of everything. One who does not know how to call Him in the measure of the middle line, but leans to the left line or to the right line, the Creator moves away from him. Happy is he who enters in wisdom and comes out in wholeness, to know the ways of the Creator.

229) Rabbi Isaac said, "When we sit before Rabbi Shimon, everything is said before him openly

and we do not need to cover the matters with names and appellations. Rabbi Shimon is not like the rest of the people, or everyone compared to him are as the rest of the prophets compared to Moses."

232) As the Creator does not forget His name, the Creator does not forget Israel, for they are gripped to His very name.

Ketuvim

[Hagiographa]

SONG OF SONGS

New Zohar, Song of Songs

87-88) The Song of Songs is the praise of praises to the king that peace is his, *Bina*, for he is the place that needs joy, where there are no anger or *Din* because the next world, *Bina*, is all joy, delighting everyone. For this reason, it sends gladness and joy to all the degrees.

As the awakening of gladness should be evoked from this world upward, joy and gladness should be evoked from the world of the moon, *Malchut*, toward the upper world, *Bina*. Therefore, the worlds stand in a different manner and the awakening rises only from below upward.

90) The one with eyes gathers embers of fire and organs of fire, which enter the palace, *Zvul*, the palace where all the praises are set to rise. It is a palace in which there are 1,006 degrees that rise by the praise of the praises. In the midst of them all is a degree that is more internal than all, where the love of that praise is sorted, the sorting of the bottom point. When it has been sorted out from among everyone, she rises in a song, and she is called "The Song of Songs."

She rises above all those praises and is sorted out from all of them.

99-100) Several times the Creator admonished Israel to return them in repentance to Him, so they would take the right path to rise among them. This is because when Israel are worthy and walk on the straight path, it is seemingly an ascent to the Creator with them from all the nations of the world, for when Israel are worthy and walk on the straight path, the Creator raises them above all the people in the world, and everyone thanks and praises Him. But not only they, even the upper ones above all thank Him for Israel. Even more, He actually rises in His glory thanks to Israel. And better yet, even Israel actually rise by the glory of the Creator above and below.

When Israel are clean, the throne above—*Malchut*—rises ever upward by several joys, several love, the worlds—ZA and *Malchut*—conjoin in gladness, all are blessed from the depth of the streams, *Bina*, and all the worlds are watered, blessed, and sanctified in several blessings, several sanctities, and the Creator delights in them with joy in wholeness.

105-106) When Solomon built the Temple, and the lower world—*Malchut*—was completed like the upper world—*Bina*—Israel were all clean and rose several high degrees. Then the throne, *Malchut* rose with joy in several joys and several measures.

Then "The song of songs, which is Solomon's" rose with joy and descended with joy, all the worlds were with joy, and the bonding was with joy. A song to the Creator is when *Malchut* sings to the Creator. The songs are to the upper and lower, to the bonding of ZA and *Malchut* through *Yesod*, which unites them with one another. "Which is Solomon's" is the bonding of all the worlds in gladness, to the king that peace is his, *Bina*.

114-117) When King Solomon came and the Temple was built, and all the worlds were of one weight above and below, and ZA and *Malchut* were face-to-face, equal to each other, then that six, *Malchut*, who receives and collects all those upper 60, *HGT NHY de* ZA, was opened.

Six was opened, *Malchut*, when those 60 upper ones were opened, *HGT NHY de* ZA. And when the six, *Malchut*, was opened, blessings came out to the world. It was opened when the slant serpent that sits by its feet was removed from it. The slant serpent is the verse of *SAM*, the source of all the *Klipot* and evil. And when this one was over, the six became a song and the good treasure was opened. It is written about it, "The Lord will open unto you His good treasure." By whose force was it opened? The heaven, the remaining 60, *HGT NHY de ZA*, who is called "heaven." The songs are *HGT NHY de ZA*, which were all opened and established to give food to all the worlds.

Then it is written, "And Judah and Israel dwelt safely, every man under his vine and under his fig-tree." And it is also written, "Eating and drinking and being merry," since six, *Malchut*, and sixty, *HGT NHY de ZA*, were opened and all the upper delights were coming down to all the worlds, and all were delighted to go up to the upper world, *Bina*, to gather blesses and delights for the worlds. Then love for the upper king, *ZA*, evokes out of them, for all to be one, *ZA* and *Malchut* without separation. At that time the praise that transcends all praises to the king that peace is his, *Bina*, is that everything will be in gladness above and below.

217-218) "Draw me, we will run after you." It is written, "And I shall place My Temple among you."

The Creator placed His Divinity among Israel so she would lay over them as a mother over the sons, protecting them on all sides. As long as the holy mother, Divinity, sits over Israel, the Creator comes to dwell with them because the Creator never leaves Divinity, and all the love above is in her.

For this reason, the Creator has placed her as a collateral in the midst of Israel, so they might know that He will not forget them and would never leave them because of the collateral within them. Divinity says to the Creator, "I was collateral amidst the lower ones, I shall be collateral with You, so you will not forget my sons. To rise before You, me and my sons will run after You."

363) Many are included in the name *Elokim*, and it is entirely one name, since the first name, *HaVaYaH*, ZA, drew the last one over there— *Elokim*, *Malchut*—and then everything is one bonding for all the upper degrees of ZA. The lower ones, those of *Malchut*, connect to one another so they are all one connection, one bonding, and one unification.

480-481) Happy are those who engage in Torah to know the wisdom of their Master. They know and look at high secrets. When a person departs from this world and repents, and only transgressions that death atones remain for him, through the death, all the *Dinim* in the world depart from him. Moreover, 13 gates from the secrets of the pure persimmon—on which high wisdom hangs—open for him.

Even more, the Creator engraves him in the garment of kingship where all the forms are engraved. The Creator plays with him in the Garden of Eden and bequeaths him two worlds: this world and the next world.

482-483) **The wisdom that one should know**: to know and to observe the secret of his Master, to know himself, to know who he is, how he was created, where he comes from and where he is going, how the body is corrected, and how he will be judged by the King of All.

To know and to observe the secret of the soul. What is the soul within him? Where does it come from, and why does it come into this body, which is a foul drop that is here today, and in the grave tomorrow? To know the world one is in, and for what will the world be corrected; to gaze upon the sublime secrets of the Upper World, and to know one's Master. And one observes all that from within the secrets of the Torah.

485-486) The soul says to the Creator, "Tell me the secrets of the sublime wisdom, how You lead and govern the Upper World; teach me the secrets of the wisdom that I have not known and not learned thus far, so I will not be shamed among those High Degrees, among which I come."

The Creator replies to the soul, "If you know not, O fairest among women," if you have come and did not gaze in the wisdom before you came here, and you do not know the secrets of the Upper World, "go thy way," for you are not worthy of entering here without knowledge. "Go thy way by the footsteps of the flock," reincarnate in the world and become knowing by these "footsteps of the flock." Those are human beings that people trample with their heels, for they consider them lowly; but they are the ones who know their Master's sublime secrets. From them will you know how to observe and to know, and from them will you learn.

496) Elijah said to Rabbi Shimon: "Happy are you that the secrets of your Master shine before you like the light of the sun. Because of it, all the words from your mouth are engraved above. I am happy that I have heard them from your mouth.

Happy are you in this world and happy are you in the next world. The meaning of that matter was hanging before the holy king, and was not disclosed to all the hosts above. Who is it who disclosed it now in this verse? It is you. Happy are you in this world and in the next world."

515) Rabbi Shimon was happy and said, "First, before these words of the Song of Songs were revealed, I was weeping and sad. Now that these words have been revealed, I am happy. I say, 'Happy am I for having been rewarded with such degrees, that sublime matters of above have been revealed.'"

630-631) "And God said, 'Let us make man in our image, after our own likeness.'"

When the Creator created the upper world, ZA, and the lower world, *Malchut*, both were of the same form—one was like the other. When the Creator wished to create the man below, He wished to make him like the two worlds, making his form similar to the two worlds.

All the secrets of above and of below are in man. The skull of the head that is on the body is the upper world with those corrections in the head. The body, *HGT*, is the body of above, whose degrees stand in organs under the head. The thighs and the legs are *NHY*, and all are in degrees below, as it should be such as above. The Creator engraved in man all the upper and lower forms so that man would be whole in everything.

632-633) When the Creator desires a person, all his steps and all his roads are set before Him and He corrects them, each one as it should be, and his way will be favorable even in worldly matters.

If a person sets his mind, will, and heart on the holy king, to walk in His ways, which He has made by Himself, the Creator desires him as if those ways were His very own.

Ruth

New Zohar, Ruth

2) Everything that the Creator created in His world, He created only for His glory, as it was said, "All that is called by My name, and for My glory I have created it, formed it, and even made it." The Creator created the man in the world and placed His name in him, *HaVaYaH*.

8-12) When a person is made out of a drop in his mother's placenta, as he grows the Creator gradually instills within him a spirit and a soul. A candle is placed over his head at night, as it is said, "When His candle shone above my head," and a pillar of light by day, as it was said, "And the pillar of cloud journeyed ... and by night in a pillar of fire ... to go by day and by night." It was said, "For a candle is a *Mitzva* and the Torah is light." *Malchut*, who governs at night, is called "A candle of *Mitzva*," and ZA, who is called Torah, governing the day, is called "And the Torah is light."

He is taught the whole of the Torah and he is taught all the *Mitzvot*, and he is told, "See that this is a winding road," which is called "night." In that place, all the souls of people shall come up, as it was said, "Small and great are there, and a servant is free from his master."

He is shown in the pillar of fire that is on his head several bears and leopards and lions, and sabotaging angels sitting there. And there is a dog there. David said about that, "Deliver my soul from the sword; my only one from the power of the dog." That place is darkness, and sabotaging angels call him in the nights. He said about it, "For fear at nights." They are actually called "nights."

He is told, "If you are rewarded with *Mitzvot*, each and every *Mitzva* will make of him a good angel for you. When you come with this hoe and are rewarded with *Mitzvot* they will say, "Build up, build up, clear the way, remove every obstacle out of the way of so and so," and the sabotaging angels will not rule over you.

Similarly, during the day they say, "If you are rewarded with the Torah, each and every letter will be an angel who will help you in this place." The Torah is called "way." Walk in this way so they do not govern you. He said about it, "To show them the way." Afterwards they will show him the Garden of Eden and each part within it for the righteous himself, and he is sworn to keep the whole Torah.

123) Rabbi Hiya said, "And the path of the righteous is as the light of dawn, shining more and more until the perfect day."

One who walks on the way should have with him one with whom to speak of words of Torah. So is the path of the righteous, shining more and more, walking, and words of Torah with him, and the Torah is light. "Until the perfect day," until Divinity partakes with him and does not move from him. We learned that wherever there are words of Torah, Divinity is there, as it is said, "In every place where I mention My name."

152) "And you shall love the Lord your God with all your heart," with both your inclinations—the good inclination and the evil inclination. All are needed as one.

155) The Creator created in man four letters *Yod-Hey Vav-Hey*, which are His holy name. He created in him a soul to a soul, which is called "man," and in which the lights spread in nine lights *KHB HGT NHY*, and *Ateret Yesod* complements them to ten. They hang down from *Yod de HaVaYaH*, and they are one light without separation.

169) Any gentile who repents and parts from idol-worship and from transgressions, the Creator will instill within him a holy spirit and a holy soul. And therefore, he has a part in the next world.

187) There is not a person in the world who does not have those two fires, which are called "the evil inclination" and "the good inclination." The Creator gave them to people to guide them with them.

217-218) "And the Lord God planted a garden in Eden on the east."

When the Creator created *Adam HaRishon*, He created him from the Temple. He took from the dust of the Temple and created him. Once He had created him and he stood on his legs, all the creatures came to bow before him.

What did the Creator do? He took him from there, placed him in the Garden of Eden, and made for him ten canopies, such as the *Yod*, canopies that the Creator would make for the righteous in the Garden of Eden in the future, and the ministering angels were descending and ascending and being merry before him, and He gave him high wisdom.

222-224) "The Lord is near to all who call Him, to all who call Him in truth." Man's desire is more important to the Creator than all the sacrifices and offerings in the entire world. When one puts his will in repentance, there is not a gate in all the firmaments that will not be open before him. Man's sacrifice depends on the heart and on the will, as it is written, "And he shall confess wherein he has sinned." He confessed to it, and it all depends on the heart. There is none closer to the face of the Creator than a man's heart. It is more favorable to Him than all the sacrifices and offerings in the entire world.

228-235) In the whole world, nothing stands before the Creator but man's repentance and prayer.

There are three kinds of repentance in that text—prayer, plea, and tear—and all are written in that verse: "Hear my prayer, O Lord, and give ear unto my plea; keep not silence at my tear."

All three are important to the Creator, but of all of them, none is as important as the tear, for in tears the heart, the will, and the entire body awaken and go, and in these 13 gates they come before the Creator.

It is written about prayer, "Hear," as it is written, "Hear my prayer, O Lord." It writes a plea in it, as it is written, "And give ear unto my plea." A tear is not like them, but more than everyone, as it is written, "Keep not silence at my tear."

A prayer, sometimes a person prays his prayer and the Creator hears but does not wish to grant his wish, and He is silent toward him and does not watch over him, for only hearing is written in regard to it.

A plea is more important than a prayer, for he cries out with the heart's desire before his Master. And because he places more of his desire, it is written about it, "Give ear," as though lending His ear to the matter. And yet He is silent and does not wish to grant his wish. But a tear is with the heart and with the desire of the entire body. This is why it is written about it, "Keep not silence at my tear."

Not all the tears come before the king. Tears of anger and tears of one who slanders his friend do not come before the king. But tears of prayer and of repentance, and those who pray out of their plight, all those breach firmaments and open gates and come before the king.

On the day when the Temple was ruined, all the gates were locked, but the gates of tears were not locked. It is written in Hezekiah, "I have heard your prayer, I have seen your tear," meaning actual seeing out of the tears.

In the future, it is written, "And the Lord God shall wipe off the tear from every face." There are tears for better and there are tears for worse. For better—when they are of the good inclination; for worse—when they are of the evil inclination. It is written about tears in plight and tears of prayer, "They shall come with weeping and with supplications will I lead them."

245) Happy are the friends who engage in Torah, and those who purify others so they can engage in Torah.

349-353) "With my soul I have desired You in the night; even with my spirit within me I seek You."

"With my soul I have desired You." The Creator has placed within man two good forms to serve in this world, *Nefesh* and *Ruach* [soul and spirit]. The *Nefesh* is to sustain the body with the *Mitzvot* that awaken from it. The *Ruach* is to awaken in the Torah and to lead him in this world. If the *Nefesh* is rewarded with *Mitzvot* and the *Ruach* is rewarded with engaging in Torah, additional *Gadlut* [greatness/adulthood] comes down on him from above—*Neshama*, *Haya*, *Yechida*—according to his ways.

With those two—*Nefesh* and *Ruach*—the man walks in this world and uses them, for that *Nefesh* exists in a body only when the *Ruach* that is on it awakens.

When a person comes to serve and to work his Master with those two, *Nefesh* and *Ruach*, a holy awakening awakens on him from above and remains in the man, surrounding him on all sides. It awakens supernal wisdom in him in to reward him with being in the king's palace.

That awakening on him is from a high place, from *Bina*. What is its name? Its name is *Neshama*. From her a man awakens to make repentance and good deeds, and she is a high force, the power of repentance, who is *Bina*, called "repentance." She is the mother of *Ruach*, who extends from ZA, and the *Ruach* is her son, for ZA is the son of *Bina*.

The *Neshama* has a supernal lover. What is his name? His name is *Neshama* to *Neshama*, which is the light of *Haya* that extends from *Hochma*. She is called "the father of the *Ruach*," from ZA, since HB are AVI to ZA. From her, fear, love, Torah, and *Mitzva* awaken to a person, as they extend from father and mother, son and daughter. Fear and love extend from HB, who are called "father and mother." Torah and *Mitzva* extend from ZA and *Malchut*, who are called "son and daughter" of *HB*. *Yod* of the name *HaVaYaH*, *Hochma*, is father. *He* [*Hey* without the *Yod*] is *Bina*, mother. *Vav* is *ZA*, son, and the bottom *Hey*, *Malchut*, is the daughter. This is the full *HaVaYaH*.

452-456) Happy are Israel, for they always excel in *Mitzvot*—when they sit, when they walk, when they lay, and when they rise.

Israel should always be crowned in Torah and *Mitzvot*, to always cling to the Creator, as it is written, "And you who cleave to the Lord your God are alive everyone of you this day." Anyone who clings to his Maker is never harmed.

Moreover, two ministering angels accompany a person, one on the right and one on the left, as it is written, "For He will command His angels for you to keep you in all your ways." Moreover, if he is always in *Mitzvot*, the Creator seemingly becomes his guardian, as it is written, "The Lord keeps you."

What does the Creator do? He takes an angel who walks to his right and places him before him, while he stands in his place, as it is written, "The Lord is your shadow on your right hand." And He places that angel, which is to his left, behind the person, and the Creator on the right and on the left, thus the person is kept from all his sides. Who can harm him?

For this reason, one should not be without Torah and without *Mitzvot* for even an hour. In his house, the Creator keeps him from the outside, and the man from inside.

642) Rabbi Akiva said, "Since the day when the Temple was ruined, champions of counsel have been cut off, the views have been faulty, the heart does not exist in full, and everything follows the appearance."

691) Happy is he who exerts to know in that world where the souls are. One who knows in it and exerts to know it, there is no measure to his wisdom.

737) Happy are they who bless and sanctify their Master each day with the heart's desire.

TRANSLATION AND EXPLANATION OF ACRONYMS AND TERMS

Acronyms & Terms	Expansion/Translation	
AA	Arich Anpin	Long Face
AB	72 in Gematria	HaVaYaH filled with Yods
ABYA	Atzilut, Beria, Yetzira, Assiya	
Adam HaRishon		The First Man
AHP	Awzen, Hotem, Peh	Ear, Nose, Mouth
AK	Adam Kadmon	Ancient Man
AVI	Aba ve Ima	Father and Mother
BON	52 in Gematria	the name HaVaYaH filled with Heys
BYA	Beria, Yetzira, Assiya	
Chazeh		Chest
Din		Judgment
Ein Sof		Infinity

ELEH	*Aleph-Lamed-Hey*	Lower part of the name *Elokim*
Elokim	God	
Gadlut	Greatness/adulthood	
GAR	*Gimel Rishonot*	First Three (*Sefirot* in a *Partzuf*)
GE	*Galgalta Eynaim*	Skull and Eyes
GE AHP	*Galgalta, Eynaim, Awzen, Hotem, Peh*	Skull, Eyes, Ear, Nose, Mouth
Gematria	Numeric value of the letters and their combinations.	
HaVaYaH	*Yod-Hey-Vav-Hey*	
HB	*Hochma* and *Bina*	
HB TM	*Hochma, Bina, Tifferet, Malchut*	
HBD	*Hochma, Bina, Daat*	
HBD HGT NHY	*Hochma, Bina, Daat, Hesed, Gevura, Tifferet, Netzah, Hod, Yesod*	
HBD HGT NHYM	*Hochma, Bina, Daat, Hesed, Gevura, Tifferet, Netzah, Hod, Yesod, Malchut*	
HG	*Hassadim and Gevurot*	

HG TM	Hesed, Gevura, Tifferet, Malchut
HGT	Hesed, Gevura, Tifferet
HGT NHY	Hesed, Gevura, Tifferet, Netzah, Hod, Yesod
HGT NHYM	Hesed, Gevura, Tifferet, Netzah, Hod, Yesod, Malchut
HS	Hochma Stimaa	Blocked (hidden) Hochma
Ibur	Conception/impregnation	
Idra Raba	"Great Circle" or "Great Assembly" This is the name of the cave where Rabbi Shimon and his students hid from the Romans and wrote *The Zohar*. Also, the title of one of the parts in *The Zohar*.	
Katnut	Smallness/infancy	
KH	Keter, Hochma	
KHB	Keter, Hochma, Bina	
KHB HGT NHY	Keter, Hochma, Bina, Hesed, Gevura, Tifferet, Netzah, Hod, Yesod	
KHB HGT NHYM	Keter, Hochma, Bina, Hesed, Gevura, Tifferet, Netzah, Hod, Yesod, Malchut	

KHB TM	*Keter, Hochma, Bina, Tifferet, Malchut*	
KHBD	*Keter, Hochma, Bina, Daat*	
Kli (plural: *Kelim*)	Vessel	
MA	45 in *Gematria*	The name *HaVaYaH* filled with *Alephs*
MAD	*Mayin Duchrin*	Male Water (Aramaic)
MAN	*Mayin Nukvin*	Female Water (Aramaic)
Masach	Screen	
Merkava (pl. *Merkavot*)	Chariot/Assembly/Structure	
MI	Mem Yod	Upper part of the name *Elokim*
Mitzva (pl. *Mitzvot*)	Commandment/Precept—correction of the desire into having the aim to bestow.	
Mocha Stimaa	Blocked (hidden) Mind	
Mochin	Lights of *Hochma*	
NE	*Nikvey Eynaim*	Sockets of the Eyes

New Zohar	Additional interpretations to the Bible that were added after the first interpretations were compiled, hence the title, New Zohar.	
NH	Netzah, Hod	
NHY	Netzah, Hod, Yesod	
NHYM	Netzah, Hod, Yesod, Malchut	
NR	Nefesh, Ruach	
NRN	Nefesh, Ruach, Neshama	
NRNHY	Nefesh, Ruach, Neshama, Haya, Yechida	
PBP	Panim be Panim	Face-to-Face
Rachamim	Mercy/mercies	
RADLA	Reisha de Lo Etyada	The Unknown Rosh (head)
Rashbi	Rabbi Shimon bar Yochai	
RTS	Rosh, Toch, Sof	Head, Interior (middle), End
SAG	63 in Gematria	HaVaYaH filled with Yods and Aleph in the Vav

SAM	Angel Sam'el	
Sitra Achra	Other Side	
TANTA	*Taamim, Nekudot, Tagin, Otiot*	Flavors, points, tags, letters
TM	*Tifferet, Malchut*	
TNHYM	*Tifferet, Netzah, Hod, Yesod, Malchut*	
Tzimtzum	Restriction	
Tzimtzum Aleph	First Restriction	
Tzimtzum Bet	Second Restriction	
VAK	*Vav* (six) *Ktzvot* (edges)	The bottom six *Sefirot* of a *Kli*
Yenika	Nursing/suckling	
YESHSUT	*Ysrael Saba ve Tevuna*	
ZA	*Zeir Anpin*	Small Face
ZAT	*Zayin Tachtonot*	Seven lower *Sefirot*
ZON	*Zeir Anpin* and *Nukva*	

FURTHER READING

To help you determine which book you would like to read next, we have divided the books into six categories—Beginners, Intermediate, Advanced, Good for All, Textbooks, and For Children. The first three categories are divided by the level of prior knowledge readers are required to have in order to easily relate to the book. The Beginners Category requires no prior knowledge. The Intermediate Category requires reading one or two beginners' books first; and the Advanced level requires one or two books of each of the previous categories. The fourth category, Good for All, includes books you can always enjoy, whether you are a complete novice or well versed in Kabbalah.

The fifth category—Textbooks—includes translations of authentic source materials from earlier Kabbalists, such as the Ari, Rav Yehuda Ashlag (Baal HaSulam) and his son and successor, Rav Baruch Ashlag (the Rabash). As its name implies, the sixth category—For Children—includes books that are suitable for children ages 3 and above. Those are not Kabbalah books per se, but are rather inspired by the teaching and convey the Kabbalistic message of love and unity.

Additional material that has not yet been published can be found at www.kabbalah.info. All materials on this site, including e-versions of published books, can be downloaded free of charge directly from the store at www. kabbalahbooks.info.

BEGINNERS

The Spiritual Roots of the Holy Land

The Spiritual Roots of the Holy Land takes you on a wondrous journey through the land of Israel. As you take in the breathtaking pictures of the holy land, another layer of the age-old country is revealed—its spiritual roots, the ebb and flow of forces that have shaped the curvy landscape that is sacred to billions of people around the world. At the end of the book, you'll find roadmaps of Israel, to help you locate each place you visit, whether in mind or in body, and more details on the forefathers who have made this land the focal point of an entire planet.

Self-Interest vs. Altruism in the Global Era: How society can turn self-interests into mutual benefit

Self-Interest vs. Altruism in the Global Era presents a new perspective on the world's challenges, regarding them as necessary consequences of humanity's growing egotism, rather than a series of errors. In that spirit, the book suggests ways to *use* our egos for society's benefit, rather than trying to suppress them.

The earlier chapters offer a novel understanding of Creation in general, and of humanity's existence on this planet, in particular. Then, we are offered a birds-eye view of history as a record of humankind's growing egotism. The final chapters address our current social and political challenges, and explain how we can use our egos to resolve them, rather than letting them ruin our collective home, as we have done so many times before.

A Guide to the Hidden Wisdom of Kabbalah

A Guide to the Hidden Wisdom of Kabbalah is a light and reader-friendly guide to beginners in Kabbalah, covering everything from the history of Kabbalah to how this wisdom can help resolve the world crisis.

The book is set up in three parts: Part 1 covers the history, facts, and fallacies about Kabbalah, and introduces its key concepts. Part 2 tells you all about the spiritual worlds and other neat stuff like the meaning of letters and the power of music. Part 3 covers the implementation of Kabbalah at a time of world crisis.

Kabbalah Revealed: A Guide to a More Peaceful Life

This is the most clearly written, reader-friendly guide to making sense of the surrounding world. Each of its six chapters focuses on a different aspect of the wisdom of Kabbalah, illuminating its teachings and explaining them using various examples from our day-to-day lives.

The first three chapters in *Kabbalah Revealed* explain why the world is in a state of crisis, how our growing desires promote progress as well as alienation, and why the biggest deterrent to achieving positive change is rooted in our own spirits. Chapters Four through Six offer a prescription for positive change. In these chapters, we learn how we can use our spirits to build a personally peaceful life in harmony with all of Creation.

Wondrous Wisdom

This book offers an initial course on Kabbalah. Like all the books presented here, *Wondrous Wisdom* is based solely on authentic teachings passed down from Kabbalist teacher to student over thousands of years. At the heart of the book is a sequence of lessons revealing the nature of Kabbalah's wisdom and explaining how to attain it. For every person questioning "Who am I really?" and "Why am I on this planet?" this book is a must.

Awakening to Kabbalah: The Guiding Light of Spiritual Fulfillment

A distinctive, personal, and awe-filled introduction to an ancient wisdom tradition. In this book, Rav Laitman offers a deeper understanding of the fundamental teachings of Kabbalah, and how you can use its wisdom to clarify your relationship with others and the world around you.

Using language both scientific and poetic, he probes the most profound questions of spirituality and existence. This provocative, unique guide will inspire and invigorate you to see beyond the world as it is and the limitations of your everyday life, become closer to the Creator, and reach new depths of the soul.

Kabbalah, Science, and the Meaning of Life

Science explains the mechanisms that sustain life; Kabbalah explains why life exists. In *Kabbalah, Science, and the Meaning of Life*, Rav Laitman combines science and spirituality in a captivating dialogue that reveals life's meaning.

For thousands of years Kabbalists have been writing that the world is a single entity divided into separate beings. Today the cutting-edge science of quantum physics states a very similar idea: that at the most fundamental level of matter, we are all literally one.

Science proves that reality is affected by the observer who examines it; and so does Kabbalah. But Kabbalah makes an even bolder statement: even the Creator, the Maker of reality, is within the observer. In other words, God is inside of us; He doesn't exist anywhere else. When we pass away, so does He.

These earthshaking concepts and more are eloquently introduced so that even readers new to Kabbalah or science will easily understand them. Therefore, if you're just a little curious about why you are here, what life means, and what you can do to enjoy it more, this book is for you.

From Chaos to Harmony

Many researchers and scientists agree that the ego is the reason behind the perilous state our world is in today. Laitman's groundbreaking book not only demonstrates that egoism has been the basis for all suffering throughout human history, but also shows how we can turn our plight to pleasure.

The book contains a clear analysis of the human soul and its problems, and provides a "roadmap" of what we need to do to once again be happy. *From Chaos to Harmony* explains how we can rise to a new level of existence on personal, social, national, and international levels.

Kabbalah for Beginners

Kabbalah for Beginners is a book for all those seeking answers to life's essential questions. We all want to know why we are here, why there is pain, and how we can make life more enjoyable. The four parts of this book provide us with reliable answers to these questions, as well as clear explanations of the gist of Kabbalah and its practical implementations.

Part One discusses the discovery of the wisdom of Kabbalah, and how it was developed, and finally concealed until our time. Part Two introduces the gist of the wisdom of Kabbalah, using ten easy drawings to help us understand the structure of the spiritual worlds, and how they relate to our world. Part Three reveals Kabbalistic concepts that are largely unknown to the public, and Part Four elaborates on practical means you and I can take, to make our lives better and more enjoyable for us and for our children.

INTERMEDIATE

The Kabbalah Experience

The depth of the wisdom revealed in the questions and answers within this book will inspire readers to reflect and contemplate. This is not a book to race through, but rather one that should be read thoughtfully and carefully. With this approach, readers will begin to experience a growing sense of enlightenment while simply absorbing the answers to the questions every Kabbalah student asks along the way.

The Kabbalah Experience is a guide from the past to the future, revealing situations that all students of Kabbalah will experience at some point along their journeys. For those who cherish every moment in life, this book offers unparalleled insights into the timeless wisdom of Kabbalah.

The Path of Kabbalah

This unique book combines beginners' material with more advanced concepts and teachings. If you have read a book or two of Laitman's, you will find this book very easy to relate to.

While touching upon basic concepts such as perception of reality and Freedom of Choice, *The Path of Kabbalah* goes deeper and expands beyond the scope of beginners' books. The structure of the worlds, for example, is explained in greater detail here than in the "pure" beginners' books. Also described is the spiritual root of mundane matters such as the Hebrew calendar and the holidays.

ADVANCED

The Science of Kabbalah

Kabbalist and scientist Rav Michael Laitman, PhD, designed this book to introduce readers to the special language and terminology of the authentic wisdom of Kabbalah. Here, Rav Laitman reveals authentic Kabbalah in a manner both rational and mature. Readers are gradually led to understand the logical design of the Universe and the life that exists in it.

The Science of Kabbalah, a revolutionary work unmatched in its clarity, depth, and appeal to the intellect, will enable readers to approach the more technical works of Baal HaSulam (Rabbi Yehuda Ashlag), such as *The Study of the Ten Sefirot* and *The Book of Zohar*. Readers of this book will enjoy the satisfying answers to the riddles of life that only authentic Kabbalah provides. Travel through the pages and prepare for an astonishing journey into the Upper Worlds.

Introduction to the Book of Zohar

This volume, along with *The Science of Kabbalah*, is a required preparation for those who wish to understand the hidden message of *The Book of*

Zohar. Among the many helpful topics dealt with in this text is an introduction to the "language of roots and branches," without which the stories in *The Zohar* are mere fable and legend. *Introduction to the Book of Zohar* will provide readers with the necessary tools to understand authentic Kabbalah as it was originally meant to be—as a means to attain the Upper Worlds.

The Book of Zohar: annotations to the Ashlag commentary

The Book of Zohar (*The Book of Radiance*) is an age-old source of wisdom and the basis for all Kabbalistic literature. Since its appearance nearly 2,000 years ago, it has been the primary, and often only, source used by Kabbalists.

For centuries, Kabbalah was hidden from the public, which was deemed not yet ready to receive it. However, our generation has been designated by Kabbalists as the first generation that *is* ready to grasp the concepts in *The Zohar*. Now we can put these principles into practice in our lives.

Written in a unique and metaphorical language, *The Book of Zohar* enriches our understanding of reality and widens our worldview. Although the text deals with one subject only—how to relate to the Creator—it approaches it from different angles. This allows each of us to find the particular phrase or word that will carry us into the depths of this profound and timeless wisdom.

GOOD FOR ALL

The Kabbalist: a cinematic novel

At the dawn of the deadliest era in human history, the 20th century, a mysterious man appeared on the socio-political scene carrying a stern warning for humanity and an unlikely solution to its suffering. In his writings, Kabbalist Yehuda Ashlag described in clarity and great detail the wars and upheavals he foresaw, and even more strikingly, the current economic, political, and social crises we are facing today. His deep yearning for a united humanity has driven him to unlock *The Book of Zohar* and make it—and the unique force contained therein—accessible to all.

The Kabbalist is a cinematic novel that will turn on its head everything you thought you knew about Kabbalah, spirituality, freedom of will, and our perception of reality. It is the first book of its kind to try to convey the inner workings and sensations of a Kabbalist who reached the highest level of attainment, a person who is in direct contact with the singular force governing all of reality.

The Kabbalist carries a surprising message of unity with scientific clarity and poetic depth. It transcends religion, nationality, mysticism, and the sheer fabric of space and time to show us that the only miracle is the one taking place within, when we begin to act in harmony with Nature and with the entire humanity. It shows us that we can all be Kabbalists.

The Point in the Heart: A Source of Delight for My Soul

The Point in the Heart; a Source of Delight for My Soul is a unique collection of excerpts from a man whose wisdom has earned him devoted students in North America and the world over. Michael Laitman is a scientist, a Kabbalist, and a great thinker who presents ancient wisdom in a compelling style.

This book does not profess to teach Kabbalah, but rather gently introduces ideas from the teaching. *The Point in the Heart* is a window to a new perception. As the author himself testifies to the wisdom of Kabbalah, "It is a science of emotion, a science of pleasure. You are welcome to open and to taste."

Attaining the Worlds Beyond

From the introduction to *Attaining the Worlds Beyond*: "...Not feeling well on the Jewish New Year's Eve of September 1991, my teacher called me to his bedside and handed me his notebook, saying, 'Take it and learn from it.' The following morning, he perished in my arms, leaving me and many of his other disciples without guidance in this world.

"He used to say, 'I want to teach you to turn to the Creator, rather than to me, because He is the only strength, the only Source of all that exists, the only one who can really help you, and He awaits your prayers for help. When you seek help in your search for freedom from the bondage of this world, help in elevating yourself above this world, help in finding the self, and help in determining your purpose in life, you must turn to the Creator, who sends you all those aspirations in order to compel you to turn to Him.'"

Attaining the Worlds Beyond holds within it the content of that notebook, as well as other inspiring texts. This book reaches out to all those seekers who want to find a logical, reliable way to understand the world's phenomena. This fascinating introduction to the wisdom of Kabbalah will enlighten the mind, invigorate the heart, and move readers to the depths of their souls.

Bail Yourself Out

In *Bail Yourself Out: how you can emerge strong from the world crisis*, Laitman introduces several extraordinary concepts that weave into a complete solution: 1) The crisis is essentially not financial, but *psychological*: People have stopped trusting each other, and where there is no trust there is no trade, but only war, isolation, and pain. 2) This mistrust is a result of a *natural process* that's been evolving for millennia and is culminating today. 3) To resolve the crisis, we must first *understand* the process that created the alienation. 4) The first, and most important, step to understanding the crisis is to *inform* people about this natural process through books, such as *Bail Yourself Out*, TV, cinema, and any other means of communication. 5) With this information, we will "*revamp*" our relationships and build them on trust, collaboration, and most importantly, care. This mending process will guarantee that we and our families will prosper in a world of plenty.

Basic Concepts in Kabbalah

This is a book to help readers cultivate an *approach to the concepts* of Kabbalah, to spiritual objects, and to spiritual terms. By reading and re-reading in this book, one develops internal observations, senses, and approaches that did not previously exist within. These newly acquired observations are like sensors that "feel" the space around us that is hidden from our ordinary senses.

Hence, *Basic Concepts in Kabbalah* is intended to foster the contemplation of spiritual terms. Once we are integrated with these terms, we can begin to see, with our inner vision, the unveiling of the spiritual structure that surrounds us, almost as if a mist has been lifted.

This book is not aimed at the study of facts. Instead, it is a book for those who wish to awaken the deepest and subtlest sensations they can possess.

Children of Tomorrow: Guidelines for Raising Happy Children in the 21st Century

Children of Tomorrow is a new beginning for you and your children. Imagine being able to hit the reboot button and get it right this time. No hassle, no stress, and best of all—no guessing.

The big revelation is that raising kids is all about games and play, relating to them as small grownups, and making all major decisions together. You will be surprised to discover how teaching kids about positive things like friendship and caring for others automatically spills into other areas of our lives through the day.

Open any page and you will find thought-provoking quotes about every aspect of children's lives: parent-children relations, friendships and conflicts, and a clear picture of how schools should be designed and function. This book offers a fresh perspective on how to raise our children, with the goal being the happiness of all children everywhere.

The Wise Heart: Tales and allegories by three contemporary sages

"Our inner work is to tune our hearts and our senses to perceive the spiritual world," says Michael Laitman in the poem Spiritual Wave. *The Wise Heart* is a lovingly crafted anthology comprised of tales and allegories by Kabbalist Dr. Michael Laitman, his mentor, Rav Baruch Ashlag (Rabash), and Rabash's father and mentor, Rav Yehuda Ashlag, author of the acclaimed *Sulam* (Ladder) commentary on *The Book of Zohar*.

Kabbalah students and enthusiasts in Kabbalah often wonder what the spiritual world actually feels like to a Kabbalist. The allegories in this delicate compilation provide a glimpse into those feelings.

The poems herein are excerpts from letters and lessons given by these three spiritual giants to their students through the years. They offer surprising and often amusing depictions of human nature, with a loving and tender touch that is truly unique to Kabbalists. Indeed, *The Wise Heart* is a gift of wisdom and delight for any wisdom seeking heart.

TEXTBOOKS

Shamati (I Heard)

Rav Michael Laitman's words on the book: Among all the texts and notes that were used by my teacher, Rav Baruch Shalom Halevi Ashlag (the Rabash), there was one special notebook he always carried. This notebook contained the transcripts of his conversations with his father, Rav Yehuda Leib Halevi Ashlag (Baal HaSulam), author of the *Sulam* (Ladder) commentary on *The Book of Zohar*, *The Study of the Ten Sefirot* (a commentary on the texts of the Kabbalist, Ari), and of many other works on Kabbalah.

Not feeling well on the Jewish New Year's Eve of September 1991, the Rabash summoned me to his bedside and handed me a notebook, whose cover contained only one word, *Shamati* (I Heard). As he handed the notebook, he said, "Take it and learn from it." The following morning, my teacher perished in my arms, leaving me and many of his other disciples without guidance in this world.

Committed to Rabash's legacy to disseminate the wisdom of Kabbalah, I published the notebook just as it was written, thus retaining the text's transforming powers. Among all the books of Kabbalah, *Shamati* is a unique and compelling creation.

Kabbalah for the Student

Kabbalah for the Student offers authentic texts by Rav Yehuda Ashlag, author of the *Sulam* (Ladder) commentary on *The Book of Zohar*, his son and successor, Rav Baruch Ashlag, as well as other great Kabbalists. It also offers illustrations that accurately depict the evolution of the Upper Worlds as Kabbalists experience them. The book also contains several explanatory essays that help us understand the texts withinIn *Kabbalah for the Student*, Rav Michael Laitman, PhD, Rav Baruch Ashlag's personal assistant and prime student, compiled all the texts a Kabbalah student would need in order to attain the spiritual worlds. In his daily lessons, Rav Laitman bases his teaching on these inspiring texts, thus helping novices and veterans alike to better understand the spiritual path we undertake on our fascinating journey to the Higher Realms.

Rabash—the Social Writings

Rav Baruch Shalom HaLevi Ashlag (Rabash) played a remarkable role in the history of Kabbalah. He provided us with the necessary final link connecting the wisdom of Kabbalah to our human experience. His father and teacher was the great Kabbalist, Rav Yehuda Leib HaLevi Ashlag, known as Baal HaSulam for his *Sulam* (Ladder) commentary on *The Book of Zohar*. Yet, if not for the essays of Rabash, his father's efforts to disclose the wisdom of Kabbalah to all would have been in vain. Without those essays, few would be able to achieve the spiritual attainment that Baal HaSulam so desperately wanted us to obtain.

The writings in this book aren't just for reading. They are more like an experiential user's guide. It is very important to work with them in order to see what they truly contain. The reader should try to put them into practice by living out the emotions Rabash so masterfully describes. He always advised his students to summarize the articles, to work with the texts, and those who attempt it discover that it always yields new insights. Thus, readers are advised to work with the texts, summarize them, translate them, and implement them in the group. Those who do so will discover the power in the writings of Rabash.

Gems of Wisdom: words of the great Kabbalists from all generations

Through the millennia, Kabbalists have bequeathed us with numerous writings. In their compositions, they have laid out a structured method that can lead, step by step, unto a world of eternity and wholeness.

Gems of wisdom is a collection of selected excerpts from the writings of the greatest Kabbalists from all generations, with particular emphasis on the writings of Rav Yehuda Leib HaLevi Ashlag (Baal HaSulam), author of the *Sulam* [Ladder] commentary of *The Book of Zohar*.

The sections have been arranged by topics, to provide the broadest view possible on each topic. This book is a useful guide to any person desiring spiritual advancement.

Let There Be Light: selected excerpts from The Book of Zohar

The Zohar contains all the secrets of creation, but until recently the wisdom of Kabbalah was locked under a thousand locks. Thanks to the work of Rav Yehuda Ashlag (1884-1954), the last of the great Kabbalists, *The Zohar* is revealed today in order to propel humanity to its next degree. Ashlag's *Sulam* (Ladder) commentary has made *The Zohar* accessible to all.

Let There Be Light contains selected excerpts from the series *Zohar for All*, a refined edition of *The Book of Zohar* with the *Sulam* commentary. Each piece was carefully chosen for its beauty and depth as well as its capacity to draw the reader into *The Zohar* and get the most out of the reading experience.

More importantly, as *The Zohar* speaks of nothing but the intricate web that connects all souls, diving into its words attracts the special force that exists in that state of oneness, where we are all connected. *The Zohar* is the bridge that connects us to that source of energy and vitality that permeates all of reality.

FOR CHILDREN

Together Forever: The story about the magician who didn't want to be alone

On the surface, *Together Forever* is a children's story. But like all good children's stories, it transcends boundaries of age, culture, and upbringing.

In *Together Forever*, the author tells us that if we are patient and endure the trials we encounter along our life's path, we will become stronger, braver, and wiser. Instead of growing weaker, we will learn to create our own magic and our own wonders as only a magician can.

In this warm, tender tale, Michael Laitman shares with children and parents alike some of the gems and charms of the spiritual world. The wisdom of Kabbalah is filled with spellbinding stories. *Together Forever* is yet another gift from this ageless source of wisdom, whose lessons make our lives richer, easier, and far more fulfilling.

Miracles Can Happen: Tales for children, but not only...

"Miracles Can Happen," Princes Peony," and "Mary and the Paints" are only three of ten beautiful stories for children ages 3-10. Written especially for children, these short tales convey a single message of love, unity, and care for all beings. The unique illustrations were carefully crafted to contribute to the overall message of the book, and a child who's heard or read any story in this collection is guaranteed to go to sleep smiling.

The Baobab that Opened Its Heart: and Other Nature Tales for Children

The Baobab that Opened Its Heart is a collection of stories for children, but not just for them. The stories in this collection were written with the love of Nature, of people, and specifically with children in mind. They all share the desire to tell nature's tale of unity, connectedness, and love.

Kabbalah teaches that love is nature's guiding force, the reason for creation. The stories in this book convey it in the unique way that Kabbalah engenders in its students. The variety of authors and diversity of styles allows each reader to find the story that they like most.

ABOUT BNEI BARUCH

Bnei Baruch is an international group of Kabbalists who share the wisdom of Kabbalah with the entire world. The study materials (in over 30 languages) are authentic Kabbalah texts that were passed down from generation to generation.

HISTORY AND ORIGIN

In 1991, following the passing of his teacher, Rav Baruch Shalom HaLevi Ashlag (The Rabash), Michael Laitman, Professor of Ontology and the Theory of Knowledge, PhD in Philosophy and Kabbalah, and MSc in Medical Bio-Cybernetics, established a Kabbalah study group called "Bnei Baruch." He called it Bnei Baruch (Sons of Baruch) to commemorate his mentor, whose side he never left in the final twelve years of his life, from 1979 to 1991. Dr. Laitman had been Ashlag's prime student and personal assistant, and is recognized as the successor to Rabash's teaching method.

The Rabash was the firstborn son and successor of Rav Yehuda Leib HaLevi Ashlag, the greatest Kabbalist of the 20th century. Rav

Ashlag authored the most authoritative and comprehensive commentary on *The Book of Zohar*, titled *The Sulam* (Ladder) *Commentary*. He was the first to reveal the complete method for spiritual ascent, and thus was known as Baal HaSulam (Owner of the Ladder).

Bnei Baruch bases its entire study method on the path paved by these two great spiritual leaders.

THE STUDY METHOD

The unique study method developed by Baal HaSulam and his son, the Rabash, is taught and applied on a daily basis by Bnei Baruch. This method relies on authentic Kabbalah sources such as *The Book of Zohar*, by Rabbi Shimon Bar-Yochai, *The Tree of Life*, by the Ari, and *The Study of the Ten Sefirot*, by Baal HaSulam.

While the study relies on authentic Kabbalah sources, it is carried out in simple language and uses a scientific, contemporary approach. The unique combination of an academic study method and personal experiences broadens the students' perspective and awards them a new perception of the reality they live in. Those on the spiritual path are thus given the necessary tools to study themselves and their surrounding reality.

Bnei Baruch is a diverse movement of tens of thousands of students worldwide. Students can choose their own paths and intensity of their studies according to their unique conditions and abilities.

THE MESSAGE

The essence of the message disseminated by Bnei Baruch is universal: unity of the people, unity of nations and love of man.

For millennia, Kabbalists have been teaching that love of man should be the foundation of all human relations. This love prevailed in the days of Abraham, Moses, and the group of Kabbalists that they established. If we make room for these seasoned, yet contemporary values, we will discover that we possess the power to put differences aside and unite.

The wisdom of Kabbalah, hidden for millennia, has been waiting for the time when we would be sufficiently developed and ready to implement its message. Now, it is emerging as a solution that can unite diverse factions everywhere, enabling us, as individuals and as a society, to meet today's challenges.

ACTIVITIES

Bnei Baruch was established on the premise that "only by expansion of the wisdom of Kabbalah to the public can we be awarded complete redemption" (Baal HaSulam). Therefore, Bnei Baruch offers a variety of ways for people to explore and discover the purpose of their lives, providing careful guidance for beginners and advanced students alike.

Internet

Bnei Baruch's international website, www.kab.info, presents the authentic wisdom of Kabbalah using essays, books, and original texts. It is by far the most expansive source of authentic Kabbalah material on the Internet, containing a unique, extensive library for readers to thoroughly explore the wisdom of Kabbalah. Additionally, the media archive, www.kabbalahmedia.info, contains thousands of media items, downloadable books, and a vast reservoir of texts, video and audio files in many languages.

Bnei Baruch's online Kabbalah Education Center offers free Kabbalah courses for beginners, initiating students into this profound body of knowledge in the comfort of their own homes.

Dr. Laitman's daily lessons are also aired live on www.kab.tv, along with complementary texts and diagrams.

All these services are provided free of charge.

Television

In Israel, Bnei Baruch established its own channel, no. 66 on both cable and satellite, which broadcasts 24/7 Kabbalah TV. The channel is also aired on the Internet at www.kab.tv. All broadcasts on the channel are free of charge. Programs are adapted for all levels, from complete beginners to the most advanced.

Conferences

Twice a year, students gather for a weekend of study and socializing at conferences in various locations in the U.S., as well as an annual convention in Israel. These gatherings provide a great setting for meeting like-minded people, for bonding, and for expanding one's understanding of the wisdom.

Kabbalah Books

Bnei Baruch publishes authentic books, written by Baal HaSulam, his son, the Rabash, as well as books by Dr. Michael Laitman. The books of Rav Ashlag and Rabash are essential for complete understanding of the teachings of authentic Kabbalah, explained in Laitman's lessons.

Dr. Laitman writes his books in a clear, contemporary style based on the key concepts of Baal HaSulam. These books are a vital link between today's readers and the original texts. All the books are available for sale, as well as for free download.

Paper

Kabbalah Today is a free paper produced and disseminated by Bnei Baruch in many languages, including English, Hebrew, Spanish, and Russian. It is apolitical, non-commercial, and written in a clear, contemporary style. The purpose of *Kabbalah Today* is to expose the vast knowledge hidden in the wisdom of Kabbalah at no cost and in a clear, engaging style for readers everywhere.

Kabbalah Lessons

As Kabbalists have been doing for centuries, Laitman gives a daily lesson. The lessons are given in Hebrew and are simultaneously interpreted into seven languages—English, Russian, Spanish, French, German, Italian, and Turkish—by skilled and experienced interpreters. As with everything else, the live broadcast is free of charge.

FUNDING

Bnei Baruch is a non-profit organization for teaching and sharing the wisdom of Kabbalah. To maintain its independence and purity of intentions, Bnei Baruch is not supported, funded, or otherwise tied to any government or political organization.

Since the bulk of its activity is provided free of charge, the prime sources of funding for the group's activities are donations and tithing—contributed by students on a voluntary basis—and Dr. Laitman's books, which are sold at cost.

HOW TO CONTACT BNEI BARUCH

1057 Steeles Avenue West, Suite 532
Toronto, ON, M2R 3X1
Canada

Bnei Baruch USA,
2009 85th street, #51,
Brooklyn, New York, 11214
USA

E-mail: info@kabbalah.info
Web site: www.kabbalah.info

Toll free in USA and Canada:
1-866-LAITMAN
Fax: 1-905 886 9697